THE
BOOK OF
DAYS

D0631845

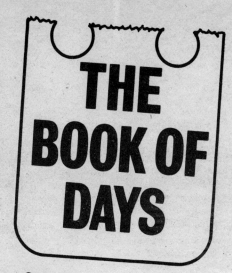

THE BOOK OF DAYS

Bob Monkhouse...

ARROW BOOKS

Arrow Books Limited
17 – 21 Conway Street, London W1P 5HL

An imprint of the Hutchinson Publishing Group

London Melbourne Sydney Auckland
Johannesburg and agencies
throughout the world

First published 1981
© Bob Monkhouse 1981
Illustrations © Bob Monkhouse 1981

Set in Times and Univers

Made and printed in Great Britain
by The Anchor Press Ltd
Tiptree, Essex

Photoset in Great Britain
by Photobooks (Bristol) Ltd

ISBN 0–09–927150–8

Dedicated to Gary
who let me do it,
Abigail who helped me
to do it, Simon who's
promised to read it,
Wendy who typed it
and Jackie who hopes
I won't do it again.

AUTHOR'S NOTE

I wrote all this in longhand in two diaries while juggling 182 reference books and 26 other sources.

I apologise for the mistakes. If I knew where they were, I'd correct them.

Where gag lines are quoted I've attributed them to the person I heard say them first.

My grateful thanks are due to all these sources of wit, especially to comedy star Ted Rogers, and US humorists John Fultz, Dan O'Day of O'Liners, Joe Hickman of Contemporary Comedy and Robert Orben, the king of the one-liners.

Special thanks to the 'Curator of Oddities' himself, Jeremy Beadle. I've tried not to duplicate facts in his fascinating book *Today's the Day* (W.H. Allen & Co. Ltd), but often Jeremy's special knowledge has been vital to my purpose and I do thank him for his generous help.

Author's profits from this little venture will be distributed to:

> The Stars' Organization for Spastics
> The Muscular Dystrophy Fund
> Heart Foundation
> Kyre Park Hall Spastics Centre
> Kidney Research
> and others

If this curious chronicle does well, I'll write a second edition. All contributions from readers will be welcome, more so when the origin of an item is also supplied.

Have a nice 365 days!

SO A NEW YEAR STARTS TODAY

Funny thing about new years. They just don't seem to last as long as they used to. January was named after Janus, the two-faced god, much worshipped by trades union bosses and cabinet ministers.

The horror film was officially born on this day in 1937. The British Board of Film Censors introduced the 'H' certificate – 'H' for horrific. Robert Orben says he saw a great horror film: 'This monster, two thousand feet high, eats Benidorm! And, in the middle of the night, he has to get up and drink the Kaopectate factory.'

The *Daily Universal Register* altered its name today in 1788. The notice hanging outside its London offices became a sign of *The Times*.

The postmaster of Lismore welcomed the new year of 1821 today – by riding in an oyster tub drawn by two cats, a badger, a hedgehog, a goose and a pig! The ninety-seven-year-old Mr Huddy won a bet by travelling like that today across the bit of Scotland between Lismore and Fermoy. The folks in Fermoy congratulated him on the improvement in his postal delivery service.

THE EUROPEAN ECONOMIC COMMUNITY WAS INAUGURATED ON THIS DAY IN 1958.

and Britain became a member on this same day in 1973. Are you pleased with the way the Common Market has worked for us? I reckon it cost us more to go into Europe than it did on 'D' day!

That was a wonderful party last night. Now, if I can only get the blood out of my eyes and back in my veins, we'll begin. . . .

Today in 1727 was the birthday of the weedy English General James Wolfe. He was the consumptive weakling who led the victorious British army at Quebec in 1759, of whom King George II said, 'Mad, is he? Then I hope he will bite some of my other generals!'

TODAY IN 1839 WE SAW THE FIRST MOON PHOTOGRAPH!

Lady Gough's Book of Etiquette was published today in 1870. It forbade the placing of books by male authors next to books by female authors on any bookshelf – unless the male and female in question were married.

It showed the surface of the moon well enough to make me feel they'd got the same gardener I've got.

2 JAN

The Football Association chose this day in 1921 to announce their ban on ladies playing soccer professionally. Women weren't allowed back into the league until 1970. Ironically, the ban came in the same year that British females got the vote. One of the big issues in Women's Lib is that women want to get out of the kitchen. George Burns says, 'My mother would never have gone along with that. There were twelve kids in my family and my mother's idea of liberation was to get *into* the kitchen. What she wanted to get out of was the bedroom.'

Today in 1901 *The Times* reported the alarming news that China had agreed to let Russia rule over Manchuria as a protectorate. Quite a scoop! Even the empress of China had not known of the agreement – until she read about it in *The Times*! Personally, I don't trust China. Any country that has 1000 million people and claims that ping-pong is their most popular indoor amusement will lie about other things too.

The first father whose three sons were senators was Joseph Patrick Kennedy. Two of them, John Fitzgerald Kennedy and Robert Francis Kennedy, were sworn in on this day – JFK in 1953 and Bobby in 1965. (Teddy was sworn in on 9 January 1963 – and has been swearing ever since.) Oddly . . .

3 JAN

The man who killed the man who killed JFK died on this day in 1967. Jack Ruby, a fifty-five-year-old nightclub owner in Dallas, Texas, and a passionate supporter of the assassinated President Kennedy, died while awaiting his retrial for the murder of Lee Harvey Oswald. Months later all charges against him were dismissed.

THE FIRST DRINKING STRAW WAS PATENTED IN 1888...

by Marvin Stone who rolled them by hand from paraffined manila paper so that they wouldn't split or crack. Was it Marvin who first said, 'Never give a sucker an even break'?

On this day of World War I the first use of tear gas was reported in 1915. My father was in France when the first shot was fired. He was in Leeds when the second shot was fired.

4 JAN

'It's impossible to make a funny joke about blindness,' someone stated flatly. Well, flatly enough to prompt Peter Cook to prove the person wrong and invent his blind BBC Radio newsreader who fluffs an announcement and says, 'I'm sorry, I'll feel that again.' Louis Braille was born today in 1809, inventor of the alphabet that bears his name, a system in which you run your fingers over a number of bumps and you get the message. In some offices, this is known as how to hire a secretary.

CHARLIE CHAPLIN turned down the New York film critics award for 'The Great Dictator' today in 1941. He said he sought 'only to please the public'. The world was his oyster. And he was its pearl.

Idle hands made heavy work on this day in 1972 when fifteen enthusiasts in oriental martial arts went to work on a six-room house due for demolition in the village of Idle, Yorkshire. They reduced the house to rubble in six hours using only their hands and feet. In my *Karate Handbook* it says stance is vital: 'To attack a twenty-stone opponent you must be perfectly balanced.' Now that just doesn't make sense. Anyone who'd attack a twenty-stone opponent has got to be unbalanced for a start.

London was snowed under today in 1867. Even the sturdy omnibuses gave up except for those which could be drawn by four horses instead of two. Under somewhat different weather conditions, the Sahara Desert Transit Authority switched from camels to cars on this day in 1924. Joe Hickman notes, 'By car you could cross the Sahara in only three days. It took nine days by camel – and even then you really had to hump it.'

The German National Socialist Party was formed today in 1919, to become better known and worse hated as the Nazi Party. Adolf Hitler called himself a strict vegetarian although he was criticized for eating pig's knuckles. He organized the deaths of six million Jews yet worried about 'the most humane way to cook lobster'.

Arsenal fullback Eddy Hapgood used his head to score a curious penalty goal this afternoon in 1935. Liverpool goalie Riley punched the ball straight on to Eddy's skull – and he scored on the rebound! Jasper Carrott hated being a goalie in his school team. He says he wasn't very good. 'After my first few games, they put a bell in the ball so I'd know when it was coming.'

5 JAN

Today is the 1938 birthday of King Juan Carlos of Spain, in Rome, Italy, designated by General Franco as his successor in 1969 when he said, 'Carlos is the Juan I want.'

EDWARD THE CONFESSOR MADE HIS BIGGEST CONFESSION

– to his maker – on this day in 1066. He was one of the four sons of Aethelred the Unready and his wife, Emma the Ever-ready, a mismatched couple if ever there was one. Edward was very pious and very dull. And I do mean dull. His personal physician was a coroner.

The world's first top hat was worn in London today in 1797. James Hetherington was promptly arrested and fined £50, reports Jeremy Beadle, for wearing 'a tall shiny structure calculated to frighten timid people'. He observed in a letter to the Irish playwright Sheridan, 'The band was tight and gave me a headache.' I've worked in a lot of nightclubs where the same thing happened.

6 JAN

He made a 'silk' purse out of a sow's ear! Wallace J. Murray who died on this day aged eighty-eight in Gorham, Maine, USA, said he made the purse 'to demonstrate American scientific abilities'. It's on permanent display at the Smithsonian Institution in Washington, DC. Aren't some proverbs silly? How about 'Still waters run deep'? If they're still they don't run . . . and if they run they're not still! Want a proverb for the 1980s? Try 'A penny saved is a penny depreciated.'

In the State Infirmary, Kampala, this morning in 1973 Dr Mabale asked for a stethoscope – and found there was no medical equipment in the entire hospital! Patients in the fifty-five beds of the government-run Ugandan infirmary were transferred to other medical centres as Dr Mabale and his staff investigated the massive theft of surgical instruments, medicines, anaesthetics – even cotton wool. The burglar turned out to be the night nurse! Nurse Shole Napurate had shifted the lot, nearly two tons in all, in only six hours. Her van (and her husband) were over the border before the first patients awoke to ask for bedpans – and they were missing too! What happened to the nurse? She's still absent without gauze.

Nothing ventured, nothing gained. Boldly upon this day in 1957 Drs V. S. Hilliard and Roberto Mann performed Britain's first prefrontal lobotomy – both had been dentists! Asked how a man who'd begun his career as a dentist could make such a radical change as to become a brain surgeon, Dr Mann should have replied (but didn't), 'My drill slipped.'

Louis Braille died on this day in 1852, aged forty-three years and two days. The French musician from Coupvray had a good incentive for inventing the raised-dot system of writing used by the blind: he was blinded himself at the age of three.

America's first flu epidemic broke out today in 1733 and affected about three-quarters of the entire population. Last 7 January I got over the flu in twenty-four hours. I think the germs froze to death.

7 JAN

The world's most southerly baby is also the only child who can claim to be the first born on any continent. Today in 1978 Emilio Marcos Palma was born at the Sargento Cabrol Base – in Antarctica! They told the mother, 'Your baby was born further south than any other.' She said, 'But don't they all come out that end?'

Errol Flynn was sued by a girl who said he was the father of her child – for the seventh time! This happened today in 1958. Within a year the star was dead, aged only fifty. At one stage Errol would lure a desirable teenager aboard his yacht by assuring, 'You'll love it. I've named it after you.' No girl could resist a pitch like that. It was only after they arrived at the marina and saw the boat bobbing beside the landing that she'd realize she'd been had. The letters on the stern read: 'After You'.

THE MACARONI CLUB WAS FOUNDED TODAY IN 1780

– a kind of eighteenth-century Gay Lib. Young Englishmen, who affected precious ways and adopted foreign foods and phrases, minced around London in fancy clothes, mocked as 'macaronis'. And that explains that curious line in 'Yankee Doodle', the pre-revolutionary marching song. Remember? 'He stuck a feather in his cap and called it macaroni' – that didn't mean Italian pasta: it meant English poofta.

Sir Thomas Lawrence died on this day in 1830. He said, 'I have painted portraits of every great face except that of God Almighty, a commission I can no longer postpone.'

The British were defeated by the Americans when the Battle of New Orleans took place on this day in 1815 . . . and Sir Edward Pakenham, who forecast his own defeat, fell between the *bayoux* and the Mississippi with a bullet in his spine. His body was returned to Ireland in a cask of rum. But how many know that the great Andrew Jackson fought this great and bloody victory two weeks after the war was over?

8 JAN

Galileo Galilei died on this day in 1642 . . . but the greatest Italian astronomer and physicist never dropped weights from the Leaning Tower of Pisa as is popularly believed. That famous experiment was performed by Simon Stevin years before Galileo's work with the laws of bodies in motion. But another scorned legend about him, long disbelieved, is really true. The story tells how, tried by the Inquisition in Rome for his heresy of teaching the Copernicus theory, he was brought to the point of denying it and admitting that the sun was not the centre of our system. The papal court demanded his agreement that the earth is the unmoving centre. Rising from his knees, Galileo said softly, 'Nevertheless – it does move.' Scholars have rejected the tale as a piece of 18th-century nonsense for years. But the statement is written on a portrait of Galileo completed in 1640 – only seven years after his trial!

Dance king Victor Sylvester opened his first dancing school in Croydon today in 1949. It had waltz-to-waltz carpeting.

MARCO POLO DIED ON THIS DAY IN 1324.

The Royal Danieli Hotel in Venice has accommodation named after Polo. It's a small white suite with a view.

The *Queen Elizabeth* was destroyed by fire in Hong Kong harbour on this day in 1972. I travelled on it once with 150 chefs! I think it was a Cook's tour.

9 JAN

Open-mouth kissing on the screen! The crowds were open-mouthed too – tonight in 1927, New York City – when real-life lovers Greta Garbo and John Gilbert gave their tongues to silent movies with uninhibited clinches in 'Flesh and the Devil'. By another of magical movieland's coincidences, this is also the day in 1951 on which America's first X-rated film was shown. Now porno movies are getting so bad, they're running these pictures with English subtitles – because the heavy breathing drowns out the soundtrack!

A MILLIONAIRE BREWER CHALLENGED A PUBLICAN TO A DUEL, SHOT & KILLED HIM AT DAWN TODAY IN 1901... AND ALL BECAUSE HE SAID HIS BEER WAS "LIKE DOG'S URINE"!

GNAT'S, JA! DOG'S...NEVER!

THEY WERE AT LAGERHEADS...

FRANZ VON EBERHARDT GOT 3 YEARS IN A PRUSSIAN JAIL FOR FATALLY WOUNDING HOST OTTO HELM... BUT THE JUDGE ALLOWED HIM "A DAILY BEER RATION"!

10 JAN

The lowest-ever denomination note was issued by the Bank of England on this day in 1828 – it was worth one penny. Jeremy Beadle comments, 'Similar in many ways to the pound in 1980!' Nowadays a person's take-home pay can hardly survive the trip. And while we're on the subject of costly matters...

The League of Nations was founded on this day in 1920. It was like a one-armed bandit. We kept feeding it money but it never paid off.

The Penny Post began in Britain today in 1840. A *penny* to send a letter! Do you realize if today's postage gets any higher, it's going to be cheaper to go yourself?

The first oil was struck in Texas in 1901. Joey Adams says, 'Our gas stations are closed on Sundays so the station owners can go to church and confess their prices.'

THE FIRST LONDON BLACKOUT - 1812!

An impenetrable fog of sooty smoke and polluted mist shrouded London so totally on this day that the sun could not get through and midday was just like midnight. So air pollution is nothing new. That's why London sparrows sleep on one foot. They use the other to hold their noses.

Fourteen-year-old Nigel Short became the youngest British chess player to be an international master. It happened when the leader at the Hastings tournament, Andersson, resigned an adjourned game today in 1980. Now Nigel won't play in the contests unless they pay him more money. He sent the organizers a telegram: 'I want a bigger cheque, mate – your move!'

TOMMY MANVILLE WEDDED HIS THIRTEENTH BRIDE TODAY IN 1960...

She was twenty-five and Tommy was sixty. His doctor told him, 'Sex could prove fatal.' Tommy said, 'So? If she dies, she dies!'

11 JAN

'Call Me Madam', Irving Berlin's hit musical, told the story of the lady who died on this day in 1975, aged eighty-four. Pearl Mesta from Sturgis, Michigan, became the most famous and popular 'hostess with the mostes' on the ball' in Washington, DC, during the 1940s. She was US envoy to Luxembourg from 1949 to 1953, where she gave her most lavish, extravagant party. To give you some idea, the Savoy made an offer for the leftovers.

The US surgeon general issued a massive report citing 'overwhelming proof' linking health hazards to smoking this morning in 1979. I know cigarettes are bad for me. My wife came home from a weekend at her parents' and found one with lipstick on it.

12 JAN

The world's most faithful dog died on this day in 1942. Jeremy Beadle writes, 'Shep was his name and he'd spent the last six years of his life waiting at a Montana railway station for his dead master to return.' I've got a dog that barks all night for no reason. I'm thinking of buying him a burglar.

GERMAN WRITER & CRITIC FRIEDRICH VON SCHLEGEL DIED ON THIS DAY IN 1829 AGED 56. ANYTHING MYSTERIOUS, DANGEROUS & INDIAN. HE'D HAVE LOVED TAKE-AWAY VINDALOO!

HE FREAKED OUT ON

WHAT A DREAMER! IF WE LIVED IN INDIA, WE'D STARVE!

IF WE LIVED IN INDIA, MY DEAR WIFE ... YOU WOULD BE SACRED!

OH, TO BE IN INDIA NOW THAT HELGA'S HERE

BOB MONKHOUSE

The first X-ray was demonstrated in 1896 by Roentgen. Mrs Roentgen said, 'Who needs it? I've always been able to see through you!'

Dame Agatha Christie died on this day in 1976. And they don't know whodunnit!

The first X-ray photograph was made in the USA today also in 1896 – by Dr Henry Louis Smith. He fired a bullet into a corpse and then took a fifteen-minute exposure which, when developed, revealed the exact location of the bullet. Everyone agreed that it was a dead shot.

Stephen Foster died on this day in 1864, aged only thirty-eight. He wrote 'Oh, Susannah!', 'My Old Kentucky Home', 'Old Folks at Home', 'Camptown Races', 'Beautiful Dreamer' and 'Jeanie with the Light Brown Hair'. He died an alcoholic, living on turnips and apples, penniless and lying in a Bowery gutter.

The first wind-screen wipers were introduced in 1921. Scottish motorists are said to have switched them off whenever passing under a bridge.

13 JAN

Tonight Wyatt Earp died in 1929, aged eighty-one! With his brothers and Doc Holliday, Wyatt had made US Western history with the controversial gunfight at the OK Corral in 1881. His last words were, 'This indigestion is killing me.' Maybe he should have sent for the Bicarbonate Brothers – Wild Bill Hiccup and Hopalong Acidity. They were among the early settlers.

The pilot of an experimental jet fighter plane pressed a button today in 1942. He became the first pilot ever to leave his plane by courtesy of an emergency ejector seat. He landed safely from 7875 feet outside Rechlin in Germany. Frank Carson tells the tale of two Irish pilots who went up in an open plane. One asks, 'If I press the button marked "Ejectors", will we fall out?' The other says, 'No, I'll still talk to you.'

63 AD

Today the Roman Emperor Nero acquired a special flock of homing pigeons. They were used to get the early results of chariot races to him!

THE FIRST COCKTAIL WAS MIXED TODAY IN 1776

14 JAN

. . . booze and feathers! The likeliest explanation dated from this day in the American War of Independence when a barmaid named Betsy Flanagan dealt swiftly with a drunken joker. The woozy wit pointed to bantam tailfeathers decorating a tavern in Elmsford, New York, and demanded a glassful of 'them cocktails', giving a coarse reason for their effect on his virility. It's said Betsy served the poor sot a mixture of various liquors and crammed the feathers in as well. A crowd of rowdy US militia mocked the man until he swallowed the awful concoction – and the term 'cocktail' became army slang for any combination of alcoholic beverages.

The Anglo-Irish philosopher George Berkeley died on this day in 1753. The great churchman fell into the habit of placing his speeches on the lectern about thirty minutes before his audience gathered so he could enter without carrying notes. An envious colleague sneakily removed his final page. Berkeley's address went well until he reached the bottom of the preceding page: 'And so, my friends, as Adam might have said to Eve . . .' For a moment he searched vainly for the missing last page, then continued 'As Adam might have said to Eve – there seems to be a leaf missing.'

Off to Wonderland went Lewis Carroll on this day in 1898 – his real name: Charles Lutwidge Dodgson, a portmanteau personality – open as Carroll, closed behind the armour of Dodgson. He looked for glamour in the prosaic. He once saw an entrancing sign he thought said 'Romancement'. Only to find, upon getting nearer, it read 'Roman Cement'.

A fifty-foot-high wave swept over the north end of Boston, Massachusetts, killing twenty-one people on this day in 1919. The single giant wave travelled at thirty-five miles per hour and covered eight buildings. It happened because a huge ninety-foot storage tank burst, releasing its contents – twenty-seven million pounds of gooey, sweet molasses! So as not to get too sickly about this, let's just say the folks came to a sticky end and forget about it.

15 JAN

The British Museum opened its doors on this day in 1759 in Montague House. The present building, immediately behind, wasn't begun until seventy-four years later. Among the earliest exhibits were socks which belonged to King Henry VIII, said to have been 'knitted' for him by Queen Catherine of Aragon, his first wife. Now lost, they are said to have measured forty inches in length! Magnificent – but a wee bit tight under the arms.

EMMA, LADY HAMILTON DIED ON THIS DAY IN 1815.

It was after one night with her that Nelson immediately named his ship *Victory*.

Civil rights hero Martin Luther King was born on this day in 1929 in Atlanta, Georgia, USA. He was assassinated in Memphis, Tennessee, on 4 April 1968. The 1964 Nobel peace Prize-winner said, 'I want to be the white man's brother, not his brother-in-law.'

Two years after narrowly missing a gold medal in the marathon at the 1964 Tokyo Olympics, Japanese athlete Kokichi Tsubmaya committed hara kiri from the shame of letting down his country. Sad, eh? I prefer the tale of the Jewish kamikaze pilot. He crashed his plane into his brother's scrapyard.

16 JAN

Today in 1936 a note was delivered to Edward, Prince of Wales, as he was shooting with friends in Windsor Great Park. His mother wrote of the illness of his father, King George, who had caught cold, 'I think you ought to know that Papa is not very well.' Edward returned to Fort Belvedere and handed the discouraging news to a lady friend, Mrs Wallis Simpson. On 20 January, four days after the urgent note, the royal physician Lord Dawson admitted to the world that 'The King's life is moving peacefully towards its close'. The national anthem rang out across Britain but the words – 'Long to reign over us' – were hardly prophetic. King Edward VIII – the jogging, penny-pinching, Buick-driving, $10\frac{1}{2}$-stone, joke-loving monarch had Lloyd's of London quoting odds against there being a queen to crown at his 1937 coronation of twenty to one. On 10 December, erratic Edward made his abdication speech. George VI became king, and a bewildered Princess Elizabeth was repeating, 'But what happened to Uncle David?'

'TIME,
GENTLEMEN,
PLEASE!'

– and the booze was banned today in 1919 as US prohibition began. (Sixty years later a survey revealed that the USA has more teetotallers – 32 per cent of the population – than any other country in the world!) The passing of the Eighteenth Amendment gave birth to an alcoholic orgy of long cars, pure jazz, Chicago 'typewriters' and bosoms that flattened to feature sensational legs in flapper fashions. As Canada went dry, except for wayward Quebec, Germany banned schnapps and even Russia stopped vodka production.

This was the 1706 birthday of Benjamin Franklin. Joe Hickman says, 'Ben thought he was smart when he discovered electricity . . . but he wasn't half as smart as the guy who discovered the meter.'

Sir William Beatty, the naval surgeon who operated on Nelson at Trafalgar, kept the bullet which killed our most famous admiral – and on this day he had it mounted in gold as a souvenir. It was inscribed, 'Would that this were yet in the enemy's chamber and Nelson still in Emma's.'

17 JAN

'SCARFACE' AL CAPONE

was born on this day in 1899 . . . in Naples, Italy. He was jailed in 1931 for income tax evasion and died on 25 January 1947, of VD. Al invented the game of Mafia Roulette. Three hats are floating in fresh cement and you bet money on which one has a corpse under it.

King Henry VIII fell off his horse today in 1536. The forty-four-year-old monarch toppled off while jousting and was unconscious for two hours. It was considered 'a miracle he was not killed'. Some experts believe the accident triggered off Henry's mental instability. He wore the same clothes for ten weeks after the fall, refusing to change into clean linen. (I suppose he could have pleaded insanitary.)

This evening in 1954 Marcel Grosse was arrested in Tangiers while directing a film about a bank robbery. During the filming, Grosse had actually robbed the bank! The Algerian film maker confessed that the film (his fourth) had been contrived as a cover for the £70,000 theft!

Captain Scott reached the South Pole today in 1912. He kept a stiff upper lip. With weather like that, it was easy. Not to mention a brittle nose.

18 JAN

LONDON'S A. A. MILNE WAS BORN TODAY IN 1882

It was when he had a house by the sewage works that he wrote his famous book *The House at Pooh Corner*. Literature could celebrate this birthday but only mourn the same date forty-four years later when . . .

Rudyard Kipling died on this day in 1936. T. S. Eliot called him 'a laureate without laurels . . . a neglected celebrity'. Perhaps the artful polish of his artistry conceals his uncertainties and subtle intuitions in finished exactness. Orwell said he worshipped Kipling at thirteen, loathed him at seventeen, enjoyed him at twenty, despised him at twenty-five – 'and now again rather admire him. The one thing that was never possible . . . was to forget him.' Fascinating to me is a comment by Sir George Younghusband, who served many years with soldiers but had 'never heard the words or expressions that Kipling's soldiers used.' Nor did his brother officers know of them. 'But sure enough, a few years later, the soldiers thought, talked and expressed themselves exactly like Rudyard Kipling had taught them in his stories . . . Rudyard Kipling made the modern soldier!'

Muhammad Ali won his fight to be born today in 1942. On this same day in 1887, the mighty John L. Sullivan surprised his many fans by fighting six rounds with Patsy Cardiff and only achieving a draw. Only afterwards did they learn that Sullivan had boxed all six rounds with a broken arm!

The creator of the first detective story was born today in 1809. Edgar Allan Poe, author of 'The Murders in the Rue Morgue', had the tale published in *Graham's Magazine* in April 1841, and launched a new genre, inspiring Arthur Conan Doyle, Agatha Christie and scores of other writers to compose detective fiction. I'm trying something new. I'm reading a murder mystery backwards! I already know the butler did it . . . now I can hardly wait to find out who he did it to!

LUCILLE BALL MAKES TV HISTORY

She had a son *on* screen . . . and *off* . . . today in 1953! Desi Arnaz the Fourth was born at the same time as 'I Love Lucy' revealed the birth of 'little Ricky Ricardo'. Too good to be true? Not for a shrewd old trouper like Lucy. She knew the value of great publicity – *and* the accuracy of Caesarean birth. As for outstanding babes . . .

Dolly Parton was born today in 1946 at Sevierville, Tennessee; a sweet and talented little country girl who's been blown all out of proportion.

JAMES WATT WAS BORN IN SCOTLAND TODAY IN 1736

He invented the first efficient steam engines in 1769 and was the first man to use a steam engine to turn a wheel. He was twice arrested for 'flashing' in the streets of Glasgow and gave his name as John Wick! (I was arrested for flashing once. The case was dropped because of insufficient evidence).

19 JAN

20 JAN

King George V died on this day in 1936. Next evening, his body was carried the slow half-mile to the Church of St Mary Magdalene in a plain wooden coffin hewn from Sandringham oak. His son and very temporary successor, Edward, had no overcoat to keep out the rain. Mrs Wallis Simpson persuaded him to wear his father's fur topcoat. During the funeral Edward found a note in the pocket in King George's handwriting; it read: 'Red Romany, 3.30, Brighton' – the name of a horse the king had intended to back before he fell ill. The record books reveal the sad fact – it won at eight to one!

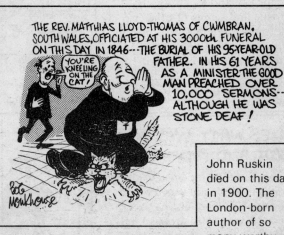

THE REV. MATTHIAS LLOYD-THOMAS OF CWMBRAN, SOUTH WALES, OFFICIATED AT HIS 3000th FUNERAL ON THIS DAY IN 1846 --- THE BURIAL OF HIS 95-YEAR-OLD FATHER. IN HIS 61 YEARS AS A MINISTER THE GOOD MAN PREACHED OVER 10,000 SERMONS -- ALTHOUGH HE WAS STONE DEAF!

YOU'RE KNEELING ON THE CAT!

John Ruskin died on this day in 1900. The London-born author of so many worthy works on art and social problems (*Modern Painters*, 1843–60; *Letters to the Workmen and Labourers of Great Britain*, 1871–84) had quite a nice line in sly wit. In an inaugural address at Cambridge School of Art he said, 'For myself, I am never satisfied that I have handled a subject properly till I have contradicted myself at least three times!'

'Big Daddy' Idi took over Uganda on this day in 1971 . . . in a coup d'état deposing President Milton Obote. By December 1980, Obote was back in power while Amin fretted in Libyan exile, saying that he foresaw another coup d'état. 'Well,' he sang, 'Ah taught Ah taw a coup d'état!'

King Louis XVI was guillotined on this day in 1793. The next in line – King Louis Philippe – who had been living in a one-room flat over a bar in Philadelphia and then had joined the army of the French Revolution, promptly deserted. In 1830, he was crowned the 'Citizen King'.

The English critical biographer Lytton Strachey died on this day in 1932, aged fifty-one. His final words were, 'If this is dying then I don't think much of it.'

TODAY IS ST VINCENT'S DAY

the patron saint of wine growers. He frowned upon Giuseppe Massmann and Benito Gatio who were accused of making and selling a totally phoney wine today in 1968. It was flavoured with all sorts of rotten fruit from Rome's street markets – dates, figs, bananas, even marrows and beans – then coloured with cochineal, clarified, neutralized and boosted with neutral spirit. They sold millions of bottles of the stuff throughout Italy for thirteen years! It was what you might call 'Little David' wine . . . three glasses and you Goliath down.

Buddy Holly made his last recordings on this day in 1959 – in a New York hotel room, on the same Ampex recorder he always used. None of Buddy's work was ever recorded in a studio.

22 JAN

The first commercial TV station west of the Mississippi opened today in 1947. Where else but Hollywood? Their first commercial was for a dog food called Woof ('Dogs ask for it by name')!

This is the day in 1596 on which Sir Walter Raleigh did *not* introduce tobacco into England. It's also the day on which he didn't introduce potatoes as well! Potatoes had already been cultivated in Italy and Cyprus and a botanist named Starling brought them to his Sussex garden in the early 1590s. As for Raleigh's famous Virginia tobacco, a Frenchman had started everyone smoking twenty-six years before in 1560. His name was Jean Nicot – and that's why we call it nicotine. Do you read all these reports that smoking can wreck your health? Made me so nervous I'm up to five packets a day. I smoke two and cough three.

THE ADVOCATE

daily newspaper of Barbados, ran this ad today in 1975: 'To the person who stole my car – you have my deepest sympathy.'

23 JAN

The biggest blue whale on record swam into the Panama Canal today in 1922. She wandered in accidentally from a cruise of the Caribbean and was killed with machine guns because her amazing size – ninety-eight feet long – was a real danger to shipping! Later, superstitious sailors swore they heard the whale's mate forlornly searching the seas and singing, 'Blubber, Come Back to Me' . . .

EDOUARD MANET WAS BORN TODAY IN 1882, IN PARIS

He painted joyously free from sterile conventions, often shocking subjects ('Le Déjeuner sur l'herbe'); his beautiful 'Rue Mosnier aux drapeaux' went for £480 in 1898 – sixty years later it fetched £113,000. I had a great idea for an art school. You don't paint the nude models, you trace them!

The man who wrote *Fanny Hill* died on this day in 1789. John Cleland wrote his classic of erotic literature while in debtors' prison, from 1748 to 1749. I've got nothing against sexual licence. I just don't know where to get one.

In the USA this is National Handwriting Day. The greatest handwriting expert in criminal history was named Hans Inck! He assisted the German police in over a hundred cases – then was arrested for forgery. He wound up in the pen I suppose.

SIR WINSTON CHURCHILL DIED ON THIS DAY IN 1965

He claimed his secret of hypnotizing both sides of the House of Commons was the length of his cigar ash. MPs became transfixed during Winnie's speeches as he puffed on a stogie and spoke at length, a four-inch ash slowly forming and remaining in place in defiance of gravity. Years later he confessed his private trick . . . a hat pin thrust through the length of the cigar.

24 JAN

The first beer in cans was sold today in 1935 . . . in Richmond, Virginia, by the Krueger Brewing Company of Newark, New Jersey. I once asked a waiter in the Beverly Hills Hotel, 'Do you serve beer in the can?' He said, 'No, but you can take it in there with you if you like.'

GOLD!

was discovered at Sutter's Mill, California, today in 1848. At the time of writing, gold has a value of around £250 an ounce. Remarkably, however, all the gold ever mined on this poor old planet would only fill a five-storey office building. That's less than two trillion dollars worth. Contrary to general belief, this gold strike was far from being America's first. A gold nugget was found in the Reed Mine, Cabarrus County, North Carolina, in 1799, the size of a 'small smoothing iron' . . . but no one knew it was gold for twelve years. The owner had used it as a paper weight!

The mad Roman Emperor Caligula was assassinated today in AD 41. His last words were, 'I am still alive!' He was right, but not for long.

TODAY
IS
BURNS
DAY...

celebrating the birth of Robert Burns in 1759 (Ayrshire) – 21 July 1796; Rossetti wrote of him, 'Burns of all poets is most a man.'

On this day in 1555 Nostradamus published his first three *Centuries* – and was summoned to Paris by Henry II and Queen Catherine to explain a quatrain predicting the death of the king. Century 1, quatrain 35 ran, 'The Young Lion shall overcome the old in single combat. He will pierce his eyes in their gilded cage . . . cause his cruel death.' Four years later in 1559 King Henry II, his emblem a lion, jousted with Montgomery, young captain of his Scottish guard. Montgomery's lance pierced the king's eye through a gold visor. He died in agony.

25
JAN

An American study of fatal heart attacks in Japan came out today in 1976. It revealed that 80 per cent of the victims died immediately after, or during, extra-marital intercourse. And a third of them were drunk. My wife said, 'If I catch you in bed with another woman I shall leave you.' I said, 'It's a deal!'

Scarface died on this day in 1947, aged forty-eight. Born in Naples, Al Capone dominated organized crime in Chicago from 1925 until he was caught and jailed in 1931. According to *The Guinness Book of Records*, Capone holds the record for the 'highest gross income ever achieved in a single year by a private citizen'. In 1927 he made $105 million! He had the rich man's curse . . . piles of gold.

The first baby sitters' insurance policy was issued today in 1950 – protecting the Missouri Employment Service against fraud and dishonesty on the part of babysitters placed in jobs around St Louis, by the frequently sued company. The Morgenthaus of Piedmont Drive had good reason to sue. Their fifteen-year-old babysitter, Mary Beth Keach, was left alone with baby Joseph for three hours long enough for Mary Beth's boyfriend, sixteen-year-old Ray Languedoc, to drive his removal van up to the Morgenthaus' bungalow, load their entire home into it and vanish, leaving only a naked Joseph behind on the bare floor. When the cops caught Mary Beth and Ray, he told them, 'She wanted to kidnap the kid too but we neither of us knew how to feed it so we just took its clothes.'

26 JAN

Baird gave the first demonstration of TV in Soho, London, today in 1926. I wonder what he'd think of his invention today. Last night I saw a programme that openly flaunted killings, beatings, violence and sex. I think it was called 'News at Ten'.

WHEN CANADIAN FARMER'S WIFE JAN STOREY FOUND HER HUSBAND'S HOME-MADE WINE TOO SWEET AND STRONG, SHE POURED IT AWAY IN THEIR GARBAGE BIN. CITIZENS OF LA BALLE TOWNSHIP SAW AN UNUSUAL SIGHT IN THEIR MAIN STREET TODAY IN 1932 --- A DRUNKEN GRIZZLY BEAR WEARING A GARBAGE BIN ON ITS HEAD !

IT'S NOT CALLED THE STENCH... IT'S CALLED THE BOUQUET...

BOB MONKHOUSE

The Cape Kennedy tragedy happened on this day in 1967. Three astronauts – Chaffee, Grissom and White – died in a ball of fire in their spacecraft. But the US space programme went on to the 1969 triumph when Aldrin and Armstrong walked on the moon on 20 July, 250,000 miles above the earth. Of course in coke-snorting circles this is known as hedge hopping.

27 JAN

Mozart was born today in 1756. I never buy his records. I'd rather get Brahms and Liszt!

Today in 1948 General MacArthur's man in Japan weighed a whale. Lieutenant Colonel Winston C. Waldon of the US Army, representing MacArthur and in charge of the 1st Fleet of the 1947/8 Japanese Antarctic Whaling Expedition, had an eighty-nine-foot female blue whale weighed piecemeal on board the factory ship *Hashidate Maru*. It tipped the scales at 300,707 pounds – that's over 134 tons. Or the equivalent in weight of 4,800,000 mice!

28 JAN

SIR FRANCIS DRAKE

died on this day in 1596, aged fifty-six. His achievements included circumnavigating the world ('Funny,' said Bernie Winters, 'it didn't look Jewish.') and defeating the Spanish Armada in 1588. He was struck in the ear by a Spanish musket ball and his deaf condition came to be known by the phrase 'Armada hearing'.

US journalist Robert Benchley arrived in Venice today in 1921 and cabled home: 'Streets full of water. Please advise.'

King Henry VIII died on this day in 1547 . . . still chuckling as he recalled the day Anne Boleyn said, 'Henry, ever had a tune running through your head and you just can't get rid of it?' – and Henry said, 'I can fix that.'

SHUDDER TIME !

On this morning – at 3 a.m. precisely – a man named Charles Davies died. He was on holiday at his sister's home in Leicester. His sister phoned his house in Leeds to tell Mrs Davies the sad news and was told that Charles Davies's wife had also died that same morning. The time of death – 3 a.m. precisely. Weird, eh? I'm used to uncanny events and deep trances ever since I started having a nightly communion with a departed person in the spirit world . . . Johnny Walker.

The Victoria Cross was instituted today in 1856. The first ones were made from guns captured from the Russians in the Crimean War. The first man to win the VC was Lieutenant Charles Lucas of the Royal Navy who threw a live shell overboard from the warship *Hecla* during the bombardment of Bomarsund in Finland. Fewer than 1400 Victoria Crosses have been awarded. Ken Dodd thinks his dad ought to have been given one of them for his courage in making scores of low-flying missions, strafing and dropping bombs on Berlin: 'The Germans used to go mad . . . well, this was 1957.'

The great American revolutionary was born today – in Thetford, England. Author of *Common Sense*, Thomas Paine was born in 1737 but went to America in 1774. He wrote, 'People don't plan to fail – they just fail to plan.'

Today in 1801 Cleopatra's Needles were rediscovered in Alexandria. Ours came to the Thames Embankment, London, in 1878. The other went to Central Park, New York City, in 1880. Isn't it strange to think they were a gift from Egypt? Even in those days the Arabs were giving us the needle.

29 JAN

SAMUEL PEPYS

went to see a play: 'Sitting in a darkened row a lady spat backwards and hit me. After seeing her to be a very pretty lady, I was not troubled at all . . .'

30 JAN

Charles I got it in the neck on this day in 1649. And this seems to be a fateful day for knocking off our leaders because . . .

Adolf Hitler was named chancellor of Germany in 1933, Seven years later, on this same day in 1940, he told a huge crowd at the Berlin Sportpalast, 'It is no use serving grass to lions. It makes them hungrier still!' How true. And it's no use serving baked beans on a cavalry charge. It frightens the horses.

US President Andrew Jackson was murderously attacked today in 1835. The would-be assassin was Richard Lawrence who believed that he was King Richard III and hated Jackson for claiming his lands. And as if that wasn't crazy enough . . .

Mahatma Gandhi was assassinated on this day in 1948. Asked Gandhi's first name in a quiz game, comedian Frank Carson suggested, 'Goosey-goosey?'

SUPERMAN'S ARCH ENEMY IS LEX LUTHOR.

He was born in the comic strip today in 1955 (thanks to Mort Weisinger) on the very same day as the film star who portrays him in the movies 'Superman' and 'Superman 2', Gene Hackman! Gene was born today in 1931 at San Bernardino, California. While in the Marines, he was demoted three times for disobedience. He likes the 'Superman' films and says, 'Superman *has* to be fast. That costume has no zipper.'

The first chimp went up into space in 1961. The launch was a little hairy.

Guy Fawkes was executed on this day in 1606. The thirty-six-year-old Yorkshireman tried to avenge the enforcing of penal laws against the Catholics by conspiring to blow up the Houses of Parliament while James I was meeting his chief ministers upstairs, 'The cellars looked like a badly run steakhouse,' said comedy writer Wally Malston. 'Full of angry Beefeaters searching for "forks"!'

31 JAN

The lions came to Trafalgar Square today in 1867. The four great bronze figures at the base of Nelson's Column were completed by the foremost English animal painter, Sir Edwin Landseer, despite failing health. Pigeons are very observant; as soon as the lions were unveiled they spotted them.

The US government ordered all Sioux Indians on to reservations on this day in 1876 – sparking off the Sioux Wars. Dan O'Day comments, 'The government said it wasn't exploiting the Indians; it was *civilizing* them . . . just like we use DDT today to civilize the birds!'

FEELING SEXY?

You've got a slim chance! Today in 1977 *Environment* magazine announced that you use up to 300 calories during the average 'romantic interlude' – and up to twelve calories in a passionate kiss! So you *can* lose weight having a quick nibble.

1 FEB

The world's most prestigious crossword was first published in *The Times* this morning in 1930. Jasper Carrott says he deeply impresses fellow passengers on the train by completing it in four to five minutes. Then he alights leaving his *Times* behind – so they can puzzle over words like ZNNPAFF and KRXDDOT!

February was the invention of the Roman King Numa Pompilius. The name derives from the Latin 'Februare' – to purify – and 'Februa', a festival of purification held on February 15. This is Purification Day for ancient Egyptians too . . . so if you know any ancient Egyptians, try scrubbing them down with a drop of Dettol in the tub.

ALEXANDER SELKIRK WAS DISCOVERED TODAY IN 1708...

. . . cast away on Juan Fernandez Island. His experiences later inspired the story of Robinson Crusoe. You may remember William Cowper's immortal poem about him:

> I am monarch of all I survey,
> My island is ordered and tidy,
> And I'm working a four-day week,
> 'Cause my work is all done by Friday!

The 'king' was born today in Cadiz. Not a Spanish monarch. This was in Cadiz, Ohio, USA – and his realm was Hollywood. Clark Gable was to be christened William when he was born today in 1901. He's in so many BBC 2 midnight movies, he keeps more people up than takeaway curry.

The Germans capitulated at Stalingrad on this day in 1943. They said, 'We'd rather die than go on fighting.' The Russians said, 'Funnily enough, that was your exact choice.'

The *Flying Scotsman* ran 186 miles in 31 hours 33 minutes 37 seconds – without a single rest break! Max Telford was born on this day in 1935 at Hawick in Scotland. He developed his running endurance in New Zealand and staged the greatest nonstop run ever recorded at Wailuku, Hawaii, from 19 to 20 March 1977. Later in the same year he ran 5110 miles in under 107 days, from Anchorage, Alaska, to Halifax, Nova Scotia. Robert Orben says, 'If you want to run ten miles a day, it's easy. All you have to do is put something around the edge of your shorts . . . lace.'

Wooden money was issued in Tenino, Washington, USA, today in 1932. They were twenty-five-cent, fifty-cent and one-dollar tokens printed on spruce and cedar wood, an emergency form of scrip to keep Tenino depositors in business after the local bank folded. What a great idea for the 1980s! If you haven't enough to pay your heating bills, at least you've got money to burn.

Today in 1967 George Humphrey, former US secretary of the Treasury, was reported in *Look* magazine as saying, 'It's a terribly hard job to spend a billion dollars and get your money's worth.'

Two Swiss mountaineers conquered the north face of the Matterhorn in the first successful winter attempt on this day in 1962. Oddly enough, one of them was named Lyons and, when he fell during the descent, he tumbled over and over for 150 feet (but was unharmed). And if you think I've got the nerve to wonder if this was the world's biggest Lyons Swiss Roll, you are absolutely right.

3 FEB

Thomas Carlyle died on this day in 1881. He said, 'If you can't bite, don't growl.'

Manchester's first waxworks exhibition opened this morning in Market Street. From all over Lancashire, thousands came to see effigies of the duke of Cumberland 'sitting in his regimentals', the actress Peg ('Of Old Drury') Woffington and 'divers Royal personages, beasts and curiosityes'. The proprietor's name was John Melter! (No one could hold a candle to him.)

Today in 1925 Gloria Swanson became the first big movie star to marry a titled foreigner. She chose Henri, Marquis de la Falaise de la Coudraye – an interpreter – and wired her studio, 'Am arriving with the Marquis tomorrow morning stop please arrange ovation.'

The American Boy Scouts were formed in 1910, just three years after Robert Baden-Powell founded the first group in England. So teenage gangs of boys with knives are nothing new.

4 FEB

The ancient Greeks shared at least one problem with us. On this day in 1957 tablets were excavated from the ruins of Chios. They were used to display warnings to the pre-Christian litterbugs, telling them not to drop rubbish in public places 'lest they incur the wrath of the nymphs'! Archaeologists digging in Herculaneum, near ancient Pompeii, uncovered an equally enlightening clue about the ancient Romans – over 900 Roman pub signs. That recalls a delightful sketch by Canada's Wayne and Shuster. In a bar in ancient Rome a customer orders a Martinus. The bartender says, 'Don't you mean Martini?' 'If I wanted two,' growls the customer, 'I'd ask for them.'

Today in 1899 the waffle iron was patented in Britain . . . for people who had wrinkled waffles.

BRRR!

It was cold today in 1947! How cold was it? Well, it was so cold that when Eskimos rubbed noses it was only because they were trying to light a fire. At a Snag River trading post in the Yukon, Canada recorded its lowest-ever temperature – 81 degrees below zero. But every Canadian Mountie was still determined to get his man – mostly hoping for a warm cuddle.

The Yalta Conference began on this day in 1945. Churchill growled, 'Nothing annoys a politician so much as the discovery that other politicians are playing with politics.'

Today is the anniversary of the Mexican constitution of 1917. I've eaten their enchiladas and drunk their tequila – and, by god, I've wished I had a Mexican constitution!

There was no need to count on your friends after this day in 1850, when Frank S. Baldwin patented the adding machine. It was twenty inches high and weighed eight and a half pounds. Nowadays, thanks to the microchip, it's the little things that count.

Prehistoric bones were dredged up off the Danish coast of Zeeland today in 1978 – an incredible 240,000 years old! That makes them 200,000 years older than Neanderthal man and 150,000 years older than Cro-Magnon. And nearly twenty years older than Les Dawson's material.

Today is the birthday of Sir Robert Peel in 1788. He organized our first proper police force, and dishonest men trembled at the thought of being caught by the peelers.

5 FEB

The first load of guano was imported from Peru to Bristol in 1833 – for use as a fertilizer. Guano is a rich deposit of bird and bat droppings which builds up in caves or on rock where no rain falls to wash it away. That was the first load of crap to come across the Atlantic. These days we get a load on TV nearly every night.

6 FEB

A BEA aircraft crashed on take off in Munich – killing twenty-three passengers, including eight Manchester United football players – on this day in 1958. Within ten years of the tragedy, Manchester United had recovered brilliantly, then to become a safe target for comedians once more with a poor 1969 season. George Roper was able to tell club audiences, 'They're at Old Trafford this Saturday . . . and it's an all-ticket match. Five for a shilling. Sir Matt Busby saw me there the other week. He said, "Are you staying to the end of the match, George?' I said, "Yes." He said, "There's the keys – lock up!"'

Queen Elizabeth II succeeded to the throne today in 1952. What a very royal occasion the coronation was – and what a gasp of admiration went up as the young queen literally *glided* into Westminster Abbey. No one had been expecting the skateboard.

King Charles II died on this day in 1685. He sired at least fourteen illegitimate kids, only one by Nell Gwynn. He was sardonic, robust and particular about the women he made love to. They had to be awake.

US President Ronald Reagan was born today in 1911. In his Warner Brothers studio dressing room he had a decorative sampler which read, 'Swallow your pride occasionally. It's non-fattening.' Isn't it weird that if he were still a film actor, he'd be too old to *play* the president?

Freddie Trueman's secret – revealed in the *Daily Express* by Jeremy Beadle – was to ensure the stump holes were well watered so when he hit them they would cartwheel through the air. Yorkshire's bluntly funny cricket star was born today in 1931. He told a Leeds audience, 'I've given up cricket for sex . . . because the scoring's easier and you don't have to change shoes.'

7 FEB

The ice cream cornet was introduced in Britain today in 1912 . . . after being a wafer a while.

The world's laziest man died on this day in 1905 in Bristol, aged eighty-two. Tom Oaksby never worked, never walked further than the nearest pub and spent forty-seven years in bed! The only reason he snored was that he couldn't get anyone to do it for him.

Skin Pix went automatic today in 1875, when Sam O'Reilly of New York City introduced the first tattooing machine. Comedian Stan Stennett said he'd always wanted to marry the fat tattooed lady in a circus: 'I'd have warmth in the winter, shade in the summer – and moving pictures all the year round.'

If it's wet, boiled, fried, brewed, pulled by a barmaid, tossed by a cook or laid by a hen – he'll eat it! England's human garbage disposal unit set another one of his highspeed consumption records today in 1975. Already the holder of *every* beer-drinking record, Peter Dowdeswell of Earl's Barton is also the world's champion pancake eater and hardboiled egg swallower. On this anniversary he downed two litres of beer in only six seconds! What a pedal bin! If you trod on his foot, the top of his head would fly open!

TODAY IS INDEPENDENCE DAY IN GRENADA

– what the Communists might call 'a chip off the old bloc'. As the tiny Russian-influenced Caribbean island accepts 200,000 tourists each year and also experiences 200 inches of rain per annum, they should know plenty about the old Communist preoccupation . . . soaking the rich.

8 FEB

Mary, Queen of Scots, got axed on this day in 1587. One of the biggest history mysteries surrounds her 'sealed box'. Mary's young husband, Darnley, was murdered in 1567 and only three months later she married the man suspected of the crime, the earl of Bothwell. Her jewel box of love letters, discovered under a servant's bed, was said to provide clear evidence, in Mary's own handwriting, that she was involved in both the murder plot and an adulterous affair with Bothwell. True or false? No one knows for sure. Mary's son was pretty busy on this date too when . . .

KING JAMES I DISSOLVED PARLIAMENT TODAY IN 1622

He was the first monarch of England to use a fork. And, according to an entry in *The People's Almanac 2* he was once so delighted with a loin of beef served to him at dinner that he knighted it and then said, 'Arise, Sir Loin.'

D. W. Griffith's film masterpiece 'The Birth of a Nation' was released today in 1915. Allowing for inflation and rising costs, it's the biggest moneymaker in movie history – and Hollywood's greatest embarrassment, with its frank hostility towards black Americans and its portrayal of the Ku Klux Klan as heroes. It was the first film ever screened at the White House. Eighteen actors were killed during the filming of the violent epic. Griffith said, 'We would have killed more but we had a film to make.'

Feodor Vassilyev's youngest child was born this morning in 1765 – it was his sixty-ninth! Feodor, a peasant from Shuya in Russia, had a wife who kept having multiple births – quadruplets four times, triplets seven times and sixteen pairs of twins. Out of her total production of sixty-nine babies, nearly all survived to adulthood.

9 FEB

The Devil's footprints appeared overnight in South Devon and were seen in 100 miles of tracks today in 1855! The inexplicable prints of a cloven hoof wove their way over fields, walls, rooftops – even haystacks. *The Times* of 16 February reported, 'Considerable sensation has been evoked in the towns of Topsham, Lympstone, Exmouth, Teignmouth and Dawlish, in the south of Devon, in consequence of the discovery of a vast number of foot-tracks of a most strange and mysterious kind.' Heavy snow had fallen overnight. In the morning the clearly defined hoofprints were found, each 4 inches by $2\frac{3}{4}$ inches, $8\frac{1}{2}$ inches apart, each in a *single line*! Birds couldn't have left these baffling steps which appeared 'clear as if . . . branded with a hot iron'. Otters, rats, badgers, seals, even a kangaroo – all manner of creatures were suggested but no known agent could account for the 100-mile path that local folks believed was walked by Satan himself one frosty night over 125 years ago.

'The most discreet travel agency' was opened today in 1955 in Tokyo, Japan. To attract only the most discerning and refined clientele, proprietor Hideki Yomonaga offered the most delicately phrased descriptions of the travel facilities and hotels in a tasteful brochure. When a tourist asked why he had been booked into a guesthouse other than the one he had requested, he received a charming letter from Yomonaga himself: 'My firm would prefer not to send such an honoured client as yourself to this inn. It is a hotel more suitable for use as a temporary rest-house for an instant couple.'

10 FEB

John Goode died on this day in 1883 . . . famous for not being the king of England, although he remained quite sure that he was. That's why his throne room was in Broadmoor Asylum. Me, I've always believed in that great saying, 'Never be ashamed of who you really are.' I'd like to tell you who said it, but it's anonymous.

GENERAL MARRIES BENEATH HIM!

Charles Lamb was born today in 1775. A punniac (that's a punning maniac), he quipped, 'Punsters are made not born, because people can't bear them.'

Lavinia Warren was three inches shorter than the bridegroom on this, her wedding day in 1863. And that took some doing because he was claimed to be exactly 2 feet 11 inches tall. You've guessed it . . . it was the marriage of P. T. Barnum's world-famous circus star 'General' Tom Thumb. Joe Hickman comments, 'They saved money at the reception by standing on the cake themselves.'

11 FEB

Soviet spies Guy Burgess and Donald Maclean appeared in Moscow today in 1956 after their escape from the UK – 'Proving that daisies may not tell,' said Max Bygraves, 'but pansies do.'

This was Ringo Starr's wedding day in 1955 when Maureen Cox became the first person to say, 'Stick with me, Starr, and I'll make you a baby!' (He didn't. They divorced ten years later.) But this wasn't the only big-name marital do on this day, because . . .

This was also Napoleon's wedding day – but it was 'Not tonight Josephine!' The emperor had given Jo the imperial heave-ho for failing to fill the Napoleonic nursery and on this day in 1810 he took unto him Princess Marie Louise, hoping for a son and heir as soon as nature would allow. As comedian Billy Bennett once remarked, 'That night they were hardly a Bonaparte!'

HAPPY BIRTHDAY

to Thomas Alva Edison in 1847. He wanted to give the Statue of Liberty a voice by installing a giant phonograph in the mouth! According to Edward Lucaire, author of *Celebrity Trivia*, Edison ('Popsy Wopsy' to his wife) was highly motivated by money, and once said, 'Anything that won't sell, I don't want to invent.' Before his death, he had been granted 1098 different patents from the US Patent Office, an unbeaten record. Among the things he tried but failed to invent were an electric piano (now commonplace in recording studios and clubs), the cigar lighter (patented by Moses Gale in 1871) and a double-sided bra for girls with saggy shoulder blades.

'Honest Abe' was born today . . . in 1809 in a log cabin on Sinking Spring Farm near Hodgenville, Kentucky, the son of a poor farmer. Assassinated on Good Friday, 1865, it's little known that the sixteenth president of the USA predicted his own death . . . and saw his ghost in a dream on the night before! Lincoln took a strong interest in psychic phenomena after the death of his son Willie and took part in White House seances in an effort to contact him. He had reported corpse-like images of himself in the mirror to his wife and, at a cabinet meeting on 14 April – the day of his murder – he told colleagues of a dream in which he saw himself dead and bound 'toward an indistinct shore'. Only a week previously, in another dream, Lincoln walked the silent corridors of the White House until soft sobbing drew him to a jet-draped coffin. He asked, 'Who is dead?' A guard replied, 'It is the President.' He died aged fifty-six, the first of four American presidents to fall to an assassin's bullet.

Lady Jane Gray gave up being queen of England after only nine days in the job on this day in 1554. She said she just hadn't got the head for it.

The great Australian gold rush began today in 1851 – when nuggets were found at Summerhill Creek. One of the first discoverers of the gold was so frightened of what outlaws would do to him to get his share, he committed suicide. His name was Frank Coward! And he *was* a coward. Some folks say he was such a coward he shot himself in the back.

THIS WAS LANA TURNER'S 1st WEDDING DAY IN 1940...TO SWING'S SUPERSTAR OF THE CLARINET, ARTIE SHAW. THE MARRIAGE DIDN'T LAST...

THEY'RE ARGUING OVER CUSTODY OF THE WEDDING CAKE!

Bobmonkhouse

Machine-gun Jack McGurn was shot to death in Chicago today in 1936. He was one of the four killers in the St Valentine's Day Massacre tomorrow in 1929, when seven members of Bugs Moran's gang were gunned down in a Chigago warehouse. In those days Chigago had a large floating population. Mostly face down in the river.

13 FEB

Jesse James robbed his first bank today in 1866. I checked the cost of my overdraft last week. I think the robbers have taken over the banks.

The first American quintuplets were born today in 1875 . . . to Edna Knaouse of Watertown, Wisconsin, although quins have been claimed for Mars Bluff, South Carolina, in 1776, where a Mrs Walter Tegg was said to have called out four times in the night for her husband to bring the lantern and each time she had a baby girl. The fifth time she called, Walter answered, 'I'll come – but I won't bring the lantern. I think it's the light that's attracting them.'

Beyond our Ken, dear Kenneth Horne left us on this day in 1969. With him, 'Round the Horne' – one of radio's funniest-ever shows – died too. 'Historically,' wrote co-writer Barry Took, '"Round the Horne" was created at a time – 1964 – when most people thought that radio was dead.' Barry and Marty Feldman wrote fifty shows in all, then Barry worked on a further twenty with Donald Webster, Johnnie Mortimer and Brian Cooke. They are all collectors' items. I always prized Ken's closing remarks each week. For example: 'Lastly, a police message. If any passer-by in Lisle Street last Saturday night witnessed a middle-aged man stagger out of the Peeperama Strip Club and get knocked down by a passing cyclist, would you please keep quiet about it as my wife thinks I was in Folkestone.'

Each year on this day, Johnnie and Fanny Craddock exchange braised hearts. 'They've been sweetbreads for years!' explains Barry Cryer.

IT'S GELETINE'S DAY TODAY!

Yes, I know it's supposed to be a special day for lovers inspired by poor old St Valentine but you just look him up. Fat lot *he* ever knew about love! He was a tragic Christian martyr, beheaded on this day – approximately – in the year 270. And, to put it delicately, my researches suggest he had very little to do with the activities of lads and lasses in romantic mood. I don't want to spread any unkind rumours but, back in those days when men were men and women were women, old Val appears to have been a bit of a novelty. No, it's much more likely that this special day celebrates the Norman word 'galentine', a word for ladies' man. I always try to do a little more for my wife on Valentine's Day. Little things, like holding the door open for her when she goes out on her paper round.

15 FEB

The first adhesive stamp was used in the USA today in 1842 by the City Despatch Post, a private concern later acquired by the government for $1200. Just like the British Post Office's adhesive stamp, we've been stuck with it ever since. And if you have a complaint the Post Office will tell you where to stick it.

US President Elect Franklin Delano Roosevelt survived an assassination attempt on this day in 1933. The *New York Times* reported, 'Just after he ended a speech at Bay Front Park, Miami, at 9.35 p.m., the gunman fired, probably fatally wounding Mayor Anton Cermak of Chicago. Four other persons were hit by five shots before a tiny woman seized the man's wrist, deflecting his aim from President-elect Roosevelt'. The *Times*'s fears were well founded. Cermak did not survive the attack by Joe Zingara, who told the police he had attempted to kill King Victor Emmanuel of Italy ten years earlier. On trial, he cried, 'As God is my judge, I should not die for this deed!' And the judge said, 'He isn't. I am and you will.'

THIS WAS DECIMAL CURRENCY DAY IN 1971!

Now the only money that goes as far as it did then is the 10p that rolls under the sideboard.

The first British Parliament of the twentieth century opened today in 1901 – with a new member for Oldham named Winston Churchill. Among his many qualities, Winston had a fantastic memory. Outside the Houses of Parliament stands a large statue to the memory of Winston Churchill. (And to the memory of that joke. May they both rest in peace.)

They auctioned off Joan Crawford's possessions on this day in 1978 . . . bringing in a total of $80,000. One buyer bid $325 for sixty-eight pairs of false eyelashes. Strange to recall how proudly she used to show callers around her house, giving the price of every possession as she guided them along. *Sunday Pictorial* columnist Rex North was one such guest in 1952. He admired Joan's new swimming pool and asked, 'But how do you keep out the riff raff?' 'My dear,' was Joan's reply, 'In Beverly Hills the riff raff have their own swimming pools!'

In Amsterdam on this morning in 1978, Antoni Przbysz petitioned the court for a legal change of his name – to Jacob Przbysz.

The Benevolent and Protective Order of Elks was founded today in 1868 in New York City. Their resident barman invented the hangover cure of two aspirins dissolved in soda water. He may have been the first man to serve an Elk-a-seltzer.

Today in 1961, *Explorer 1* was launched. Personally, I don't believe there is intelligent life on other planets. Why should other planets be any different from this one?

Nylon was patented by a Du Pont Chemical Research team today in 1937. The name 'Nylon' is composed of 'NY' for New York and 'Lon' for London . . . the two cities where it was developed. Within thirteen months the first nylon stockings went on sale. There was a run on them, of course.

17 FEB

They founded the British League of Mothers in the UK today in 1882. Al Burnett of London's Stork Club loved to tell his crowd, 'We're holding a mothers' meeting backstage at midnight. So all you girls who want to become mothers, DON'T . . . BE . . . LATE!'

French ski champ Jean-Claude Killy won his third gold medal at the 1968 Winter Olympics. His fractured English is charming. When blizzards put a temporary stop to his skiing, he said he had been 'winterrupted'. He describes his mania for skiing as 'sloping sickness'.

Witty beauty Prunella Gee was born today in 1950. Before appearing on ATV's 'Celebrity Squares' she showed the producer the blouse she was going to wear. Paul Stewart Laing gaped as she held it up. 'But you can see right through it!' he exclaimed. With genuine female logic Prunella replied 'Not when I'm in it.'

The first ship passed through the Suez Canal today in 1867. As if anticipating future events, the ship's name was HMS *Perilous* and her captain's middle name was Eden!

CHINA INVADED VIETNAM TODAY IN 1979.

Joey Adams says he opened a fortune cookie in a Chinese restaurant. It said, 'Better tip big – we've got the bomb too.'

It was on this evening in 1904 that Winston Churchill dined at the country estate of Lord and Lady Salisbury. Asked by the amorous but elderly hostess how he had enjoyed his stay, he replied, 'If the soup had been as warm as the champagne, and the champagne as old as the chicken, the chicken as plump as the maid, and the maid as willing as you, madam, I should have had an excellent visit.' Well, that's the way I heard it.

Today in 1564 Michelangelo died. It's hard to believe that he painted the Sistine Chapel on his back. I suppose he must have used a mirror.

The first Canadian Lumberjack's Union was founded today in 1862 . . . by a splinter group, I expect.

Thomas Edison patented his phonograph today in 1878 – although he hadn't set out to invent that machine at all! His original intention had been to invent a telegraph repeater and he'd given directions for building it to one of his mechanics the previous August. Tom realized he'd hit upon a moneymaker; the device earned £1 billion in only fifty years! Not a lot? Well, if you had spent £1000 a day every day since the birth of Christ, you still wouldn't have spent £1 billion even now!

They burned Isobel Cockie at the stake in Scotland on this day in 1596. She'd been found guilty of 'twelve points of witchcraft'. One of these was 'materialyzing . . . objekts and eviedence of certaine unknowne matters from the future'. She shouldn't have let them see her flying around on her vacuum cleaner.

19 FEB

GEORGE WASHINGTON WAS BORN ON 12 FEBRUARY TODAY!

Not clear? Let me simplify it for you. The father of the United States of America and the first US president was *actually* born on February 12th in 1732 . . . but when the calendar was revised in 1752, 12 February became 22 February – which is why Americans celebrate his birthday today on 19 February. Got it straight now? No? That makes two of us.

The Mercedes car was named in 1901 – after Mercedes Jellinck, the daughter of a director of the Daimler Company. The new 35-horsepower Cannstatt Daimler was called the Mercedes while the firm's Austrian branch adopted her sister's name for their new item, the Maja. Guess which I bought. In all fairness, my Maja Sedan three-wheeler does do over fifty miles to a gallon. Over fifty miles per gallon! It gets towed a lot.

20 FEB

A nine-year-old boy was crowned king of England today in 1547. He was Edward VI, only child of Henry VIII by his third wife, Jane Seymour. The duke of Somerset's brother used to bribe the young king with pocket money. The earl of Warwick was said to have hypnotized him into a trance and so taken over the court. But the boy king reigned only six and a half years before dying of consumption. Archbishop Thomas Cranmer said, 'So short a life, but he never lost an enemy.'

The first performance of Oscar Wilde's *Lady Windermere's Fan* was given tonight in 1892 and drew applause with the third-act line, 'We are all in the gutter, but some of us are looking at the stars.' Like Nigel Dempster and William Hickey.

WHIRLED AROUND THE WORLD!

The historic orbit made by John Glenn today in 1962. Has it ever occurred to you – an astronaut is the only bloke who's really glad to be down and out?

Who said lightning never strikes twice in the same place? Barnum perhaps, fooling some of the people all of the time? Or 'Evita', Señora Eva Perón, The President of Argentina's second wife who never gave a sucker an even break. Anyway, you'll recall how Eva and her hubby milked Argentina dry, robbing the state-run charities to fill their bottomless Swiss bank accounts? That was way back in the 1950s. Today in 1978 a judge indicted Señora Isabel Perón, Perón's third wife and herself the ex-President of Argentina, for fraudulent use of $8 million from the funds of the state-run charity known as the Solidarity Crusade. But Argentina still owes a lot to the Perón family – ulcers, starvation, headaches . . .

MARY WOLLSTONECRAFT SHELLEY DIED TODAY IN 1851. SHE WROTE 'FRANKENSTEIN'...

IT'S A BOOK ABOUT BODY-BUILDING.

BOG MOUSEHOUSE...

MARY WAS ONLY 20 YEARS OLD WHEN SHE WROTE HER CLASSIC!

This evening in 1966 my first wife said to me, 'I think you ought to go to the doctor. Other men don't come home too tired to argue.'

On this day in 1613 Michael Romanov, son of the patriarch of Moscow, was elected tsar of Russia – and so founded the house of Romanov. When Tsar Michael paid his first official visit to the newly built harbour at Odessa, the streets were swarming with cheering boys and girls, lining the route taken by his coach. 'My goodness,' the tsar cried in wonder, 'where do all these children come from?' 'Your Imperial majesty,' said the mayor, 'we have been preparing for this great day for years.'

21 FEB

Prime Minister Ramsay MacDonald had lunch today in 1931 with Charlie Chaplin. There's a difference between a British prime minister and a clown. A clown acts like an idiot and gets paid a lot for doing it. Whereas . . . on second thoughts, there's no difference.

Group Captain Sir Douglas Bader was born today in 1910. The legless air ace of the RAF in World War II once told BBC radio's Peter Duncan on 'Roundabout', 'There are two types of people . . . those who divide people into two types and those who don't.'

'The Academy of Human Achievement' gave up and collapsed today in 1928. This distinguished 'Society of Scholars' lasted only six years and was also founded on this day in Bloomsbury, London, a curiously significant date for its twenty-two members. They asserted, for example, that Man invented both the wheel and fire on this symbolic day in prehistory. But consider *that* old chestnut for a moment. How could the wheel have been 'invented'? Round objects are natural. Only the axle makes them practical to man's needs. As for fire, poor primitive mankind had enough lighting and volcanic flame to make extinguishers a much more urgent discovery.

Footnote: Listed as a member of this goofy group was G. K. Chesterton, a literary giant who adored eccentrics. Could he have 'invented' the whole thing as a real-life counterpart to his fictional 'Club of Queer Trades'?

22
FEB

Frank W. Woolworth opened his first five-cent store in Utica, New York, today in 1879 – and almost went broke! Then he moved to Lancaster, Pennsylvania, opened a ten-cent store and made millions. Motto: When in debt, change your address and raise your prices. Frank first tried his idea on 24 September 1878, during the country fair in Watertown, New York, by originating a '5 cent table' in the store of Moore & Smith. He knew he was on to something when everyone offered him five cents for the table.

The Reverend Sydney Smith died on this day in 1845. His conclusions about us: 'Man is certainly a benevolent animal. A never sees B in distress without thinking C ought to relieve him directly.'

23 FEB

Today in 1953 US comedian Jack Benny tried to cash a cheque for $50 at a London bank where he wasn't known. He had no identification, and the bank manager said, 'I suppose the only way you can prove you're Jack Benny is by telling me a few jokes. Jack pocketed the cheque. 'If I were to tell you jokes for fifty dollars,' he said, 'you could be sure I wasn't Jack Benny.'

At 5 feet 7 inches, a world heavyweight champ measured up today in 1906. He was Canada's Tommy Burns from Hanover, Ontario – the only one of his countrymen ever to win the title, and the shortest. His regular sparring partner wound up with a cauliflower naval.

Jug-eared Clark Gable took off his shirt, exposed a bare chest – and millions of men stopped wearing undervests! The movie 'It Happened One Night', won Best Actor and Best Actress (Claudette Colbert) Oscars for its stars and opened tonight, across the USA, in 1934. Said Milton Berle, 'Gable's wrecked the US underwear business' but called him 'the best ears of our lives'.

Importing opium was outlawed by the USA today in 1887. Personally, I've never been able to get along with drugs. I tried 'snorting coke' but the straw kept getting stuck up my nose. And I prefer Pepsi anyway.

Henri Landru was executed in France on this day in 1922 – better known as 'Bluebeard'. He was convicted of killing ten of his thirteen fiancées. His last wish was to have his feet washed – but it was refused. Charles Chaplin based his film 'Monsieur Verdoux' upon him, and told biographer Jean-Pierre Malcolm, 'I discovered Landru was homosexual. But then it's only thanks to Adam's rib that we're not all fairies!'

Charles Le Brun was born today in 1619. He was the great French court painter and once, when he was working on a portrait of the ageing Louis XIV, the Sun King suddenly asked him, 'Don't you think I'm looking much older?' Too honest to lie but too smart to tell the truth, Le Brun answered, 'Sire, I can detect only the traces of a few more victorious campaigns on Your Majesty's brow.'

'The world is running ten days late!' said the pope in 1582. And so Pope Gregory produced his new calendar. It took the British 170 years to get around to adopting it. The Russians switched to it in 1917 and the Arabs, Japanese and Chinese are still thinking it over. What hope is there for world peace when half of the nations can't even agree on what day it is? The same problem eventually obsessed a French monarch . . .

The holy Roman emperor was born today in 1500 at Ghent in Flanders. Emperor Charles V killed thousands who refused to conform to his religious beliefs. Defeated, he abdicated and retired to a monastery where he amused himself trying to make twelve clocks run precisely together. Failing again, he said, 'How absurd – to think I could make all men think alike about God when I can't make two clocks agree about time.'

The first rocket was sent into space today in 1949. The Russians hinted that their first satellite would contain cattle but it didn't. Shame. It would have been 'the herd shot around the world'.

Khruschev attacked Stalin in a secret speech at the Communist Party Conference on this day in 1956. As Soviet leader, Joseph Stalin once paid an official visit to his birthplace at Gori. A helpful aide briefed the virtual dictator of all Russia about each man in line to shake his hand. Halfway through, the aide whispered, 'Comrade Premier, the next man is Sergei. He was your teacher in mathematics, geography and history. He once caned you for disobedience. You ran errands for his wife who paid you in biscuits and apples.' So Stalin greeted the man with, 'So, my dear Sergei, one of your pupils at least made good!' Sergei stared at him blankly. 'You taught me the history of our great Mother Russia,' said Stalin. Still no response. 'Don't you remember?' Stalin pleaded, 'You beat me once. I was disobedient. I ran errands for your wife. She gave me biscuits and apples . . .' Remembrance at last dawned on Sergei. 'Oh, yes,' he said. 'The Dzhugashvili's boy. Are you here to meet this madman Stalin too?'

25 FEB

Auguste Renoir was born today in 1841 in Limoges, France. Leader and founder of the French impressionist movement, he was once invited to a dinner party by a pushy and ignorant hostess. He telegrammed, 'Apologize I cannot attend your party tonight. Contrived excuse follows.'

CASSIUS CLAY

hammered Sonny Liston on this day in 1964 – becoming world heavyweight boxing champion. Interviewing Liston, Michael Parkinson commented, 'For a while during that fight I thought you had him scared.' Liston nodded, 'Yeah – that's when he thought he'd killed me.'

COME CLEAN!

They did – today in 1976 – when a survey was released on the world's hygiene habits. Those cleanliness addicts, the US population, did well. Only 3 per cent of Americans do not buy soap. Hey, wait a minute . . . that's six million people! Phew! I'd hate to be stuck in a broken lift on a warm day with those six million gamey Yanks. So which country do you suppose uses more 24-hour anti-perspirants and deodorants than any other? It's Japan – and the men use them more than the women! Personally, I use a 23-hour deodorant. I like an hour to myself every day.

26 FEB

The queen joined a union today in 1976! When Elizabeth II started the new printing presses of the *Daily Express*, she was told that only union members were allowed to operate the machinery – so her majesty joined NATSOPA. Now what happens if they go on strike? Would she have to take industrial action? That's a laugh . . . how can a ruler work to rule? Ted Rogers suggested that she could always withdraw her labour for a while . . . like taking her head off all the stamps.

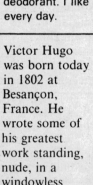

Victor Hugo was born today in 1802 at Besançon, France. He wrote some of his greatest work standing, nude, in a windowless room in Guernsey, his writing paper pinned to the wall! Throughout his prodigious working life, he used to write 100 lines of verse or 20 pages of prose every morning. One piece of his advice I never forget: 'When a woman is talking to you, listen to what she says with her eyes.'

27 FEB

A bird brought London to a standstill – when Goldie the eagle escaped from Regent's Park Zoo today in 1965. Cyril Fletcher said he'd seen it flying overhead – and it spotted Cyril too. 'I think it wanted to buy my hat .... it put a deposit on it.'

The man who discovered the condition reflex, Ivan Pavlov, died today in 1936. The Russian physiologist won a Nobel prize in 1904 for his work on the digestive system. As a private experiment, Ivan secretly lived on only beans for eight weeks but his friends soon got wind of it.

The Indians seized Wounded Knee, South Dakota, today in 1973 . . . and they occupied it for seventy days in protest at the federal treatment of native American redskins. They were led by a great chief. 'Him have ten squaw and forty-five papoose.' They didn't name him Chief Spread Eagle for nothing.

The Central Criminal Court at the Old Bailey was opened today in 1907. In those days the average case took five hours! Today our judges are so far behind in trying cases, if you commit a crime, chances are it'll take you longer to get *into* jail than it will to get *out*.

Many happy returns of the day to Elizabeth Taylor (1932, London), wife of Virginia Senator John Warner, who tells the tale of how he cut himself shaving because he had been thinking about an upcoming speech. 'Well,' said Liz, 'you ought to think about your face and cut your speech.'

On this day in 1618 Maurice of Nassau succeeded as prince of Orange – upon the death of his brother, Philip William. Orange was a bit of Holland then. Now it's a bit of France. You're not going to believe this, giving the k.o. to the House of Orange, a dynasty founded by William the Silent. I don't know who William the Silent was. He didn't say.

The final cuppa in the US? The American Congress, rebelling against unfair taxes, outlawed tea-drinking today in 1775. 'It's wicked stuff,' said Ken Goodwin who claims his brother went blind drinking tea. 'The spoon poked his eye out!'

My late lamented pal, US comedian Zero Mostel, was born today in 1915. An outrageously funny man, he used to drive his car with a ghastly rubber mask fixed to the *back* of his head. Then if a road hog attempted to overtake him at high speed, Zero would lean out of the car window. The overtaking driver would be totally unnerved to see what seemed to be a leering, cross-eyed lunatic staring back at him while still going at over fifty miles per hour!

Today in 1900 they relieved Ladysmith. The British had lost over 1200 men against the Boers' 200 in the Battle of Ladysmith on 30 October the previous year – and the town had been besieged ever since. When General Sir Redvers Buller broke the siege up on this day, the place was in a pretty bad state. People were so hungry, the rats would only go around in pairs. All the population had to eat was stuffed cockroach. Still, at least a family of six could have a leg each.

Finally, the strange story of the grey-eyed Indians of North Carolina. Explorers travelling inland on the Lumber River on this day in 1744 were amazed to come across a tribe of 'Lumbee Indians' with pale eyes, many of them blonde and all speaking a degenerate form of English. Many believed they were descended from Sir Walter Raleigh's 'Lost Colony' which vanished without trace in 1591 from an abandoned fortress less than 200 miles from the Lumber River! I always feel very sorry for the American Indians, don't you? They were the only ones ever to be conquered by the US and not come out ahead.

29 FEB

Gioacchino Antonio Rossini was born today in 1792 in Pesaro, Italy. He wrote thirty-nine operas, including 'The Barber of Seville' in 1816 and 'William Tell' in 1829. When his 1826 opera 'The Siege of Corinth' received a derogatory review, Rossini wrote to the critic: 'Sir, I am sitting in the smallest room of my house. I have your review before me. In a moment it will be behind me.'

Last leap year over sixty girls proposed to me. *Over sixty*! (They were *all* over sixty!)

TODAY IS BACHELOR'S DAY EVERY FOURTH YEAR

But just because it's a leap year doesn't mean you can leap on anyone you fancy.

Quite truthfully, a rather beautiful singer who was a musical stage star really *did* propose to me on this day in 1960. I said I couldn't marry her but I'd always admire her taste.

1 MAR

The Profumo scandal broke on this day in 1963. Exactly forty years earlier, on this same day, another leading politician named John Perryman (same initials as John Profumo) was accused of appropriating Liberal Party funds to build a house for his lady friend. Most senior politicans have an official limousine. What they need is a getaway car.

The whistle blew for Dixie Dean, legendary British footballer, today in 1980. Thousands lined the Birkenhead streets for the funeral of the seventy-three-year-old soccer hero. Many years before jogging became such a fad, Dixie advised me to try it. He watched me guzzling and smoking and flirting with waitresses at a 1960 charity dinner in Blackpool, then told me; 'Bob, you must do more to keep fit. Jog round Stanley Park every morning.' I did, throughout that year's six-month summer season. For what good it did me . . . thanks, Dixie! He also said, 'You burn up the same amount of energy making love as you do jogging round the park.' I asked, 'Why do you want me to waste it jogging?' Dixie replied, 'Because, Sunny Jim, after a couple of laps round the park, at least you don't want a cigarette.'

The first practical typewriter was produced today in 1873 – by E. Remington and Sons, Ilion, New York. It had a lever on it which said 'Firmer Writing'. I want one with a lever that says 'Funnier Writing'.

ST DAVID DIED ON THIS DAY IN 601

It was way back when the Welsh were fighting the Saxons that David devised a way for his soldiers to recognize their own side in battle. He told them to have a leek in their hats.

D. H. Lawrence died on this day in 1930. My grandfather took out a copy of his most controversial novel, *Lady Chatterley's Lover*. The librarian said, 'I thought you never read anything except history.' He said, 'At my age, dearie, this *is* history.'

Gustav Mahler's Eighth Symphony had its American première in Philadelphia tonight in 1916. A 110-piece orchestra, 8 soloists, a 150-member children's chorus, and an 800-member mixed chorus performed the massive work . . . and the critics didn't like it! The critic for the *Philadelphian* was Oscar Fettering, a dwarfish man with a bald head and a high-pitched voice. He told Mahler, 'I express my views as an impartial outsider.' 'In that case,' said the composer, 'you must tell me what you think of the human race.'

2 MAR

General Sam Houston, who led the brilliant victory over Santa Ana for the control of Texas, was born today in 1793. When served his first-ever helping of vanilla ice cream, Houston is reputed to have expostulated, 'Madam, it is not my intention to slander your hospitality, but this here pudding is froze.'

The world's smallest national branch of 'Alcoholics Anonymous' was founded in Luxembourg today in 1948 with only two members. 'Alcoholics Anonymous' – that's a sort of Ad Hic Committee.

CONCORDE

made its maiden flight from Toulouse, France, on this day in 1969. Elaborate precautions had been taken to prevent a skyjack. Everyone was so nervous. Every time the stewardesses opened a bottle of champagne, the pilot changed course.

The *Liverpool Echo* today in 1961 carried the text of the lord mayor's speech on the inauguration of a fluoridation programme, including this classic paragraph: 'Let Liverpool – the first city to appoint a Medical Office of Health – again give a national lead to other great cities by fluoridating her water and let the slogan be, '''What Liverpool drinks today – the rest of the country drinks tomorrow''.'

3 MAR

Apollo 9 set off for its moon landing today in 1969 and for the **first time we heard Houston control counting,** '10-9-8-7 . . .' It was nothing new to me. My wife had been counting her birthdays like that for years.

Bank robbers John Dillinger and Herbert Youngblood escaped from prison on this day in 1934. Dan O'Day asks, 'Have you noticed that criminals seem to be getting younger these days? The other day a mugger came up to me on the street and said, "Give me all your money or I'll hold my breath till I turn blue!"'

A personal birthday greeting to cartoonist Ronald Searle, 1920; I once showed him one of my oil paintings and mentioned how difficult it was to sell them. 'If it's so hard,' Searle advised, 'why don't you try just selling the canvas? I'll give you a note to some tentmakers I know.' That's when I took up telling my jokes instead of drawing them. So, for my gratifying career: thanks, Ronald!

The first electric fans went on sale at Selfridge's in Oxford Street, London, today in 1909. Electric fans do not cool a room, all they do is redistribute the air. In fact, the heat from the fan's motor actually increases the room temperature!

Dan O'Day writes from Fresno, California, to show that 4 March can prove an inspirational day – William Henry Harrison always had the last laugh. People said he'd never make a successful politician, but in 1840 he ran for president of the USA. People said he'd never be elected, but on this day in 1841, he was inaugurated. People said he wasn't made of tough enough stuff to be president, but he dumbfounded them by standing bareheaded throughout the inauguration in a drenching rainstorm. People said he was just a hypochondriac when he caught cold . . . but four weeks later he even proved them wrong about that. He died.

The largest winetasting ever held took place today in 1978 . . . when 1737 lovers of the grape gathered at Nederburg, South Africa, to sample 2012 bottles of wine. My uncle Cliff is a professional winetaster. He's the only man I know who's unsteadily employed.

4 MAR

The world baked bean eating record was set in Petersfield, Hampshire, on this day in 1978 by John Lawrence who consumed 2353 baked beans in thirty minutes. *The Guinness Book of Records* accepted his speed as exceptional despite a following wind.

She carried her victim's head in a black bag . . . and sold her boiled-down remains as dripping to the local pub! Kate Webster, alias Catherine Lawler, was the 'Irish Butcher' tried at the Old Bailey in July 1879, for the grisly murder of her employer, a Mrs Thomas of Richmond. Poor Mrs Thomas's disappearance from her lonely riverside cottage might have gone unavenged but for the chance discovery made on this day in 1879 – the Thames at Hammersmith washed up a wooden box full of human flesh – all neatly sliced and boiled!

POPULAR DEATHS
– JOSEPH STALIN 1953

All Russian workers got a holiday . . . two minutes of sighing with relief.

The stapler was patented today in 1868. Misleading things. My son used to spend his teens looking at the centrefold girls in *Playboy*. The first time he went to bed with a woman he thought she was deformed. No staple in her navel.

Two absolute rulers came to power on this day. Adolf Hitler was elected chancellor of Germany in 1933. He offered Germany the return of her pride. And the value of her currency. One mark in 1921 was worth four million marks in 1933! And Marshal Tito took charge of Yugoslavia in 1945. He was born Josip Broz but changed his name to Tito in 1934. Why Tito? Well, it was a popular and fondly used name in his native region. I used to do cabaret at a famous nightspot in Cardiff, called 'Tito's'. They had a big neon sign outside saying: 'Tito's' . . . and one night the letter 'O' failed to light up. The joint was packed within three minutes.

Nano Philip Chowl of Bangkok was seven years of age when he was kidnapped in 1900. The child was returned to his parents unharmed three days later with a curious design tattooed on his left forearm. It depicted the symbols of an ancient Siamese religious sect known to have worshipped Satan and practised black arts. The tattoo bore the word 'Promised' and  this date – 6 March – in 1917. His father, a well-known Indian doctor and leading Christian teacher, attempted to have the tattoo removed without success. The seventeen-year-old Nano fell ill just before the date stated in the tattoo and gave every appearance of approaching death. Today in 1917 Nano's father and older brother, also a doctor, amputated Nano's left forearm. The boy recovered.

The skull of Swedish philosopher Emanuel Swedenborg was sold at Sotheby's in London today in 1977 – for $2850. A professor of the Royal Swedish Academy of Science bought it in order to reunite the head with the rest of the body, buried in 1772 at Uppsala, Sweden.

They say that on this day in 1926 the great Kent bowler Alfred 'Tich' Freeman pointed to the left bail on the opposing wicket in an Australian friendly cricket match in Brisbane – and then clipped that bail off exactly, without even rattling the stumps. Some say this is only a legend and that it never really happened. But my research reveals that, even if it didn't happen, it didn't happen on this day in 1926.

Clarence Birdseye sold his first packaged frozen foods on this day in Springfield, Massachusetts, USA. Now he's responsible for teaching 100 million kids that fish have fingers. And cod have crispy balls.

The Japanese launched their major offensive across the River Chindwin in Operation U-Go today in 1944. American and Chinese troops surrounded 2000 Japanese in the Hukawng Valley. In the midst of the fighting there suddenly appeared a traditionally dressed Japanese warrior who succeeded in killing twelve soldiers with his sword before gunfire cut him down! Pretty suicidal, the Japanese. I heard of a Tokyo businessman who lost a fortune in the wholesale trade, gave it all up and committed cash-and-carry.

7
MAR

John and Bill Kellogg served the first cornflakes today in 1897 – to patients at their Battle Creek Sanitarium! Which recalls the story of the orphan Rice Crispie. It had snap and crackle but no Pop.

Liberal MP Cyril Smith was ordered into hospital today in 1971 with instructions from his doctor to stick to a strict diet and lose some weight. When his office staff sent him a big basket of flowers, the twenty-two-stone Cyril acknowledged the gift with this telegram: 'Thank you for the flowers. They were delicious.'

Sir Malcolm Campbell's *Bluebird* became the world's fastest car on this day in 1935 when he raced it across Bonneville Flats, Utah, USA, at 277 miles per hour. My wife drives to the shops faster than that. The motorway police stopped her for speeding down the hard shoulder. She told them, 'I'm allowed to drive like that! It says on my driving licence "Tear along the dotted line".'

8 MAR

The bomb dropped on the Café de Paris in London tonight in 1941 . . . killing several fine musicians and their Trinidadian bandleader, Ken 'Snakehips' Johnson. Ken was a happy-go-lucky man who nursed few grudges, but he did resent the success of bandleader Geraldo who had insulted him more than once. Gerry was no racist but he had taken an eccentric dislike to Ken. Both bandleaders attended a Tin Pan Alley Band in 1939. Gerry stood to make a speech and a cloud of dense smoke was blown across him from Ken's Jamaican cigar. The crowd went silent. Gerry snarled, 'Don't you ever inhale?' 'Not while you're in the room, I don't,' said Ken. By the time I came into show business, the story was such a legend even Geraldo was telling it. And that's how I heard it.

THE 1st U.S. GROUND COMBAT UNIT LANDED IN VIETNAM TODAY IN 1965...

"QUIET SECTOR? HOW YA THINK I BEEN STRIKIN' MATCHES ALL DAY?"

One disgusted newspaper condemned the film as 'a thunderbolt of salaciousness!' In the historic shocker, copyrighted today in 1900, John C. Rice swept back his moustaches and planted a thirty-second plonker on the lips of mature May Irwin. I wish my stupid son would learn from training films like that. The pretty girl next door phoned him up and whispered, 'I want you to give me something which begins with a K, ends with an S, and will bring a tingle to my lips.' He went over there with a pair of kippers.

9 MAR

THIS IS ST FRANCES DAY

On this day in 1942 the Dutch and Allied Forces on Java capitulated . . .and the Japanese took 60,000 prisoners. When things got tough on Java, Japanese General Tomogama called his starving troops together and said, 'Men, I've got good news and bad news. First, the bad news – there's nothing left to eat on these islands but sea gull droppings. Now the good news – there isn't enough to go round.'

St Frances of Rome is the patron saint of housewives, motorists and *bachelors*. The USA ought to be grateful to single people. Columbus would never have discovered America if he'd been married. Can't you just hear her? 'You're going *where*? With *whom*? To find *what*? And I suppose Queen Isabella is giving you those three ships for *nothing*?!!!'

Boozed with beer, Jumbo was exported to the USA – when his sale to Phineas T. Barnum was declared legal today in 1882. The giant elephant so loved by visitors to London Zoo had to be stunned with beer before he'd quit our shores unprotestingly. I wonder if, in a drunken delirium, he saw pink people.

On a busy street in Portsmouth, a thirteen-year-old girl screamed for help as men dragged her into a car today in 1968. Not one bystander tried to help the girl or even took down the car's number. One man said afterwards, 'Yes, I heard the girl screaming but I didn't take any notice.' Later, people *did* take notice. The incident was one of several that had been filmed by Southern Television and shown on national TV screens. It had been staged to illustrate the astounding public apathy towards crime. The abductors were local policemen!

10 MAR

Lincolnshire's Charles Frederick Worth died on this day in 1895, aged seventy. He'd left England for Paris when he was nineteen to open his own ladies' tailor shop, soon to become the first fashion house to create and display a collection in advance. Worth founded Parisian *haute couture*, the first man to achieve significance in women's fashions. The garment biz is tough today. One manufacturer told me, 'Business is so bad that people are returning things they didn't even buy.'

SOMETHING REALLY DUMB FOR THE DEAF

Two attempts to crack the problem of camouflaging deaf aids came along on this same day. In 1891 a US patent was issued for the Hearing Aid Hat. The topper had a built-in ear trumpet! Great if you have friends who usually talk through their hats . . . you could invite them to talk through yours for a change. Several years later the Audio Bangle Company of Hong Kong appeared in the world press announcing a transistorized deaf aid disguised as a 'pearl-drop' to fit pierced ear lobes only. Don't say it, let me . . . it was the world's first ear-ring aid.

The shortest theatrical run took place tonight in 1930. At London's Duchess Theatre 'The Intimate Revue' ran into Murphy's Law. Everything that could go wrong did. Also Murphy's Revised Law: 'Whenever one thing goes wrong, everything goes wrong at once.' At the Duchess Theatre they'd have told you that Murphy was an optimist. Costumes split, curtains jammed, the performers had amnesia, and what was meant to be a swift succession of brief witty scenes was held up by twenty-minute scene changes. The management cut frantically as the debacle dragged on, abandoning seven scenes entirely in an effort to stage the finale before midnight. Jonathan Dubert, critic for *Adam and Eve*, wrote, 'The only expression of amusement occurred when a harassed compere asked the house, denied any refreshments during the interval by some crisis in the catering arrangements, if there was "anything else at all you would like"; and a florid old gentleman in the second row retorted, "Yes, sir! Euthanasia!"'

11 MAR

The Flower sisters were burned at the stake in Lincoln, England, in 1618. Margaret and Philippa Flower, convicted of witchcraft, were said to have put a curse on the man who condemned them, Judge Charles Holiment. When he was told of it, Holiment laughed and laughed . . . and then died in 'an histerickal fit'!

Golda Meir became prime minister of Israel on this day in 1969. 'She's the toughest politician I've ever encountered,' said German statesman Willy Brandt. 'She not only demands a tooth for a tooth, she expects yours to have gold in it.'

James Boevy, Warden of Exmoor Forest, died on this day in 1965. He slept every night for forty-three years with a burning candle on a table beside his bed together with paper, pen and ink – so that he could jot down every dream! And talking of odd notes . . .

12 MAR

The lowest note ever put into song is 'D' by singer Tom King (of King's Langley, Hertfordshire), assuring him a place in *The Guinness Book of Records*. Tom denies that he's been offered a starring role in the remake of 'Deep Throat'.

The world's fastest chicken plucker was unveiled today in 1972 by Canadian inventor Leonard Scheltgen. My wife plucked a chicken last week, put it in the oven for dinner and forgot to turn on the oven. An hour later the chicken opened the oven door and said, 'Can I have my clothes back? It's freezing in here.'

The ballet 'tutu' was used for the first time this evening in 1832 – at the Paris Opera. It consisted of a white muslin costume with a low neckline, no sleeves, and a skirt that reached halfway down the calf. My daughter could have been a great ballet dancer but for two things that stood in her way. Her feet.

This morning's edition of the *Sunday Despatch* in 1958 ran this headline,

'BALLOON RACE
        – SIX DROP OUT'

The Gutenberg Bible was printed on this day in 1462. Have you seen the new Bible? They've completed updating the twenty-third psalm: 'The lord is my automatic, sheep-feeding, herding machine.'

Halley's comet came into its perihelion today in 1758 . . . just as Halley had predicted in 1682!

13 MAR

Coincidentally . . . on this same day in 1781 . . . Sir William Herschel discovered Uranus. But he didn't tell anyone because he wasn't too sure how to pronounce it.

Three heavenly events make their conjunction today – astronomer Clyde Tombaugh discovered Pluto in 1930 – which was amazing because Walt Disney didn't invent him till 1931.

Earmuffs were patented today in 1877 . . . by Chester Greenwood of Farmington, Maine, who had invented his 'ear mufflers' four years earlier. He put them on and said, 'Wow! I've just discovered stereophonic silence!'

Today in 1980 the biggest fast-food chain in Scotland claimed to have sold over eight million hamburgers. That's not bad for forty pounds of meat.

Jockey Bill Shoemaker rode his 7000th winner today in 1976! That brought lifetime winnings to $58 million. I dreamed about a race once. Woke up, gave the wife £100 and said, 'Go and put it all to win on a horse in the two-thirty at Kempton Park today . . . I can't remember the horse's name but it has something to do with a hat!' I rushed off to work, she rushed off to Ladbroke's and when I got home she said, 'There were two horses in that race, one called Hatband and the other called Blue Bonnet, so I put fifty pounds on each and they both lost!' I said, 'Damn it! Which horse won?' She said, 'Oh, some hundred to one shot called Sombrero.'

14 MAR

Remember the old line – 'Please don't shoot the pianist'? Well, nobody laughed at it in Chicago after today in 1929. The pioneer of boogie-woogie, Clarence 'Pine-top' Smith, was killed by a gunman's bullet on this night – a bullet not intended for him – and he died at his piano keyboard, aged twenty-four. Only a few days earlier he had written a letter to his friend, composer Jack Logan, in which he said, 'When I say I don't drink or smoke or mess with dope, folks wonder what the hell I'm going to die from.'

Charles Charlesworth's first years of life were quite normal after his birth today in 1829. Then at four he began to grow body hair and a beard. Liver spots appeared on the backs of his hands, his veins stood out like those of an OAP and he stooped. Wrinkled and white-haired, Charles died during his eighth year on earth. The coroner's verdict: he died of old age.

Odoacer was slain by Theodoric, King of the Ostrogoths, today in 493. Odoacer, son of Idico, was either of the Sirii nation or else a Rugian. After storming Ticinum (or Plavia), he executed Orestes in Placentia, deposed his son Romulus, recognized the overlordship of Zeno (but not Nepos) and refused to help the usurper Illus. Then he defeated the Rugi, capturing King Feletheus and his wife, Giso (he executed them at Ravenna), ordered his brother Onoulf home from Kakark, repulsed the Visigoth King Euric, recovered Cocosteron and Zixo but not Obfa, then died in the Potium when Theodoric slit his trachea. As history, it's pretty confusing – but wait till they use it as the plot for the next 'Star Wars' movie.

15 MAR

Attila the Hun died on this day in 459. Having survived countless battles and put thousands to the sword, Attila went to a wedding and died of a nosebleed! He told his wife, 'I'm dying; farewell, my heart, my beloved!' and she said, 'So long, hun!' And thirty-four years later . . .

`BIG JULIE BUMPED OFF!`

Yes, this is the Ides of March upon which Julius Caesar was stabbed to death in 44 BC. When Shakespeare's play was performed in New York City recently, half the audience left as soon as the stabbing scene took place. They said they didn't want to get involved.

The first blood bank was established in 1937. Said topical comedian Naunton Wayne, 'I popped in to make a deposit. I stood behind Bela Lugosi. He made an awfully large withdrawal and then said, "Nearly daylight, I must fly!"'

16 MAR

The oil super-tanker *Amoco Cadiz*, carrying 230,000 tons, went aground on the coast of Brittany, France, and broke in half. By noon tomorrow in 1978, five miles of coastline were mucky with oil. By 1 April, sixty miles of French coastline were similarly greased up. While North Sea rigs searched for oil under the sea, holidaymakers searched for sea under the oil.

Aldo Moro, five times prime minister of Italy, was kidnapped by members of the Red Brigade, killing his five bodyguards and seizing him from his car, on this day in 1978. His body was found eight weeks later on the following 6 June, and six persons were charged with the crime. Sometimes I think the world has so many painful problems, if Moses came down from Mount Sinai today, the two tablets he carried would be aspirin.

BARNEY OLDFIELD DROVE HIS BENZ CAR AT 131·724 MPH -- AND SET A NEW LAND SPEED RECORD TODAY IN 1910. MACK SENNETT STARRED HIM IN A 1913 SILENT FILM HIT IN WHICH HE RACED TO SAVE MABEL NORMAND FROM DEATH ON THE RAILWAY LINES! IMAGINE TRYING TO KILL YOURSELF LIKE THAT ON B.R.---

POOR SOD DIED OF STARVATION WAITING FOR THE 9·45 TO BLETCHLEY.

John Florence Sullivan died on this day in 1956. For seventeen years – 1932 to 1949 – he had attracted twenty million listeners to his radio half-hour and his feud with comedian Jack Benny was one of the most delightful stunts in US comic history. As a vaudeville juggler he'd adopted the name Fred Allen and used his dry, wry wit to punctuate his act. Some of his lines are comedy classics, like – 'Jack Benny couldn't ad-lib a belch after a Hungarian dinner' – 'He always had a chip on his shoulder that he was ready to use to kindle an argument' – 'the first Sunday I sang in the church choir, two hundred people changed their religion' – and the oft-quoted 'If criticism had any real power to harm, the skunk would have been extinct by now.'

17 MAR

A mother of six was arrested today in Marrakech, Morocco, in 1970 – for parking in the middle of a main street traffic jam. She said it was a case of emergency: baby's nappy needed changing.

Eight thousand visits to the doctor! That's how often chronic hypochondriac Walter Thurson was said to have called on GPs in the Birmingham, Glasgow and London areas over twenty years of 'wasting the time and resources of our National Health system'. For these and other offences Walter was sentenced to sixty days in prison today in 1974 . . . and promptly applied for admission to the prison hospital! I go to the doctor fairly regularly. I'm not ill. It's just that I've converted the wife to a Jehovah's Witness and now I'm trying to get him to give her a major operation.

The first space walk was taken today in 1965 – by Lieutenant Aleskey Arkhipovich Leonov when he floated in space for twelve minutes, nine seconds, while attached to the Soviet spacecraft *Voshkod 2* by a sixteen-foot nylon cord. During those twelve minutes Leonov travelled 3000 miles at 16,500 mph! 'I think those Russian space scientists are fantastic,' said US comedian Robb Wheeler, 'and if I spoke German, I'd go over there and tell them so.'

18 MAR

QUESTION:

When Henry Wells and William Fargo started their business in 1850, what did they call the company? Did you answer Wells-Fargo? Wrong! Beleave it or don't, they named their company American Express! Two years later they decided nobody would ever get any business with a duff name like American Express! (Those wooden credit cards must have been a fire hazard anyway). So in 1852 the firm became Wells-Fargo and a thousand B-picture Westerns became possible.

EMI discontinued the production of 78 rpm records in 1959. Strange! I made one for them in 1960. (It was in the shops so long, the hole in the middle healed up.)

Farouk, former king of Egypt, died on this day in 1965. He was only forty-five years old. He told girls that he was a reincarnation of Casanova! (They say that, when they got Farouk between the sheets, Casanova was still pretty dead.) Talk about strange delusions; I heard of a girl who thought she was a Vauxhall just because she was made in Luton.

Today in 1954 Howard Hughes bought RKO Pictures for $23,489,478. He became the first sole owner of a major studio. Hughes was so rich he didn't wear elevator shoes. He just had America lowered.

I'll never forget the night Tommy Cooper drank my champagne! We shared a dressing room at the Cambridge Theatre with Norman Wisdom in 1950. We were all in a show called 'Sauce Piquante' and Tommy (who was born today in 1921 in Caerphilly, Wales) helped me celebrate *my* birthday by drinking my entire magnum of champagne while I was on stage. It made Tommy so drunk he went on to do his act and accidentally got three of his tricks right!

19 MAR

The world's widest bridge was opened today in 1932, spanning Sydney Harbour. The widest bridge ever built – and the crowd's attention was diverted by a child's balloon floating across the bay and the efforts of some boys to hit it with rocks! That's Australians for you. Remember the tale of the Aussie who dreamed he was alone in a boat with Bo Derek? His pal asked, 'How did you make out?' He said, 'Great, I caught a fourteen-pound bass.'

On this day in 1813 . . . the explorer to whom Stanley said, 'Dr Livingstone I presume?' was born. David Livingstone shares this birthday with that other great traveller Sir Richard Burton, born exactly eight years later in 1821. Once after they'd slogged across a particularly dusty stretch of African desert Burton sent their porters all the way back again to fetch some soap. 'That,' said Livingstone, 'was a pretty dirty trek.'

The first US bank was robbed in 1883. The banks were very impressed and have been in the robbery business themselves ever since.

A five-year study of 3094 athletes was revealed today in 1976, showing that 22 per cent wear glasses and 11 per cent wear contact lenses. My eyesight's getting worse. I keep running into pubs.

DEATH OF A PIRATE!

20 MAR

Radio Caroline, the pop pirate which launched Tony Blackburn and changed the face of British radio, died in stormy seas off the Kent coast today in 1980. The 274-ton ship *Mi Amigo*, the station's home, ran aground and sank after sixteen years of illegal broadcasting. The first voice heard from the historic rust bucket when it opened for business at Easter 1964 was DJ Simon Dee. Other famous graduates: Johnnie Walker, Emperor Rosko, Dave Lee Travis. For the first time in British radio, they brought irreverence and unbridled high spirits to the mike, with inspired nonsense like 'Please have a paper and pencil ready . . . in case you get a sudden urge to wrap up a pencil' . . . and 'Here is a message for all listeners to this programme: Wake up, it's over!'

Direct from his escape from Elba, Napoleon entered Paris on this day in 1815 without a shot being fired in anger. The only blow struck on King Louis XVIII's behalf was by an old woman selling chestnuts. When she shouted, 'Vive le roi!' a man yelled back, 'Vive l'empereur!' – and she hit him on the head with her ladle. A classic and witty account of Bonaparte's march from his Elba gaol was supplied by a Paris broadsheet:

The tiger has broken out of his den!!!!!
The ogre has been 3 days at sea!!!!
The wretch has landed at Frejus!!!
The buzzard has reached Antibes!!
The invader has arrived in Grenoble!
The general has entered Lyons.
Napoleon slept at Fontainebleau last night.
The emperor will proceed to the Tuileries today.
His Imperial Majesty will address his loyal subjects
   tomorrow.

The man who found his family – on a rubbish tip!
Antonio Tomás, employed on the Lisbon City garbage tip
as a labourer, saw something unusual amongst the
rubble today in 1954 . . . a silver picture frame. In it was
a photograph that caused Tomas to cry out and collapse
in a faint. The picture was of a Portuguese family at a
wedding – and the bridegroom was Tomás himself.
About five years after the happy photo had been taken, a
boating accident off the coast of the Algarve resulted in
the drowning of his brother, and, everyone supposed,
Tomás as well. Although his body
was lost, a double funeral was held.
Meanwhile Tomás had been saved
by some fishermen an inexplicable
twelve miles from the scene of the
accident. He was in deep shock and
had total amnesia. His memory
remained a complete blank until this
chance discovery of his own wedding photograph in the vast ocean of
rubbish that is Portugal's biggest
dump. Nearly eight years after the
boating accident had robbed him of
his identity, Tomás recovered his
memory in a single day and was joyfully reunited with
his mother, wife and children in Coimbra. The cutest
thing I've ever seen on a tip was a sign: 'Help beautify
our rubbish dumps! Throw away something lovely!'

Bleak House indeed! Twelve-year-old Charles Dickens
was taken by his mother to see his father in
Marshalsea Debtors' Prison today in 1824. It was a
very long visit – the whole family ended up as inmates!
One thing I learned about money matters. It certainly
does.

Pierre Delamcabout, forty-two-year-old French resistance fighter, tonight shot and killed his father and his uncle – and didn't know it for two years!
Delamcabout, a respected hero of the World War II Maquis in Paris, carried out the routine assassination of two Nazi officers on leave this afternoon in 1944. It wasn't until he was reunited with his family in 1946 in London that he learned the truth. The German officers, both colonels, were brothers. The older man was Gert Von Greicher, a prewar member of Germany's embassy in France and the lover of Delamcabout's mother. Pierre was their son. He wrote the details of the extraordinary story in his memoirs, without guilt or self-pity in the words; but Pierre Delamcabout's suicide in Paris in 1958 occurred today – on the fourteenth anniversary of his tragic assignment.

22 MAR

Thomas Hughes died on this day in 1896. The Berkshire-born reformer founded the working men's clubs which gave so much employment to itinerant comics like me. He also wrote *Tom Brown's Schooldays*.
Don Maclean, Birmingham's funniest son, says in his schooldays near Rugby there was absolutely no sex instruction: 'We had to find out the facts of life from ancient carvings. On the back of the bike sheds.'

'The Barber of Seville' had its first performance tonight in 1816. Perhaps the sign outside the theatre said '"The Barber of Seville". 3000 chairs. No Waiting.'

Helen Porter Mitchell gave a toast to the world today in 1901. The Australian opera singer liked her bread sliced so thinly you could see through it, then toasted to a golden wafer. Once people had crunched on her narrow nibbles, everybody wanted some. So, since the operatic star was world-famous as Nellie Melba, they named it Melba toast. Of course, if King Richard hadn't had a mysterious illness after he ate that suet pudding, we'd never have had Spotted Dick.

23 MAR

SCOTTISH SURGEONS REMOVED A PADLOCK FROM A WOMAN'S THROAT TODAY IN 1837.

FUNNY WAY TO GET LOCKJAW!

Tennessee outlawed the teaching of evolution in 1925. Man hasn't entirely evolved from living in trees. His eyes still swing from limb to limb.

The four-minute mile was run for the first time by Britain's Roger Bannister in 1954. In the long run he was beaten.

Shiruh, Caliph of Eygypt, died of indigestion today in 1169. He'd been wolfing down the twelfth-century Egyptian equivalent of the modern doughnut . . . and the only thing digestible about those damn things is the hole.

24 MAR

Oxford and Cambridge officially drew the boat race for the only dead heat in its history in 1877. Cambridge caught up at the last minute when Oxford broke an oar. When I went out rowing with the Dulwich College old boys, we had eight of us middle-aged gents on the oars and one stroke. By the time we got back, all eight of us had had a stroke.

Cristobal Balenciaga died on this day in 1972. The Spanish fashion master of Paris popularized flowing gowns and capes in the 1950s. Comedian Tony Peers says he admires the way most women dress these days: 'But some of them ought to be investigated for deceptive packaging.'

A gang got away with four million pounds' worth of silver bullion on this day in 1980. In Britain's biggest robbery, the hijack of a lorry loaded with 321 silver bars imported from Germany was accomplished on a main road in Barking, Essex, in broad daylight and in one minute flat. A supergrass talked . . . and 10 weeks later 309 ingots were found by detectives in a lock-up garage at Oakwood, Enfield, Essex. Just one dozen were missing – on-the-spot payment for the robbers in the gang – leaving the insurance company to sing the twelve-bar blues.

The world's rarest stamp was sold today in 1970 for £115,666. Today it's valued at £500,000! It's the British Guiana one-cent black-on-magenta. Soon the cost of a stamp to send a first-class letter should equal that. I've already reached the point where I put a 50p stamp on my postcards in case the postage goes up in transit.

ILL YOU PICK UP THE NEWSPAPER? OR WILL YOU HAVE IT SCENT? HIS MORNING IN 1937 THE WASHINGTON DAILY NEWS BECAME THE 1st O USE A PERFUMED PAGE! IT DISPLAYED PICTURES OF FLOWERS TO PROMOTE HE "PEOPLE'S DRUG STORE"--- CAN YOU IMAGINE HOW THAT IDEA COULD GROW? MAXWELL HOUSE ADS WOULD SMELL OF COFFEE, CADBURY ADS OF CHOCOLATE, THE GARDENING PAGE OF BLOSSOMS, THE SPORTS SECTION OF FRESH AIR, THE SHOW BIZ PAGE OF GREASEPAINT--- AND THE PARLIAMENTARY REPORTS OF POLITICIANS' SPEECHES WOULD SMELL OF....

PHEW! WHO DID THAT?

Bob Monkhouse

On this day in 1769 a young man from Long Witton, Northumberland, was admitted to an infirmary in Newcastle upon Tyne, suffering from hiccups. They could be heard from over a half mile away! Sounds pretty close to my brother-in-law on Saturday nights. When he hiccups, he spills his booze. He's spilled so much he suffers from cirrhosis of the shoelaces.

25 MAR

It was on this day in 1959 that my first wife left a note for the milkman which said: 'Don't leave milk today. Of course when I say today I mean tomorrow because I am writing this yesterday.'

Sir John Vanbrugh died on this day in 1726. Apart from writing some glorious Restoration comedies (*The Provok'd Wife, The Relapse*), he was the architect of Castle Howard in Yorkshire, Blenheim Palace and many massive castles and giant houses. His epitaph reads: 'Lie heavy on him, earth, for he laid many heavy loads on thee'.

Ludwig Van Beethoven died on this day in 1827. He was so deaf he thought he was painting.

26 MAR

During a missile firing display in honour of Prince Philip's visit to HMS *London*, the ship's prize aimer shot down the target with a direct hit. Impressed, Prince Philip said, 'That man deserves a coconut!' A few weeks later – on this morning in 1967 – a parcel arrived from Buckingham Palace containing a prize coconut. The coconut still takes place of honour in the ship's trophy cabinet!

One hundred and twenty gallons of milk in twelve hours! That was the world milking record set today in 1937 by Andy Faust of Collinsville, Oklahoma. The cow was udderly exhausted.

THE IRON MAN OF STONE

Popeye the sailor became the first cartoon character to have his statue erected. Today in 1937 the grateful residents of Crystal City, Texas, unveiled a monument to Segal's spinach-eating hero in Popeye Park. Why? Much of the local wealth comes from agriculture and their principal crop is . . . that's right . . . spinach. Popeye's statue is fixed in place with 'a foundation of spinach, blended with cement'. And I always thought he was stuck on Olive Oyl.

27 MAR

This morning the first 'long distance' phone call was made between Boston and New York City in 1884. My wife even gossips long-distance. At our house, opportunity *has* to knock – if it phoned, it'd get the engaged signal.

HE HAD HIS TWIN BROTHER REALLY CLOSE TO HIS HEART

For thirty years, Tyko Asplund of Nedervetilaenaera, Finland, had breathing trouble. Eventually he had to stop working and go into a nursing home where lung cancer was diagnosed. He had an operation in Helsinki today in 1956, but instead of a cancer the surgeon found Tyko's twin brother! The male foetus was six inches long. (I was one of triplets, you know. It was dad's fault for going to bed with the hiccups.) And on that topic . . .

Faith, Hope and Charity were all born on this day in 1868. They became the world's oldest surviving triplets; born in the Caughlin household, Marlboro, Massachusetts. *The Guinness Book of Records* for 1980 reported the death of only one – Mrs (Ellen) Hope Daniels on 2 March 1962, when she was ninety-three. Victor Borge reckons he's got three and a half brothers. He says, 'It's true! I have three half brothers – that's one and a half, right? And then two regular brothers, making a grand total of three and a half!'

Newcastle upon Tyne University students covered a house with 4000 feet of toilet paper today in 1962. They would have covered it with 5000 feet but that would have been foolish.

Inge Simonsen, a twenty-one-year-old Norwegian, 'officially' won the first London Marathon today in 1981 . . . but he went over the finishing line hand in hand with Dick Beardsley of America. They said they were just good friends. A seventy-eight-year-old storeman with seventeen grandchildren and seven great-grandchildren finished proudly and last . . . in just over six hours. He said, 'Age is all in the mind. I feel like a twenty-year-old.' As luck would have it, there wasn't one around.

28 MAR

The world trembled at the nuclear accident at Three Mile Island, near Harrisburg, Pennsylvania, USA, on this day in 1979. The atomic core began to melt down. Remember the old song, 'He's Got the Whole World in His Hands'? Well, at that point, He nearly let go.

Douglas Fairbanks was Hollywood's most eligible bachelor to his millions of adoring fans – so he kept this 1920 wedding day a secret as he married America's sweetheart Mary Pickford. (Well, they did invite a few friends – Charles Chaplin included.) But there was no need to worry. 'Douglas Fairbanks and Mary Pickford came to mean more than a couple of married film stars,' wrote Alistair Cooke. 'They were living proof of America's chronic belief in happy endings.' It was called Hollywood's first royal wedding (although it was only Douglas Elton Ullman marrying little Gladys Smith). On their honeymoon they were mobbed in Oslo, Paris – and nearly crushed by star-crazy crowds in London's Kensington Gardens! At breakfast in the Savoy, Doug ordered a large green salad and everyone heard Mary say, 'So you *eat* like a rabbit as well!'

In 1939 the Spanish Civil War was still unfinished. Forty years later, Spanish hotels had the same problem. Seriously though, folks, General Franco and his fascist forces scored the major victory on this day, deciding the war's outcome! As his views on the war, Ernest Hemingway wrote his great novel called *For Whom the Bell Tolls*. And you always thought it was about the life of an Avon lady, didn't you?

29
MAR

The independence of Canada began on this day in 1867 when the British Parliament created the dominion of Canada. Fact: the average Canadian has an IQ several points higher than the average American. Why? Could it be the weather? Or the fact that Canadians eat larger amounts of fish per capita? Sort of a cod-given gift? And so to a man who could make even a joke as awful as that sound funny . . .

Comedian Jack Benny made his debut on radio in 1932. Regarding his theatrical debut, his great radio rival Fred Allen said, 'It was so far back in the woods, the manager was a bear. Benny's salary was paid in honey.' Of Benny's golf, Allen commented, 'By the time Jack could afford to lose a ball, he couldn't hit it that far.' Verbally, Benny had no superior in comedy timing. His valet Rochester asked, 'Boss, who was the last one you rented your tuxedo to?' Jack said, 'Why?' 'Well, boss, every time I lay the coat down, the arms fold.' It was Jack's reaction that doubled the laugh . . . 'Oh, yes . . .'

Coca-Cola was invented in 1886. Only seven men have ever known its formula since John Styth Pemberton brewed up his first pot of the stuff in his backyard. That very first formula had to be changed – it contained cocaine.

MUHAMMED ALI — CHAMPION PAINTER?

TODAY IN 1979 A PAINTING BY 'THE GREATEST' WAS AUCTIONED FOR UNICEF IN NEW YORK.

IT FETCHED A VERY GENEROUS $1,800.

Bob Monkhouse

30 MAR

Russia sold Alaska to the USA for less than two cents an acre! On this day in 1867, his fellow Americans disparaging the deal as 'Seward's Folly', the US secretary of state paid $7,200,000 for the snowbound, oil rich, future forty-ninth state. The only explanation for the high price of oil is that the earth has begun to charge storage.

On this day in 1947 the beloved star of 'The Crazy Gang', Charlie Naughton, was in the saloon bar of the Flag, a St John's Wood pub, when a huge drunken tough squeezed Charlie's bald head and sneered, 'It feels like my wife's arse! – and little Charlie felt his head with interest and said, 'By Jove, so it does, so it does!'

Today Liberal leader David Steel was born in 1938. He's a promising boy wonder. When he makes his promises, boy! do you wonder!

On this day in 1857 Madeleine Smith, eldest daughter of one of Glasgow's most prominent citizens, was arrested. Her crime: a love affair with a lowly clerk, forbidden by her eminent architect father, had led to passionate letters of devotion, letters which the clerk threatened to send to Madeleine's father – so the loving Madeleine bought some arsenic and poisoned her sweetheart. When police looked in her bureau drawer they found faint traces of arsenic, cyanide, belladonna and strychnine – but the packets were never found! (Don't say it, let me. It was the Bureau of Missing Poisons.)

At dawn on this day in 1940 a fresh, sweet spring sun warmed the soft little waves on the beach of Dunkirk, France. Luftwaffe raids began. German artillery started shelling. But the achievement of the day fulfilled the promise of the lovely dawn. More than a fifth of all the troops evacuated from their helplessly vulnerable situation on Dunkirk's beaches were in England before night . . . an incredible 68,014 men! The crews of the little ships earned themselves lasting glory as every kind of seaworthy craft set out to save allied soldiers . . . including the lighters of Pickfords, the moving firm!

The Eiffel Tower was completed today in 1889. The French pronounce it 'Ee-fell', after the man who built it. The British call it 'Eye-full' because if you stand beneath it and look up at the pigeons, that's what you'll get.

Three hundred and sixty-one eggs in 364 days – from one laid-out hen! A Black Orpington named Princess Te Kawau completed this Eastertide record in Taranaki, New Zealand, today in 1930. They doubled her egg production by a sneaky trick. They put a sign on her hen house that said, 'An egg a day keeps Colonel Sanders away!'

1 APR

Today in 1800, mathematician Claude St James published his treatise on *How to Win at Poker* – and lost £500,000! Claude was an outstanding scholar and wrote widely respected textbooks; but gambling was the downfall of this Cambridge chancer. One of his calculations still stands unchallenged – that the odds against a royal flush in poker are 650,000 to 1! He was heavily financed by a group of London backers but lost them half a million over four years of employing his systems at cards and roulette. People who go to casinos are very religious. You see them coming out saying, 'Oh, God! Oh, God!'

Today happened on 1 January . . . until 1564! Up until then 'All Fool's Day' shared its status with New Year's Day – but that didn't work out because on New Year's Day all the biggest fools are still unconscious from New Year's Eve.

THE BRIGHTON STRIP OPENED TODAY IN 1980

Sunlovers bared their teeth at the mist and rain as the South Coast resort opened its nudist beach. Shivering birdwatchers reported a few blue tits.

WHO WAS THE FIRST 'APRIL FOOL'?

According to a well-supported legend, it was an anonymous soldier who allowed the duke and duchess of Lorraine to escape from prison disguised as peasants. A village woman spotted the fugitives and alerted the soldier, but he was too smart to fall for a corny gag like that and arrested the woman instead, taking her prisoner as 'the first fool of April'. Sort of rebounded on him, didn't it?

This was the day of Casanova's birth in 1725. The Venetian adventurer was a spy, gambler and – yes – multiple seducer. His favourite contraceptive devices included a sheath made from a sheep's intestine, half a lemon used as a Dutch cap and two ounces of gold balls, also for use by his partners. I'm no Casanova. Recently I caught a Peeping Tom booing me!

2 APR

TODAY IN 1792 THE US MINT WAS CREATED

Ours was in the Tower of London in those days, a prison from which few escaped. I'm finding it just as hard to get my bank to release some money. The manager says my bank account is suffering from 'withdrawal symptoms'.

Red Rum won the Grand National for the third time in 1977. And if that's not enough of a fairy tale come true for you . . .

The first cinema – The Electric Theater – opened in Los Angeles, California, today in 1902, admission ten cents. On the programme: 'The Capture of the Biddle Brothers' and a four-minute drama titled 'Ruined by Hard Drink'. I've never seen it. I think it shows a man sitting on an icicle.

This is the 1805 birthday of Hans Christian Andersen. He inspired one of my favourite crosstalk exchanges between the radio comedy team of Murgatroyd and Winterbottom (Tommy Handley and Ronald Frandau): 'Have you read Hans Andersen?' . . . 'No, they're white. And why call me Andersen?'

Today is Day Day! Doris Day Day! America's favourite snubnosed dream was born little Miss von Kappelhoff on this day in 1924 in Cincinnati, Ohio. According to Edward Lucaire, Doris Day's friend and co-star Rock Hudson calls her Eunice and she calls him Ernie for reasons unknown. Me, I'd like to call her Frequently.

3 APR

Jazz lost a great exponent on this day in 1935 – and all because he had a sore throat. Bennie Moten was a legendary ragtime piano player and led his famous band in Kansas City. A persistently sore throat caused Bennie to call in at a nearby hospital for a throat spray. A young doctor talked him into having his tonsils out. The operation was botched, complications set in and loss of blood resulted in Moten's death . . . aged forty. His name lives on in numbers like 'Moten Swing' and 'Moten's South'. Bennie's personnel included Hot Lips Page, Jimmy Rushing and Count Basie. It was to Basie that he once said, 'No one should be allowed to play the saxophone until he knows how.'

The first jeans were made commercially in 1782 by Sam Wetherill of Philadelphia, Pennsylvania – along with 'fustians, everlastings, and coatings'. On BBC-TV's 'The Two Ronnies', fears were expressed, 'You can't help worrying about that harsh cotton material for making men's jeans – denim, and wondering if it can erode our differentials.'

DEATH BY HOT CROSS BUNS

At Kilburn in Scotland, a Miss Finch wolfed a dozen buns to celebrate Easter, 1888 . . . and dropped dead.. Her epitaph: 'She would rather die than diet'.

The NATO treaty was signed today in 1949. That's the one where the US promised to give everybody tanks, bombs and guns . . . and everybody promised not to use them. It made about as much sense as taking your wife to a brothel and paying corkage.

4 APR

Faisal II acceded to the throne of Iraq today in 1939 and, amazingly for the time, actually warned the world to conserve oil! Carpooling is an excellent petrol saver . . . just drive your car into a pool and leave it there.

A big day for music lovers . . . this is the birthday of composer Elmer Bernstein, born 1922. And also of the world's highest paid conductor, Herbert von Karajan, born 1908. Herb is so wealthy, when he walks in his sleep, he hails taxis.

Millionaire author Arthur Hailey was born in 1920. He's also rather rich. To give you some idea, he hires Vidal Sassoon to cut his grass.

THE BANKRUPTCY ACT WAS PASSED BY THE U.S. CONGRESS TODAY IN 1800...WHICH MEANT YOU NO LONGER WENT DIRECTLY TO JAIL WHEN YOU COULDN'T SETTLE YOUR DEBTS. THAT DIDN'T MAKE IT ANY EASIER TO GET A BANK LOAN THOUGH---

MANAGER

"I'D LIKE TO COMBINE ALL MY LITTLE OBLIGATIONS INTO ONE BACK-BREAKING LOAD."

THIS IS TOMB SWEEPING DAY IN TAIWAN AND HONG KONG --- WHEN GRATEFUL CITIZENS HONOUR THEIR ANCESTORS --

5 APR

Pocahontas married John Rolfe today in 1614 – and so brought peace to Pilgrims and the Chicahominy Indians. She was the daughter of an Indian chief named Powhatan. Only her real name wasn't Pocahontas; it was Matoaka. And her father's real name wasn't Powhatan; it was Wahusonacock. No one knows why he changed it. Dan O'Day speculates it's because people kept assuming he was Polish.

Charlie Chaplin became the world's highest paid star – aged twenty-six! Today in 1916 he signed a contract with the Mutual Film Corporation for $675,000 for twelve month's work. He became so rich he had a roll of $100 bills. I know lots of people have rolls of $100 bills – but Chaplin had 'em in his toilet.

The first round-the-world airplane flight took off today in 1924. Around 27,000 miles and 175 days later, the pioneers and 2 of the 3 planes returned to the starting point . . . Seattle, Washington, USA. One of the pilots, Lieutenant Leigh Wade in the *Boston*, was forced down near the Faroe Islands in the North Atlantic . . . struck by a meteorite! The chances against that happening have been calculated at 8,000,800 billion to 1, about the same as my hopes of having Bo Derek approach me on a lonely tropical beach and ask me if she can help me overcome my incipient impotence.

PAYE was introduced today in 1944. 'Pay As You Earn' – that's what it meant then. Now it means 'Pay All Your Earnings'.

For 7 hours 19 minutes they boxed . . . and ended in a draw! The longest-ever recorded boxing match with gloves was fought today in 1893. The place: New Orleans. The combatants: lightweights Jack Burked and Andrew Bowen. The draw was declared after 110 rounds. On a re-match three months later, Jack knocked Andrew out in the very first round! It's not true that Jack attributed his new good fortune to his carrying a lucky coin in his shoe, a lucky rabbit's foot in his shorts and a lucky horseshoe in his glove.

Here's a bank that really has overheads . . . the Canadian Bank of Commerce which opened a new branch today in 1968 . . . on a DC-3 plane! The fly-by-night operation was established to serve outlying communities in the Yukon. Hear that cold wind whistling round the old homestead? It's just the bank roaring by . . . making another damned overdraft!

7 APR

On 7 April 1770, the poet Wordsworth was born. Wordsworth wrote my favourite poem about the battle of the sexes:

> When the dew is falling fast,
> And the stars begin to blink.
> Ladies turn to gentlemen.
> And gentlemen turn to drink.

On 7 April 1924, they opened the aquarium in London Zoo. There was a terrible accident there one day. The head keeper fell into a tank of eels and got caught by the congers.

Queen Victoria was given chloroform to ease the pain of childbirth on this day in 1853. She was having her seventh child . . . but the significance of easing a birth was tremendous. Until this royal acceptance of the idea, decreasing the agony of delivery was regarded as a sin. I suppose the only time a woman wishes she were a year older is when she's pregnant.

A TON OF POTATOES WILL YIELD OVER 28½ GALLONS OF ALCOHOL...BUT WOE BETIDE ANYONE IN OKLAHOMA WHO TRIED IT UNTIL THE U.S. STATE REPEALED PROHIBITION. AMAZINGLY, THAT DIDN'T HAPPEN UNTIL THIS DAY IN 1959! PEOPLE WERE DESPERATE----

BOB MONKHOUSE

PETER STUYVESANT WAS ALWAYS A LONG DRAG

On this day in 1664 the last Dutch governor defied the Dutch citizens of Manhattan by refusing them any rights in the running of municipality. So they defied him right back . . . by refusing to defend the province against British invasion. That's how Colonel Richard Nicolls was able to march in on 8 September and seize the place without firing a shot – and New Amsterdam became New York. Stuyvesant complained, 'These soldiers make too much mess.' New York City still has that problem. The NYC Sanitation Dept. is very religious. They take up a collection once a week.

8 APR

Oleomargarine was patented on this day in 1873 by Alfred Paraf of New York City. It was already on sale in Britain, manufactured in France and sold for one shilling per half pound. A shilling; that's 5p . . . and it still goes a long way these days. You can carry it around for miles and miles before you find something you can buy with it.

The fire escape was patented today in 1776. I bought one of those smoke detectors but I think it's faulty. It goes off every time I've eaten curried beans.

This morning's issue of *The Sun* in 1964 carried this news item: 'LONE BELLA DIES ON SARK . . . Bella, the only female dog on the Channel Island of Sark, had been destroyed. She was thirteen and belonged to the Dame of Sark – who refuses to have any other bitch on the island.

On this morning in 1940 the commanding officer of a RN gunboat, returning from night patrol, decided to follow a dredger through the treacherous sandbanks off the Norfolk coast. He went potty when thirty minutes later both ships suddenly went aground. From his bridge the captain could see a man in oilskins coming out of the dredger's wheelhouse. The man stared at the gunboat for a moment and then yelled out, 'I've come 'ere for sand, cock. What the 'ell are you 'ere for?'

MAYBE EDISON WAS RIGHT

Thomas Alva E. announced today in 1898 that the new 'wonder battery' he was developing would put the petrol car out of business and introduce the age of the clean, noiseless electric car. As it turned out, his nickel-alkali battery was scorned. Pollution makes me wonder if Tom had the real answer. Did you know that the electric car was the first road vehicle to exceed sixty miles per hour? Recently British Leyland have developed an electric car that will go from London to Glasgow at forty mph at a cost of only £5 for the electricity. Mind you, you have to fork out another £740 for the flex.

9 APR

James Cook discovered Botany Bay on this day in 1770. He observed that the Australian aboriginals appeared, 'Open to reason'. How true. It recalls the swagman who asked the aborigine, 'How did you like the bottle of wine I gave you?' The aborigine said, 'It was just right, boss.' . . . 'What do you mean, it was just right?' . . . 'Well, boss,' said the reasonable Australian native, 'if it had been any better, you wouldn't have given it to me. And if it had been any worse, I couldn't have drunk it. So it was just right.'

THE LAST WOMAN HANGED IN BRITAIN

10 APR

David Blakely, a twenty-four-year-old racing driver, was shot dead outside a pub in North London on this day in 1955. The killer: waitress, factory worker and call girl Ruth Ellis. 'When we execute a murderer,' wrote G. C. Lichtenberg, 'we probably make the same mistake as the child who strikes a chair it has bumped into.'

The safety pin was patented in the USA today in 1849 . . . by Walter Hunt of New York City. Hunt invented the device in three hours flat in a hurry to raise enough money to settle a $15 debt. He sold the safety pin outright for $480! But don't worry about him. He had lots more good ideas like that. Hunt also invented the paper collar, the ice plough, a repeating rifle, dry dock, nail-making machine, sewing machine, explosive bullet – and, for all I know, reversible roller skates for backward children, double-decker baths for people who like to sing duets, and a bridge that went halfway across a river, turned and came back. It's for people who change their minds.

On this day in 1257, Aibex, Caliph of Egypt, was murdered by his wife. Well, he deserved it. When she asked, 'Can you explain how this lipstick got on your collar?', Aibex answered, 'No, I can't. I distinctly remember taking my shirt off.'

A Radio 4 announcer described a course for radio operators today in 1968, concluding: 'Take advantage of this opportunity. It could open up a whole new field of unemployment for you.'

On this day in 1905 Albert Einstein announced his theory of relativity of time and space. Did you know that Einstein didn't speak until he was three years old? Well, it's true. My cousin Egbert didn't speak until he

was twenty-three. He suddenly looked up from the breakfast table and said to his parents, 'This porridge is lumpy.' They wept with joy! His mother cried, 'Egbert, you can talk! Why have you never spoken before?' And Egbert said, 'Up till now, the porridge has been okay.'

US President Ronald Reagan went home to the White House today in 1981 twelve days after the attempt on his life. The Secret Service revealed today that seven would-be assassins had been arrested since John Hinckley shot Reagan. Normally the agents handle more than one thousand death threats against the president – and up to eight arrests each month!

Napoleon quit the throne on this day in 1814. He said, 'In love, a man is only victorious when he runs away.'

Sailing past Gibraltar today in 1943, the *Queen Mary* received a signal from the garrison, 'What ship? What ship?' Her immediate reply was, 'What rock? What rock?'

During a stirring address to his old school, Prime Minister George Canning painted a rosy picture of the hereafter . . . and a bold boy held up his hand to ask, 'How do you know what heaven is like if you have never been there, sir?' Canning answered, 'I have never known anyone came back because he didn't like it.' The statesman was born today in 1770.

Greta Garbo said she wanted to be *left* alone – at tonight's movie premiere in 1932 – 'Grand Hotel', co-starring John Barrymore, Wallace Beery, Lionel Barrymore, Lewis Stone, Jean Hersholt and Joan Crawford. The flick won the Oscar as best production. Garbo's English was frequently uncertain during her early days in Hollywood. After her passionate love affair with the great silent film star John Gilbert, his career suffered with the coming of sound and she was still fond of him. 'Please,' she begged MGM's executive producer Irving Thalberg, 'make a picture with John. He's as broke as the Ten Commandments.'

Yuri Gagarin became the first man in space on this day in 1961. The Russian space programme later wanted to send Yuri to the moon but he said, 'You couldn't get me on the moon if it was the last place on earth.'

12 APR

FRANKLIN D. ROOSEVELT DIED ON THIS DAY IN 1945

. . . as predicted only a few months earlier by the US psychic Jean Dixon. Dixon, a professional real estate agent, also predicted the 1947 partition of India, told Winston Churchill he would lose the 1945 general election but would be prime minister again, and correctly predicted four more historic deaths – those of Joseph Stalin, UN Secretary-General Dag Hammarskjöld (foreseeing the plane crash), J. F. Kennedy (also forecasting that the assassin's name had the initial O), and Senator Robert Kennedy. And only BBC TV's 'The Two Ronnies' can claim to know of an even more amazing fortune teller: 'She got a divorce on the grounds of her husband's adultery next weekend in Brighton.'

13 APR

Isabel de Soto became the first woman governor in the new world! Yes, she was the wife of the great Spanish explorer Hernando de Soto, a conqueror of Nicaragua and Peru and the first European pioneer to clap eyes on the Mississippi River in 1539. While he was off looking for Ol' Man River he designated Isabel to act as governor of Cuba, and she remained on the job until he got back in 1542. That sort of women's lib was quite unusual in those times. Today we're used to it. My neighbour's mother is now encouraging her son to marry a doctor.

On this day in 1912, the Royal Flying Corps was constituted by royal charter and those wonderful old aircraft are still in service. They were bought by Ugandan Airways. Every time a plane touches down in the jungle, all the natives run up shouting 'Oh, de meals on wheels am arrived!' I was in the RAF and it's true what they say. All the nice girls love a sailor but the airmen get the naughty ones.

The *Beckenham Journal*, my home-town newspaper in Kent, ran this in its personal column in 1949: 'Dear Julian, come home, forgive and forget. I have destroyed that prune pie recipe. Love—Ann.'

The man who had no nerves died on this day in 1911. Henri Pachard, the eccentric Parisian millionaire, won and lost fortunes at the Monte Carlo gaming tables without turning a hair. Accused of secret nervousness, Pachard offered to display his indifference to tension. On 9 May 1903, he stood in a circus cage with eight lions and, ignoring their roars of antagonism, fired six shoots accurately into the inner rings of a target. No one guessed he was wearing his St Michael self-cleaning Y-fronts.

The first film stuntman of importance did his thing today in 1912, when Frederick Rodman Law jumped from the Brooklyn Bridge. He was on Pathe's payroll to double Pearl White's co-stars in her famous action serials and he relished danger. A former steeplejack, he achieved fame giving parachute exhibitions. In February 1912, he'd jumped from the arm of the Statue of Liberty. Later he leapt from a New York skyscraper into a net and became the second man in the world to jump from an aeroplane to the ground, a fall of twenty-five feet, without any protective aid whatever. He did that jump for a movie called 'Man's Proudest Possession'. Luckily for Mr Law, he didn't hurt his own. He joined the Signal Corps as a balloonist in 1917 and taught recruits how to use their parachutes. In 1921, Law made his last jump. To avoid getting his feet wet, he hopped over a rain puddle – into the path of a speeding car on Piedmont Drive. He was killed at once. In his pocket was a contract for $250 to do stuntwork in another serial. Its title: 'Death on Wheels'.

14
APR

ABE LINCOLN GOT THE BULLET TODAY IN 1865

Did you ever hear about the actor who wanted to play the role of Honest Abe in a new play about the sixteenth US president? He bought a stovepipe hat, wore dark clothes just like Lincoln's, put on exactly the same beard, made himself up till the resemblance was uncanny. Then he went to the audition . . . and on the way to the theatre, he was assassinated.

Dr Samuel Johnson's dictionary was born today. From 1747 until 1755, eight and a half years of work by Johnson and his amanuenses went into the preparation of his 40,000 masterly definitions. Some words are open to more varied interpretations, e.g. his (a pronoun which means hers), tomorrow (today's best labour saving device), lovable (what a cow does for her sex life), red head (the gents on a Russian trawler), forefather (what you yell just before you hit a priest with a golf ball), alimony (disinterest, compounded annually), underdog (where you'll find yesterday's newspaper), thistledown (raining very heavily), and coincide (what you do when the rain's beginning to thistledown).

Victor Lowndes was sacked this evening in 1981. The colourful millionaire who headed Europe's Playboy empire for fifteen years was unceremoniously told to quit his penthouse flat in London's Park Lane. The move followed the lodging of official objections by police and the Gaming Board to the licences of Playboy's three West End casinos. I enjoyed the lavish style of the parties he gave at his sumptuous country estate, Stocks. We played 'Chef's Knock'. It's the same as 'Postman's Knock' but you make more of a meal of it.

Chang and Eng Bunker, the most famous Siamese twins, were born today in 1811. Anatomically conjoined, bound together by a five-inch ligament at their breastbones, they married two normal sisters, Adelaide and Sarah Yates, in North Carolina in 1843. One might have supposed that their sex life would be difficult – but they had twenty-one children to prove that one was wrong!

Who do you suppose had the smallest brain ever measured in a normal, working genius? It was the great French writer Anatole France whose non-atrophied grey matter weighed only 35.8 ounces, without the membrane (the average bloke's brain weighs between two and a half to three pounds!) With that miniature equipment, Anatole (born Jacques Thibault today in 1844) won the 1921 Nobel prize in literature. And staying in literary vein . . .

The first book-of-the-month selection was made today in 1926. Of course, it was American (who else would have dreamed up a book-of-the-month club?) The first choice was *Lolly Willowes, or The Loving Huntsman* by Sylvia Townshend – and 4750 club members got it. Comedian and actor Alfred Marks sent one book club selection back: 'It was called *Teach Yourself Surgery* . . . I just hope they don't notice I've taken out the appendix.'

PETER USTINOV WAS BORN TODAY IN 1921.

He's often teased about his beard but won't give it up, explaining, 'People can hear me better when I speak above a whisker.'

16 APR

'It gives me great pleasure and no money to be here tonight,' said the thin wild-eyed unknown – and nobody laughed at Spike Milligan, born today in 1918 at Ahmaddnagar, India. Before he had even dreamed of becoming a Goon, he did his act as a 'warm-up' for BBC's radio success 'Variety Bandbox'. The producer Brian Sears thought Spike was the worst thing he'd ever seen on a stage. The year was 1949, and Spike was very new at the game – but even then, he instinctively broke the rules. He told the people, 'I'll never forget when the producer took me on one side. And left me there.'

Early this morning in 1941, the greatest of all 'British' vocalists – Al Bowlly – was killed by a land mine. The handsome forty-three-year-old star made more records

with more top British dance bands than any other vocalist. He was so extravagant with the large income he earned that he once had to send all his clothes to a pawnbroker to raise the money to pay his hotel bill. Stuck in his room with no clothes and no more money, he had to find a way to attend a recording in the studios in Maida Vale. Al ran through the streets in vest and underpants for three miles, posing as a long distance runner. Then he recorded eight love songs in his underpants, collected his fee in cash and ran to the pawnshop to reclaim his suits.

On this day in 1524 a Florentine navigator named Giovanni da Verrazzano first discovered New York Bay and the Hudson River. Of course, he didn't know it was the Hudson River because Henry Hudson hadn't discovered it yet. Hudson didn't show up until his *Half Moon* sailed from England into New York harbour in 1609. He'd find New York very different today. It's the only city where the shortest distance between two points is always under construction.

Ben Franklin died on this day in 1790, aged eighty-four. The Boston-born US statesman invented the Franklin stove, the lightning rod and bifocal spectacles. Ben's first instructor was a teacher in English in Albemarle County, Virginia, named Benjamin Sneed (1721–1819) who taught his students for seventy-one years! For the last five of them he taught while seated upon a commode. If he didn't like what you had written, he made immediate and dramatic use of the pages.

18 APR

The great French symbolist painter of erotic subjects, Gustave Moreau, died on this day in 1898. He taught Matisse and Rouault, and left his house to France with its 8000 pictures, all forming the Moreau Gallery in Paris. Travelling in Brittany in 1875 he encountered an old peasant whose weatherbeaten face fascinated him. Moreau told him, 'I'll give you twenty-five francs if you'll let me paint you.' When the peasant hemmed and hawed, Moreau added, 'Come now, thirty francs, and that's a lot of money.' 'Ah, non, monsieur, it's not a matter of how much,' the peasant replied earnestly, 'I was just wondering how I get the paint off afterwards.'

The great San Francisco earthquake happened today in 1906. In 1966 the city finally came up with the perfect early warning system for the first signs of another tremor. It's called topless waitresses.

'THE SOUND OF MUSIC'

included the ring of cash registers. Today in 1966 film history's biggest musical moneymaker won its Oscar – while effortlessly bringing $60 million into the box office in its first year. It received an almost universal panning from the critics! Kenneth Tynan said it: 'A critic is a man who knows the way but can't drive the car.'

On this April morn in 1949 a Liverpudlian lady pedestrian was bowled over by a speeding car. Witnesses were relieved to see the driver stop and reverse to the fallen female. They then saw the motorist steal the woman's handbag and speed away again.

Insult experts of all time were not nightspot comedians like me, but statesmen like Disraeli and Gladstone. Benjamin Disraeli, Earl of Beaconsfield, who died on this day in 1881, once met the stuffy old statesman in the Commons and heard him state, 'Sir, you will come to your end either upon the gallows or of a venereal disease.' Disraeli replied, 'That depends, sir, on whether I embrace your principles or your mistress.'

19 APR

Cannabis plants were found growing in Dawlish Wood, Devon, today in 1979 . . . and many of the plants had been extensively nibbled by wild rabbits. A Torquay CID man said, 'If anyone sees a rabbit that looks as if it doesn't know whether it's coming or going, then at least they'll know where it's been.'

Grace Kelly wed Prince Rainier III of Monaco today in 1956, becoming the first American to wed a reigning monarch. Shortly before, she had won an Oscar for her performance in 'The Country Girl'. Bob Hope remarked, 'Now the girl has her own country.'

'ALCOHOL WILL KILL YOU'

quoth the seer . . . and it flaming well did! Duke Antonio Fernando of Italy was a superstitious man. When his family's famous clairvoyant warned him that spiritous liquors would cause his death, Antonio forswore all booze from that day forth. The teetotal duke still enjoyed his hunting, however. After a day in the saddle, his sore muscles craved a rubdown . . . with alcohol. A spark from the logfire lit the massage rub and, just as predicted, he died . . . burned to death. It's said his spirit still haunts the lodge.

The first legal use of the term 'trial separation' occurred in the divorce proceedings brought by a battered husband at Inverness in 1808. James Gregory Dyas accepted the opportunity to move away from his ill-tempered and violent wife Moragh and stay for six months at his sister's house in Largs. After three days of peace, James's wife arrived at his refuge and broke his legs with a plough share, crying, 'Now run off some more!' James got his divorce. More recently a teenager was telling her friend that her parents had decided on a 'trial separation'. The friend wanted to know what that was. 'It's like having a telephone disconnected,' the teenage girl explained. 'You see if you can live without it.'

20 APR

Captain James Cook discovered New South Wales today in 1770. The former grocer's apprentice from Marton-in-Cleveland, Yorkshire, observed kangaroos but didn't know what they were. He also saw an Australian aborigine who asked, 'You Cook?' . . . 'Yes' . . . 'Good – kangaroo stew twice, please.' He made a note in the ship's log: '*Aborigine*: a native Aussie and very bad comic. *Kangaroo*: a woolly jumper with 1 pocket.'

TODAY ADOLF HITLER WAS BORN IN 1889

It was comedian Harold Berens who told the story of how Hitler is found, alive and well, living in South America. Prominent German politicians fly there to see him and ask him to return to Germany as their leader. After some reluctance, Hitler says, 'OK, I'll come back, but this time, no more mister nice guy!'

JEAN RACINE DIED ON THIS DAY IN 1889

France's greatest tragic poet, Racine, never hit a man who was down. He kicked him. When he had his famous quarrel with Molière, he not only took his hit play 'Alexandre le Grand' away from Molière's stage troupe, he also gave it to a rival troupe to perform – and stole Molière's mistress as well! She was a sexy actress named Mlle du Parc, an intimate friend of the sorcerer and poisoner La Voisin, one of the foulest criminals of her age. Under torture, La Voisin testified that, tiring of his demanding lover, Racine had done away with Mlle du Parc by poison. In 1677 he married a wealthy but ugly woman several years his senior. The following day he received word that the king wished to bestow a well-paid title upon him that would free Racine from all his money worries! 'Just my miserable luck,' screamed the dramatist, 'twenty-four hours too late!'

21 APR

It was on this day in 1911 that the famous explorer Amundsen, heading due south for the pole in a blizzard, passed his first snow-ball.

Two hundred thousand pounds for a washing powder campaign – down the drain! Today in 1972 a big launch to sell a new detergent in Saudi Arabia was opened by the nationwide display of eye-catching posters with the illiteracy rate in mind. Beneath the product's headlined name were three simple, dramatic pictures. On the left – filthy washing. In the middle – its immersion in the new powder's suds. On the right – the same washing, sparkling white. As days passed, orders were cancelled and sales almost stopped. Then the desperate marketing staff realized why: Arabs read from right to left!

The first religious inscription was put upon US coins today in 1864 – when the motto of the state of Florida was inscribed: 'In God We Trust'. Much friendlier than the coins issued by the eccentric King Mwala of Angola, Africa. During his reign Mwala had the words 'Mwala's Money' stamped on all the coinage and his 'portrait' on both sides. But since he feared that publishing his own likeness would enable assassins to identify him, he had his brother's face on the coin instead!

The first known roller skates were worn today in 1760. This earliest record of 'foot-wheelies' describes a performance at a London party by a Belgian instrument maker who played the violin while circling the floor on skates.

He fell and wrecked his violin . . . but history doesn't reveal what he was playing. Could it have been wreck'n'-roll?

President George Washington went to America's first circus today in 1793 . . . in a building erected especially at Twelfth and Market Streets, Philadelphia, Pennsylvania, USA, for John Bill Ricketts' Circus. It's not true that a performing mule kicked out George's teeth although he did wear false ones. They were known as the George Washington Bridge.

Stas Szezesniak finally stopped playing his accordion today in 1979. He'd been doing it nonstop in West Chester, Pennsylvania, for 64 hours 13 minutes! Before that, he practised during the days on his accordion and nights, folding road maps. After breaking the record, Stas Szezesniak went back to his old job as an optician's eye chart.

Rupert Brooke died on this day in 1915. The Rugby-born poet wrote his two famous volumes in the early months of World War I, then died of blood poisoning while serving in the Royal Navy. He was twenty-seven.

Among his lighter couplets: 'Some weekend guests I view in sorrow . . . they're here today, and here tomorrow.'

23 APR

Miguel Saavedra died on this day in 1616, a soldier, a slave . . . and then a condemned man who was sentenced to death four times in Algeria. Giving up his unsuccessful business career, he took up writing and, at the age of fifty-eight, produced his masterpiece under the nom de plume of his middle name . . . Cervantes. His *Don Quixote* has inspired operas, a ballet and the Broadway musical smash 'Man of La Mancha'. When his finger was cut off during a fight in prison, Cervantes cooked it and ate it! (My agent once got so worried about the money I was earning, he ate his heart out. Broke a tooth.)

WILL SHAKESPERE DIED ON THIS DAY IN 1616

This matrimonial ad appeared in this morning's edition of the *Hindustan Times* in 1977: 'A 25-year-old Madras Nurse, 158.67 centimetres tall in her late 27s is seeking doctor in his early divorces.'

– just three days before his fifty-second birthday. He was only eighteen when he married Anne Hathaway. She was six years older and their first child, Susanna, was born only six months after their wedding. In those days however, the engagement was regarded as legally binding and any children born nine months after the betrothal were considered legitimate.

'He's done it again!' shouted the *Daily Mail*'s headline this morning in 1981 . . . 'Biggs is freed by legal loophole.' The runaway Great Train Robber ran out of court in Bridgetown, Barbados, yelling, 'It's back to Brazil for Ronnie Biggs!' as a crowd of West Indians cheered. Biggs was kidnapped from Brazil a month before, jailed in Barbados on 23 March and expected to be extradited to Britain to resume his thirty-year prison sentence. He served only two years of it before escaping from Wandsworth in 1965. What changed a petty crook from South London into a world celebrity was a late phone call in 1963, when an extra hand was needed at Leatherslade Farm. He was only brought in on the crime because he knew a man who could drive the royal mail train after the hold-up! His share of the £2½ million loot was to have been £140,000 – but when his wife Charmian blew a fortune on a mindless spending spree, a shop assistant became suspicious and called the cops. Asked if he would marry his fiery Brazilian girlfriend Raimunda de Castro, he replied, 'Marriage is just another kind of jail.' He shows himself up at weddings. As the bride goes by, out of force of habit, he holds up the train.

24 APR

Barbra Streisand was born today in 1942 in Brooklyn, New York City. From Japan came this compliment to her in 1967: 'Your records are selling like raw fish'.

Today in 1973 'Peterborough' of the *Daily Telegraph* saw a Kensington street-singer's card which announced woefully: 'Failed to live within income. Trying to live without'.

Queen Elizabeth II and President Eisenhower together opened the St Lawrence Seaway on this day in 1959 . . . linking the Great Lakes and the Atlantic. The arrival of a huge white whale in the Gulf of St Lawrence was regarded as a tribute to the drawing power of both heads of state. It caused unexpected trouble to a witless tourist. He watched the huge creature surface, heaving its vast bulk through the foam, then said to his wife, 'By the way, how's your mother?'

25 APR

Russia's Alexander III personally wrote the death sentence of a Jewish leader today in 1885 with these words: 'Pardon impossible, to be sent to Siberia.' His Danish wife Dagmar sympathized with the prisoner. She saved his life by delicately transposing the comma. The sentence then read: 'Pardon, impossible to be sent to Siberia.'

Wayne Morse spoke for 22 hours 26 minutes . . . and he still lost! Despite giving the longest speech ever in the US Senate (against the restoration of offshore oil reserves to individual states), Morse failed to prevent the passing of the bill. During the twenty-two-and-a-half-hour speech he drank twenty-three glasses of water. As a result, Morse finished on the dot and made a very quick dash.

'America' got its name in 1507. In a geography book, Martin Waldseemüller wrote, 'I do not see why anyone should by right object to name [the New World] America . . . after its discoverer, Americus.' Dan O'Day explains, 'He mistakenly thought Americus Vespucius discovered the New World . . . which is why to this very day it's better known as the United States of Vespucius.'

Dame Cicely Courtneidge died on this day in 1980, aged eighty-seven. Her lifelong love for her dashing husband Jack Hulbert didn't prevent her from punishing him for his occasional indiscretions. Once, during a tour of a drawing-room comedy, she hatched a plan to embarrass Jack on stage, charming the stage manager into ringing the telephone bell in the middle of Jack's best speech. She knew he'd be beside the phone at that point and unable to ignore it. The plot worked out perfectly. Just as Jack was in full flow the phone began to ring. Jack spoke louder. The phone rang on. He finally succumbed, picked up the receiver and muttered a helpless, 'Hello?' Then a flash of inspired revenge lighted his eyes. He passed the phone to Cicely: 'It's for *you*, my dear.'

Madame Tussaud's new building opened in London today in 1928. No truth to the rumour that they recently boiled down Liberal MP Cyril Smith and made the Nolan Sisters out of him.

Peter the Great, Tsar of Russia, made all the members of his court with beards and moustaches shave them off today in 1689 – and that applied to the men as well.

DANIEL DEFOE DIED ON THIS DAY IN 1731. THE PIONEER JOURNALIST WAS 59 BEFORE HE WROTE HIS 1st NOVEL! 'ROBINSON CRUSOE' TOLD OF A MAN CAST AWAY ON A DESERT ISLAND FOR YEARS WITHOUT A WOMAN...

YET I NEVER WENT TO WORK ON FRIDAY...

BoBMONKHOUSE

27 APR

The funeral service for Benjamin Disraeli was held today in 1881. Being Jewish, his body had been buried the day after his death on 19 April. When he was dying he refused to see Queen Victoria. He said, 'She would only ask me to take a message to Albert.'

Expo '67 opened in Montreal today – in 1967, of course. When Indian exhibitors wanted to include a live elephant in their display, permission was refused because of mice in the Expo buildings 'which could cause an elephant to panic and do damage to property and persons'. That's a popular fallacy. Elephants aren't scared of mice at all. In zoos and circuses mice are commonly found in the straw of Jumbo's quarters and are treated with indifference by the rightful tenants. And in the unlikely event of a mouse crawling up an elephant's trunk, it would merely be blasted out in no uncertain manner.

They shouted at him, shook, pinched and burned him . . . but William stayed fast asleep! As comatose as a backbencher, William Foxley dozed off today in 1546 . . . and did not wake up until two weeks later! He said he felt fine but had weird dreams. Mostly about being shaken, pinched and burned.

Sierra Leone became independent on this day in 1961, just one year after Togo did the same thing. Sylvanus Olympio, who led Togo to independence, was murdered by the army. The man who is alleged to have been Olympio's assassin became president seven years later – Colonel Eyadema. A slogan of his new policies was seen on posters in the capital city of Lomé. It said simply, 'Smash violence!'

The windiest place in the United Kingdom is Tiree in Argyllshire with an average wind blowing over seventeen mph! On this day in 1974 weathermen believe that a severe gust broke all existing records when it blew at over two hundred miles per hour! They weren't absolutely sure. The wind blew their recording equipment away.

They held a mutiny on the *Bounty* today in 1789. Fletcher Christian led the crew in their rebellion against the legendary Captain Bligh. One hundred and eighty years later my divorce came through on this same day in 1969 and I started paying alimony. That's what's called 'The Bounty on the Mutiny'. And on that same sad topic . . .

Muhammad Ali was stripped of his title for refusing to enter the army – on this day in 1967. They wouldn't take me because I've been married twice. I haven't got any fight left.

Claudia and James got married in Cape Town, South Africa, today in 1932. Hearty laughter was evoked by their surnames – Ball and Chayne!

In Amsterdam, Norbert Tossel began sneezing today in 1931 – and about 3000 'bless yous' later, he finally stopped on the morning of 2 May! The custom of saying 'God bless you' when people sneeze became common in the fourteenth century because one of the first symptoms of the Black Death was a sneezing fit.

Today in 1980 the British lost the only director who was a star in his own films. He never forgot his first experience with terror. He was just thirteen, living in Leytonstone, East London, when the daughter of his dance instructor was convicted of murdering her husband and was hanged. Her name: Edith Thompson.

29 APR

Her memory haunted him through his life as a gossip, wit, gourmet and the greatest British film-maker in Hollywood. In 1928 he made Britain's first talking picture thriller, 'Blackmail' . . . the tale of a female murderer. Famous for suspenseful slaughter *of* women *by* women and *for* women, he remained ideally married to screen scripter Alma Reville for over fifty years. Asked if his knighthood in 1979 would change his life with her, he replied, 'Oh, I *do* hope so.' Even his knighthood at the age of eighty was unnerving. He knelt, the queen walked slowly towards him with the ceremonial sword – and stabbed him through a shower curtain. (If the suspense is killing you, he would have approved. He was, of course, Sir Alfred Hitchcock.)

'ALL QUIET ON THE WESTERN FRONT'

academy award winning war classic, opened tonight in 1930 starring Lew Ayres. Twelve years later Ayres refused to fight in World War II, declaring himself a conscientious objector. He's a pacifist. That's a man who believes that fighting to save your country is a spectator sport.

The zip fastener was patented in the US today in 1842. A speculator bought the manufacturing rights for only $550! He was a fly customer.

At 11.30 a.m. today in 1980 terrorists seized the Iranian Embassy in London . . . and a London bobby! PC Trevor Locke was reunited with his family on 6 May after an ordeal which ended when sixteen masked SAS men stormed the embassy and rescued the nineteen hostages. The SAS heroes remain anonymous – 'The Un-mentionables'. Alan Coren insists they were really Balaclava helmet salesmen forcing an unwelcome sale.

30 APR

Queen Juliana gave herself a special seventy-first birthday present today in 1980: she abdicated! The house of Orange has given the Netherlands three queens in succession – the doughty Wilhelmina, who became a worldwide symbol of resistance to the Third Reich; the warm Juliana, who preserved the monarchy by winning the hearts of her people; and now Beatrix, intelligent but impatient and may not take well to being called 'Queen Bea'.

Casey Jones died at the throttle of the *Cannonball* – slowing down the train to save the passengers' lives – on this day in 1900. His courageous deed inspired a song that earned the composers the sum of $250,000! They sent Casey's widow a gift in appreciation – of a biscuit barrel! Widow Jones told the *Philadelphia Examiner*, 'I'm grateful and wish them no more harm than that, in the next world, they should be coals in the furnace of my late husband's locomotive.'

HITLER COMMITTED SUICIDE ON THIS DAY IN 1945

With him died thirty-three-year-old Eva Braun, made Mrs Hitler only a few hours earlier. Eva was a keen golfer. This was one bunker she never got out of.

1 MAY

'No matter which way up a cat falls,' said the Reverend Spooner, 'it always manages to pop on its drawers!' One lucky puss who managed to drop on its paws was named Gros Minou. Today in 1973 she fell twenty storeys from a Montreal apartment building – and lived! Windsor Davies says his cat is very sociable but shortsighted: 'He runs along the middle of the main road at night saying to the cat's eyes, ''Hallo, Fred! Evening, Gladys . . .'''

US pilot Gary Powers, flying a U-2 reconnaissance plane, was shot down by a Soviet missile near Sverdlovsk on this day in 1960. Powers was luckier than most spies. He was eventually returned to the USA. Alfred Marks enjoys espionage thrillers and once enthused, 'I'm reading a smashing one where James Bond rescues a gorgeous girl from being cut in two by a sort of light ray thing.' Someone suggested, 'Laser?' 'I haven't got that far,' said Alfred, 'but I'm sure he will.'

'The complete man of letters' died on this day in 1700. He was John Dryden, Poet Laureate for thirty-two years. Who can forget his immortal lines, 'When you shake the ketchup bottle, None'll come and then a lot'll.'

Japanese explorer Naomi Vemura walked to the North Pole alone! He arrived today in 1978. He paid curious Eskimos to keep away from him lest they endangered his solo claims. I wonder what he paid them with? Iced lolly, I suppose.

ONE HUNDRED YARDS OF SPAGHETTI IN TWENTY-NINE SECONDS

That's the faster-pasta eating record set on this day in 1977 by Steve Weldon of Austin, Texas, USA. Five minutes afterwards he belched and lassoed the judges.

Spiro Agnew was disbarred today in 1974. Comedian Joey Adams said, 'There is bad news, worse news and Agnews.'

Be proud, Peterborough! You can rock on with pride in your daughter, Maureen Weston – who set a world record today in 1977. She rocked nonstop for eighteen days! Well, to be honest, she took a few naps in her chair while her friend kept it going . . . and took turns singing 'Rock Around the Clock', I expect.

Lady Astor died on this day in 1964 The first woman to sit in our House of Commons, she was an American from Virginia. She campaigned for temperance and women's rights, saying, 'Feminists don't want to see women deprived of their rights – that's why we cry at weddings.'

2 MAY

Leonardo da Vinci died on this day in 1519. (His name was Leonardo and he was born in Vinci, Italy. Adds up, doesn't it?) He once painted a picture of dead fish so real it attracted flies! (He used a real fish when mixing the ingredients for the paint.)

FIELD MICE PUT ON TRIAL !

The official hearing took place in Glurns, Switzerland, today in 1520. Charged with damaging crops they were sentenced to eternal exile, writes Jeremy Beadle. We've got a field mouse in our vegetable garden. He sits on the beans and peas. Other days he runs into the cabbages and leeks.

This is a good day to be born if you want to be an athlete. Henry Cooper entered the world today in 1934 and, when the doctor slapped him, Henry hit back. Allan Wells, Britain's fastest runner, sprinted to his cot today in 1952 at Edinburgh. And the black US athlete and film star James Brown shares his 1934 birthdate with Henry Cooper. Walker Smith weighed in at eight pounds this morning in 1920, changed his name, and became world welter- and middle-weight champion Sugar Ray Robinson. England International footballer Len Shackleton kicked off today in 1922, to achieve fame as the 'Clown Prince of Soccer'. And British golfer Peter Oosterhuis was born today in 1948. Peter once told me that a golf ball has 336 dimples. I prefer Goldie Hawn's.

Cartoonist Norman Thelwell was born today in 1923; famed for his chubby little girls on chubby little ponies, he doesn't keep his own paintings on his walls. When his wife told him she wanted something in oils for the kitchen, he gave her a tin of sardines.

Sir Francis Bacon was impeached on this day in 1621. The lord chancellor was fined £40,000 for corruption, imprisoned and declared incapable of holding office . . . but Bacon was pardoned by James I the following November and his family took him home. This is history's first significant instance of bringing home the Bacon.

The enthusiastic crowds cheered at the public execution of John Price as he swung on this day in 1718 for the crime of murder. No wonder they enjoyed it. Price was the ex-public hangman!

'TOP OF THE TOPPEDED'!

4 MAY

They finally settled the Wars of the Roses today in 1471 – with a gigantic bloody punchup at Tewkesbury. That's the last exciting thing that ever happened in Tewkesbury. The town's so dull the all-night restaurant closes at 4.30 in the afternoon.

He walked 18,500 miles in 81 weeks! That was the world record set by David Kwan who left Singapore for London today in 1957. On this same day in 1960 student Piers Goddard hopped from Regent's Park to Piccadilly on one leg. Asked, 'Why on one leg?' he replied, 'I was saving the other leg for hopping back.'

Margaret Thatcher became our first female prime minister today in 1979. It was said that the Thatchers immediately settled down at no. 10 and that Denis was the one who wore the trousers in that house. Not only wore them, but washed and ironed them as well. 'The Iron Lady' might do well to remember this day in 1926, when . . .

BRITAIN COMES TO A FULL STOP

The nine-day General Strike began this morning. It was nothing compared with the world's longest running strike, the end of which was announced on BBC TV's *The Two Ronnies*: 'President Sadat has stated that work on the pyramids will be resumed tomorrow.'

Six to four favourite Diomed won the first Derby horse race this afternoon in 1780. The toss of a coin between Lord Derby and Sir Charles Bunbury determined the name of the most popular classic on the racing calendar. Had Sir Charles called correctly – the race would always have been called 'The Bunbury'!

5 MAY

The world's first train robbery took place today at North Bend, Ohio, USA, in 1865. The robbers derailed the Ohio and Mississippi Railroad engine, looted the express car, and 'robbed the male passengers'. No truth to the story that one elderly spinster sighed, 'Thank the Lord they never searched me and my money is safe'; whereupon the bandit leader turned back and searched her thoroughly for twenty minutes; then said, 'I can't find any money.' And she said, 'Don't stop now – I'll write you a cheque!'

The Nazis had their last U-boat success of World War II off America – when the U-853 sank the SS *Blackpoint* – and then was sunk herself by the USS *Atherton* today in 1945. The U-boat commander's name was Sackgasse . . . German for 'dead end'!

Today in 1980 the St John's Wood Synagogue displayed a sign in their car park: 'We forgive those who trespass against us, but they will be towed away just the same.'

And today was the birthday of Nellie Bly, 1867 (Cochran's Mills, Pennsylvania) – 27 January 1922; real name Elizabeth Cochrane Seaman, the fearless reporter for the *New York World* travelled around the world in 72 days 6 hours 11 minutes, beating the fictional record set by Phileas Fogg (1889–90). She feigned madness to expose grisly conditions in Blackwell's Island Asylum, 'acted as a prostitute' to report on corrupt policemen living off New York streetwalkers – and missed being a passenger on the *Titanic* by fifteen minutes because her taxi had a puncture!

Alan B. Shepard became the first American in space on this day in 1961. He *really* went out to launch, didn't he?

Did the last survivor of the *Mary Celeste* tell the truth on this day in 1929 – and explain the greatest sea mystery of them all? According to London's *Evening Standard* Mr Pemberton exposed the truth at last, fifty-seven years after the brigantine had been found in full sail in the Azores without a living soul on board. Pemberton was ship's cook and claims to have been right there on the *Mary Celeste* when Captain Moorhouse of the *Dei Gratia* sighted and boarded the otherwise deserted ship. He says he had to keep the truth quiet because Moorhouse wanted to tow the vessel in and claim the salvage money. But what became of the *Mary Celeste*'s crew, her captain and his wife? Pemberton's vivid tale tells how Captain Briggs had plotted with his pal, Moorhouse, in a New York tavern. The two crafty seadogs planned to abandon Briggs's craft and split the salvage. Things went badly wrong at sea. Storms caused a heavy piano belonging to Briggs's wife to slide across the room – and crush her to death. Briggs lost his mind and jumped into the sea after his wife's corpse. The crew of both ships fought each other and three were killed. Then the first mate and the remaining crew set off for Africa in the only lifeboat, leaving the ship's cook abandoned, alone until Moorhouse 'found' the brigantine and the 'Legend of the Ghost Ship' was born. It all sounds pretty far-fetched to me. I think there's a much simpler explanation of what happened to the crew. I believe Lord Lucan kidnapped them in his Time Machine.

6 MAY

One hundred and thirty hours of kissing. Today in 1978 the world kissing record was 'bussed' when Pittsburgh's Bobbi Sherlock and Ray Blazina puckered up for nearly five and a half days. They say kissing makes germs spread. But who cares if we have fat germs?

7 MAY

This morning in 1945 they woke Winston Churchill with the news of the surrender of Nazi Germany. A New York publisher was the next to speak to Churchill when the PM picked up his phone to call his wife. 'My name is Day and I'm bidding one million dollars for your memoirs!' said the publisher, amazed at his luck in having his 2 a.m. (in New York) call put straight through to the great man. Churchill rumbled, 'Can we discuss this later, sir? Just now my time isn't really my own.' 'That's OK,' said Day. 'The million isn't really *my* own either.' Personally I find very little humour in this story but it seems Churchill thought it was very funny and, when he repeated it, everyone laughed. But they would, wouldn't they?

The world's largest pearl was found in the Philippines today in 1934. According to John Fultz, 'It was huge – the oyster even had stretch marks!'

The first Catholic Mass in an airship over the ocean was conducted in the Zeppelin *Hindenburg* today in 1936: the Feast of the Apparition of St Michael the Archangel by Father John Schulte. He was the man who described the rhythm method as 'Off-season planting'.

HE MURDERED NEARLY 200 WOMEN...

. . . but hanged for murdering one. On this day in 1895 Herman Webster Mudgett, most prodigious lady killer in US history, went to the scaffold. His last words: 'I'd have been all right if it hadn't been for the women in my life.' Yes, and the absence of life in his women.

Affidavits were signed on this day in 1897 by Sheriff J. Sumpter Jnr and his deputy John McKenzie of Garland County, Arkansas, telling how their horses shied at the presence of a UFO! They clearly saw a cigar-shaped craft about 600 feet long and were told by a bearded stranger that he was on a journey in an airship, at present conserving propulsive energy. The lawmen returned forty minutes later for further confirmation but the illuminated cylinder was gone. And I just figured out why these flying saucers don't stay too long. It's some package tour agency – nine-planet tours in fourteen days!

Coca-Cola was invented today in 1886. John Pemberton mixed the multimillion pound marvel at Jacob's Pharmacy in Atlanta, Georgia. If you like a really stiff drink, try mixing it with plaster of Paris.

THE STRANGEST REPRIEVE?

The Martinique volcano Mount Pelée erupted over the town of Saint-Pierre today in 1902. Jeremy Beadle reports that there were only two survivors . . . one was a convicted murderer waiting to be hanged!

This was V-E Day: the end of World War II in Europe! I remember how we all sang and danced and held street parties, eating up all our previous food rations, drinking and making love all night long. They'd better not expect me to do all that again at the end of World War III. I'm at the age when it takes me all night to do what I used to do all night.

Colonel Blood attempted to steal the crown jewels today in 1761. Deprived of his estate when Charles II came to the throne, the Irish-born adventurer led a plot to seize Dublin Castle and kidnap Ormonde, the Lord Lieutenant. All his main accomplices were seized and executed but not our Thomas Blood. He had it away on his toes to Holland. Seven years later he led another gang of cut-throats to England with a view to grabbing old Ormonde again and hanging him! That plan went up the spout too. Then came this wild lark. Of course, he got caught this time – with the crown stuffed down his trousers! Well, that would make running for it a bit risky. Razor-sharp edges has that crown. He and his three mugs were bunged in the Tower – but Charles II gave him a full pardon and £500 a year as a pension. Was Blood a lucky bloke? Bloody lucky, if you ask me.

9 MAY

The world's biggest silver vein was struck today in 1903 – by a hammer! It should have been 'Maxwell's Silver Hammer' for a perfect song cue, but in fact the tool belonged to Fred LaRose of Cobalt, Ontario, and he chucked it at a fox. It missed. But the Canadian blacksmith had found another kind of fox. Sharp operators talked Fred out of the legendary lode he'd found. He sold it to them for a ludicrous $30,000, a tiny fraction of its true worth. Fred had spent the lot within three years. Fred was a loser. If he'd been a Hindu snake charmer, his cobra would have been deaf.

The notorious London-gang bosses the Kray twins were arrested early this morning in 1968. They proved that crime doesn't pay. They forgot to pay three police superintendents and a chief constable.

A giant squid dragged a 150-ton schooner down into the sea on this day in 1874, reports Jeremy Beadle. The *Pearl* was 'embraced', eye witnesses claimed, by tentacles as thick as a barrel. Russ Abbott's most painful pun involves a squid that falls ill. So a passing whale grabs him under one fin, rushes over to a shark and says, 'Remember I borrowed ten pounds off you and only paid back four pounds?' He's a loan shark, you see, and he says, 'Yes – where's the six quid you owe me?' – and the whale gives him the sick squid.

THE COURAGE OF HOWARD LEE HALE IS WORTH SALUTING.

He died on this day in 1976, never less cheerful and pleasant than he'd always been – after nearly thirty-two years in an iron lung! Hale, born in 1912 in Virginia, USA, is recorded in *The Guinness Book of Records* as the longest surviving patient ever sustained in that life-preserving device – thirty-one years and nine months. And he never grumbled. There are two kinds of patients in every hospital . . . those who are ill and those who complain about the food.

You have to thank Tom Lipton for that soggy limp old bag that provides your tea at breakfast every morning. Well, you have to if she buys Lipton's. The famous tea merchant was born today in 1850.

She had 16 children, 114 grandchildren, 228 great-grand-children and 9 great-great-grandchildren . . . and she met them all! On this day in 1620 Mary Honeywood died in Kent, aged ninety-three, leaving a total of 367 descendants during her lifetime. She saw every single one of them including the youngest, born only three days before her death. By that time, of course, she was on the pill.

11 MAY

Paul Tully set a crisp record today in 1969. He consumed thirty bags of salted potato crisps in twenty-four minutes at Brisbane University, Australia. A few minutes later he failed in an impromptu attempt to drink the city reservoir in a single gulp.

The world's most famous fictional liar really lived. That gloriously implausible tale-teller of Rudolph Raspe's classic book *Adventures of Baron Munchhausen* (1785) was a real German soldier and huntsman: Baron Karl Friedrich Hieronymus Munchhausen from Bodenwerder. Among his tall tales was a challenge from the king of England as to which of the two could tell the biggest lies. 'Go ahead,' said the baron and leaned back. For the next few minutes the king earnestly related how he had required soft stuffing for the queen's bed, described some searches for suitable materials, then topped it all off with, 'I waited till there was a gap in the cloudy sky, climbed up a sunbeam, plucked some fluffy cloud, and stuffed the mattress with that!' 'I know,' nodded Munchhausen. 'I saw you.'

Britain's first Nudist Congress was held today in 1910 at Wembley. It received little coverage.

Question: How many British prime ministers have been assassinated?
Answer: Not enough. No, sorry . . . I mean, one. On this day in 1812, in the lobby of the House of Commons, a merchant named Bellingham whose business had been ruined by the war with Napoleon, shot dead the prime minister, Spencer Perceval.

A dinosaur – shot by five bullets – in prehistoric times? At least two distinguished experts believed that it happened. Professor K. J. Almeida and Dr Juan-Carlos Esperanza made their amazing finds and claims today in 1939. From the Triassic period, the largest-known turtle that ever lived – eleven feet long and twelve feet wide – was found by their excavations in northern Germany. Within the skull and neck bones of the seagoing cryptodire, the two men found traces of five metal pellets, of unknown origin, perhaps meteoric. One of their theories seriously attributed the source to 'hunters from outer space'.

12 MAY

The Lady with the Lamp was born today in 1820 – and named Florence after the city of her birth. Daughter of wealthy British parents, she defied them to study nursing (a profession tending to occupy drunken prostitutes), and achieved marvels in Turkey during the Crimean War in 1854. Florence Nightingale founded the Nurses' Training Institution at St Thomas's – and in 1907 became the first woman to receive the Order of Merit. I do admire nurses. They're always carrying the can for someone.

Alcoholics Anonymous was founded in Akron, Ohio, USA, on this day in 1935. I've never been drunk in my life and I never intend to be. Because I always feel so rotten the next morning.

Historical footnote: The crouching start was first used in a foot race in the USA by Charles Sherrill of Yale University this morning in 1888. Asked, 'What was your best time?', Charles recalled, 'On a dirty weekend at a hotel in Albany.' Asked, 'Have you ever carried the Olympic flame?', he said, 'Yes, I took her to this hotel in Albany.'

The human geyser of the London and Southwark subway! That was George Monroe, a workman on the 1886 tunnel who survived the most amazing accident on this May morning. A leak developed in the advancing shield, newly designed by twenty-five-year-old James Greathead, later to become a famous

tunnel engineer. Greathead was also using another new idea – compressed air to remove gases and heat from the working men's digging area, far beneath the river bed. The tiny leak ballooned into a huge cave-in. The explosion sucked Monroe into the wall of the tunnel, a prisoner in a massive bubble. Carried by the force of the high-pressure air surrounding him, Monroe was squeezed upwards through thirty-five feet of clay and slime to the bed of the Thames. Then he was shot a further thirty feet through the water and flung twenty-five feet into the air, only to plunge back into the river. Rescued by a barge, Monroe's only damage was a temporary tendency to see double. Is that what they mean by 'tunnel vision'?

CHIEF WAMAIKAH SUPPLIED U.S. TROOPS WITH 4 MONTHS OF MEAT RATIONS IN EXCHANGE FOR $3000 IN GOLD. HE WAS GONE TODAY IN 1834...WHEN THE ARMY FOUND OUT THEY'D BEEN EATING THEIR OWN HORSES!

"THE TREATY ISN'T BINDING...HE DIDN'T INHALE."

Britain's Tommy Godwin bicycled 75,065 miles in 1939 . . . and then completed 100,000 miles in 500 days in the saddle today in 1940. That saddle-sore endurance won Tommy his place in *The Guinness Book of Records*. He wore out seven bikes, took them apart and made three new ones out of the parts. That's what's known as re-cycling your waste.

Queen Elizabeth II bequeathed three acres of Runnymede to the US – in memory of JFK – on this day in 1965. Runnymede's significance in the history of democracy dates from the signing of the Magna Carta. Only it wasn't signed at all because King John could not write! (He merely placed a seal upon it. Being a trained seal, it applauded and balanced the Magna Carta on its nose.)

14 MAY

Ss-ssch!

YOU KNOW WHO WAS CREATED TODAY

Schweppe and Company was formed on this day in 1798. The only reason Schweppe put bubbles into his simulated mineral water was to make it more like the curative natural spa waters – and during the cholera epidemic of 1832, they found out that carbon dioxide had a germicidal action – so Schweppe was accidentally right. His carbonated water *was* an aid to health after all. Perhaps he knew all the time. After all, he was a fizzicist. (And now for the most amazing fact in this book: that wasn't the worst joke in it. So watch out!)

John Eric Bartholomew was born today in 1926 in Morecambe, Lancashire – under the sign of Taurus the Bull – which Ernie Wise claims was appropriate enough. They became the beloved comedy team of Morecambe and Wise.

Sir Robert Menzies died on this day in 1978. Prime minister of Australia from 1939 to 1941 and then for seventeen consecutive years from 1949 to 1966, he was eighty-three. An Irish fellow lived in Australia most of his life and when he went home to Ireland for a visit, his old mates said, 'What are dey loike, dem Australians?' He said, 'Jasus, dey're wonderful people, Aussies, kindness itself. If you're skint, dey'll give you a bed and a meal without hesitatin', I'm tellin' ye, de real Australian is a gentleman, his wife is your wife, his house is your house, dat's the *real* Australian for ye! It's dem white fellas we don't get on with!'

The first nylon stockings were sold today in 1940. In less than eight hours, 72,000 pairs were sold in New York City alone. Within twelve weeks a house burglar had used one, pulled over his head, to disguise his appearance. He abandoned it during his escape. It was the first time a stocking had been found in a ladder.

"THE GHOST WITH A HAMMER IN HIS HAND!"
THAT'S WHAT THEY CALLED WELSH WORLD CHAMPION FLY-WEIGHT BOXER **JIMMY WILDE**, BORN TODAY IN 1892. AT ONLY 6½ STONE, HE COULD HAVE BEEN A JOCKEY----IN A GREYHOUND STADIUM.

Bob Monkhouse

The first 'Oscars' were awarded today in 1929. The then nameless statuette was awarded to an epic film of war, romance and daring in the air, 'Wings', with Gary Cooper, Clara Bow, Charles 'Buddy' Rogers and Richard Arlen. It was silent. Significantly a special Oscar went to Warner Brothers for producing 'The Jazz Singer' – 'the pioneer talking picture that has revolutionized the industry.' They say an Oscar is worth $5 million to the winning movie. Perhaps they ought to call them the Academy Rewards.

16 MAY

Dr Johnson met Boswell on this day in 1763. The first book Boswell published about 'the Great Bear' was the *Journal of a Tour to the Hebrides* with Samuel Johnson. Horace Walpole called it 'the story of a mountebank and his zany', and said, 'It were better for all had these two never met.' The times I've heard that said of my parents!

WHO IS MRS JUNKO TABEI ?

She's the Japanese lady who climbed Mount Everest, the first woman ever to do so . . . today in 1975. A small step for man – but a hell of a lot of little ones for a Japanese.'

The *Lame Duck* flew this morning in 1919 – – and landed on 27 May. It was a lame and luckless sort of duck, this one. Just before take-off, one of the five-man crew lost a hand when he caught his arm in the propeller. During the flying boat's flight from Newfoundland two of the engines broke down and the aircraft spent nearly as much time on the ground and water as in the air. They should have called it the 'Dead Duck' – except for one thing. The fact that it reached Plymouth Sound to complete the first-ever transatlantic flight.

The world's first telephone exchange took its first calls today in 1877 – from only six subscribers! Devised by Edwin Holmes it worked as a phone switchboard by day and a burglar alarm system by night . . . so Ed's first half-dozen customers were banks. I remember my first telephone. I made my first call and a voice told me I had the wrong number. I said, 'Are you sure?' And the voice said, 'Have I ever lied to you before?'

Birgit Nilsson is a world-famous Wagnerian soprano, a nationally famous wife of the owner of a Swedish hotel chain – and a wicked practical joker! In the finale of a performance of 'Siegfried', the hero leaned tenderly over Birgit who was playing the warrior maiden Brunnhilde. His intention was to wake her with a kiss. He was slightly taken aback to find on her breastplate a sign taken from a Nilsson hotel: 'Do not disturb'. (Birgit was born today in 1918 at Karup in Sweden.)

Today in 1980 the *Retford, Gainsborough and Worksop Times* carried this ad: 'Single girl groom required to work under stud groom. Ability to ride essential.'

17 MAY

The government introduced the British Summertime Act today in 1916 – but they didn't fool anyone. We still didn't get a summertime in Britain. I rented one of those caravans on the beach at Skegness. On a clear day, you can see the sea. On a rough day, you're in it.

Henry Waldegrave strangled his wife today in 1667 – and for nearly 300 years after! The site of the murder was Borley Rectory, 'the Most Haunted House in England' . . . and the ghosts of Henry and his wife were said to re-enact the ghastly scene every few months for the next 288 years until a priest performed an exorcism. That's what my TV set needs to stop all those repeats, is it?

Napoleon became emperor of France on this day in 1804. If he had conquered Europe, he would have tried to dig a canal at Suez for better access to the riches of India in his bid to seize it back from the British (who grabbed it from France in 1763). He was very hot on new ideas was old Bonaparte. He encouraged Robert  Fulton to develop the submarine and torpedoes. And he jumped at the idea of using a semaphore telegraph to send visual messages as far as the eye could see, gaining a terrific edge over his enemies. He could send a message from Paris to Rome in four hours. If the phone box vandals carry on at their present rate, there might be a market for them again. Fancy signalling to the wife that you'll be late home with a quick flash?

SQUASHED BY A STEAMROLLER AND LIVED – UNHURT!

In 1953, seven-year-old Michael Stavvides stood hypnotized by the three-ton steamroller flattening the asphalt of the Limassol street in Cyprus where he lived. Little Michael edged up behind the huge machine to get a better look – when the driver suddenly reversed. Michael vanished under the crushing rollers into the black road surface. Panic stricken, bystanders rushed to help the shaking driver recover the child's corpse – but the Savvides boy was completely unharmed. He had been pressed into the soft, warm asphalt. Beneath it, recent heavy rains had softened a channel in the soil forming the road bed *only fifteen inches wide* – just enough to make a safe groove for the child exactly where he fell.

Queen for a thousand days, Anne Boleyn was given the chop today in 1536 . . . the second wife of Henry VIII, who had wives like other people had mice. After the twenty-nine-year-old queen was beheaded for adultery and incest with her brother, her heart was stolen and secretly concealed in a church near Thetford, Norfolk. It was found again in 1836 and reburied under the church organ.

Britain's most evasive politician died on this day in 1898. I know the competition for that title is overwhelming but consider what statesman William Gladstone replied when Queen Victoria asked his opinion one day on a controversial matter of foreign policy: 'Well, ma'am, some say this and some say that, but I must strongly advise your Majesty that neither action nor inaction can be appropriate unless a firm grip can be taken on elements of these affairs as yet unrevealed, and mark my words, ma'am, I'm right.'

Today in 1978 the Sexual Olympics began in New York City – and went on for forty-eight hours. The lads did their best although the girls hoped they'd keep it up for longer. A prize of $4800 – plus a phallic gold sceptre – was awarded to Joe 'The Pole' Scarlatti, who is an Italian. He made love to twenty-seven women in four and a half hours. I'd like to go to more orgies but I can never think of anything to say.

In Greenwood, Virginia, USA, Britain's first female MP was born on this day in 1879.

She was that great advocate of women's rights, Viscountess Nancy Witcher Astor. In 1942 she said, 'I refuse to admit that I am over fifty even if that does make my sons illegitimate.'

She was Helen Reddy's 'Delta Dawn', Charles Dickens's Miss Haversham in his novel *Great Expectations* and a hundred other famous jilted brides in fiction, films and TV – but she was also *real* . . . and she died on this day in 1886. Thirty years before, Eliza Donnithorne put on her elaborate wedding gown in Sydney, Australia, and prepared for the greatest day of her young life – her wedding to her handsome lover. When hours of waiting at the church for a groom who had deserted her finally took their toll of Eliza's emotions, she fled to her home, stopped every clock and remained there in the decaying gown for three decades, the remains of her wedding cake still upon the table.

20 MAY

America's first car driver to be arrested for speeding was booked today in 1899. New York City cabman Jacob German was apprehended for hurtling his taxi along the streets at a murderous twelve m.p.h. 'This will teach you obedience,' said the judge. Now my wife is an obedient driver. If she see a sign that says, 'Pass both sides', that's just what she tries to do.

He went to bed today in 1790 for a rest – and stayed there for seventy years! When the lazy Jeremiah Carlton took to his mattress he was nineteen years old. He died aged eighty-nine – and had never left his bed for a moment. Heir to a merchant's fortune, the Sloth of Southwark was fed and washed by a team of over forty servants. Personally I love to lie in bed . . . if I can find a girl who'll believe those lies.

French novelist Honoré de Balzac was born today at Tours in 1799. He spent twenty years writing his masterpiece *La Comédie Humaine*. When his stingy uncle left him a sizeable sum, he wrote to a friend, 'Yesterday at five in the morning, my uncle and I passed on to a better life.'

21 MAY

One hundred thousand Parisians went wild when 'Lindy' completed his New York-Paris solo flight today in 1927. Charles A. Lindbergh left five children on his death in 1974, all leading intensely private lives, dictated by the kidnapping and murder of the Lindberghs' first-born son in 1932 and the resulting sensational publicity that traumatized the family. Lindy's widow is called 'Grannymouse' by her thirteen grandchildren. The family, though far-flung from Hawaii to France, is very close in mutual devotion. Unlike his dad, Scott Lindbergh doesn't fly – but he gamely posed in an open cockpit in Lessay, France, upon the 1980 renaming of their airport for his father. He said, 'I prefer my feet on what I call "terror firmer" – and the firmer it is, the less terror for me!'

And today in 1932 Amelia Earhart ended the first woman's trans-atlantic flight – from Newfoundland to Wales. She made as many headlines as when, seven year later, she flew solo from Honolulu to Oakland in 18 hours 16 minutes.

A chicken named 'Kung Flewk' flew 297 feet today in 1977, setting the world chicken flying record at the annual flying chicken meet in Ohio. His owner did a smart thing. He had the race started by Colonel Sanders!

LITTLE FLINGS MEAN A LOT!

Today in 1846 Queen Victoria received the famous Highland midgets Mary, John and Finlay Mackinlay – and in celebration the trio danced a frenzied Scottish reel. The young queen was utterly fascinated by performing dwarves and midgets and gave audience to all she could. Odd really, since Victoria herself was barely five feet tall. Just the right height for undersealing dachshunds.

Was this the date of the world's first public showing of a motion picture – in 1891? Arguments still rage but most film historians now agree that Thomas Alva Edison's workshop display of a man waving, bowing and raising his hat rates as the first 'public exhibition of a motion picture'. George Bernard Shaw came to loathe the flicks. 'Films bore me,' he explained, 'because they show interminably people getting in and out of limousines, trains and buses. I am not interested in how people get to different places but what they do when they get there.'

22 MAY

The *Repository*, the newspaper of Canton, Ohio, today in 1959 told its readers, 'Michigan motorists are warned to leave accident victims at the scene until police arrive. Until then, though, it would be considerate to visit them daily.'

He smoked 110 cigarettes simultaneously! On this day in 1974 in Los Angeles, Scott Case set a world smoking record by holding all 110 burning fags in his mouth and puffing them for 30 seconds. Later, he sneezed and had a fall of soot.

THERE'S NO POLICE LIKE HOLMES...

. . . although the writer who created the legendary Sherlock Holmes came to hate the detective and tried to kill him off in *The Memoirs of Sherlock Holmes* (1898). The clamour of his admirers forced him to resurrect the character for several more volumes – just as the author believed that he could resurrect himself through the power of spiritualism. Sir Arthur Conan Doyle was born today in 1859 at Edinburgh. It's untrue that his affection for the most painful puns drove him to instruct a decorator named Watson to paint his front door and porch a sour yellow, so that when asked what he was after, Doyle could reply, 'A lemon entry, my dear Watson, a lemon entry.'

Alexander the Great fell ill today in the year 323 BC . . . to die of fatigue and fever only twenty-one days later, aged thirty-three. He had conquered Thrace, Illyria, Persia, Tyre, Goza, occupied Egypt and taken control of all Greece. It's not widely known that Alexander invented a crude timepiece for his soldiers – a chemically treated cloth worn on the left forearm which, under the heat of the sun, changed colours every hour. This gave the Macedonian warriors the world's first wristwatch – or a device which historians call, 'Alexander's Rag Timeband'.

23 MAY

Both his parents were born at 11 a.m. today in 1934. Both are university professors. And their incredible son is Kim Ung-Yong, the Korean genius with an IQ of 210! On Tokyo TV's 'World Surprise Show', he performed integral calculus, spoke four languages and composed original poems – at the age of four years and eight months!

Benjamin Franklin's diary records this day in 1785 as the day on which he invented bi-focals. Two hundred years later, so many people are wearing glasses, if you've got perfect eyesight, they call it 'prescription eyeballs'.

CAPTAIN KIDD WAS HANGED TODAY IN 1701

The pirate from Greenock in Scotland had started out as a privateer commissioned to protect English ships from buccaneers like himself. He soon faced a mutiny and quelled it by promising to take prizes. It was when he decided to return to London and defend himself against the charge of piracy that they strung him up. He said, 'Is this what they mean by "a suspended sentence"?' The Captain was Kidding.

24 MAY

Sam Morse sent his first telegraph message in 1844 . . . between Washington and Baltimore, USA. In Morse code, an S is three dots, an E is one dot, F and L both include three dots; whereas an O is three dashes, a W uses two dashes, a Y has three dashes and so forth. So you see something like 'Sheets with Fleas' will be covered in dots. But 'Honeymoon with two rooms' will involve a lot more dashes.

Duke Ellington died on this day in 1974. 'Playing good jazz is like an act of murder,' he explained. 'You play with intent to commit something. Begin with a plan of what's going to happen. Break the laws a little. And don't wait around to get arrested.' He seldom went to bed before 6 a.m., loved to eat, adored women, invariably kissed close friends four times, twice on each cheek, and could compose fast. He dashed off 'Mood Indigo' in a quarter of an hour before a recording session. The secret of his security was constant move-ment, he never stood still; but Count Basie said, 'He didn't have to move an inch – Duke is definitely a statue in American music.' From a Count about a Duke, that's noble talk.

VICTORIA WASN'T SO VICTORIAN!

She was born today in 1819 and had a strictly pro-tected life. Until she became queen in June 1837, at the age of eighteen, she always slept in her mother's bedroom and was not allowed to speak to any adult unless her mother or governess was present. Small wonder that the release of such repression resulted in roguish ruderies with Prince Albert, involving nude drawings and smutty jokes! According to Folmer Webb, a favourite riddle between them was: 'Who's the greediest glutton for love in a bed?' The answer was: 'Look in the mirror, your face is red.' We are not amused.

25 MAY

The devilish doings of the duchess of Devonshire! Tonight in 1878 a dense London fog concealed gentlemen burglar Adam Wroth as he broke into the famous art dealers Agnew and Agnew and stole Gainsborough's masterpiece 'The Duchess of Devonshire'. Adam only wanted the painting as a hostage, a priceless item to bargain for the release of his friend, George Thompson. (George was in jail for forging cheques.) When he found that George was free on some technicality, Adam hid the world-famous painting in the USA. After twenty-five years the great painting was considered lost or destroyed by the art world. Then Adam, broke and dying from TB, sold the 'Duchess' back to the firm of Agnew and Agnew for a huge but secret amount. The treasure had been hidden in New York and Boston warehouses and – for six years – displayed on sale in a Boston art shop! When Gainsborough had painted it, the bitchy marchioness of Grays said, 'Knowing the subject, this can be never be called an old master . . . only an old mistress!'

The world's fastest animals ran a race today in 1937 – at Romford Greyhound Stadium in Essex . . . but the promoters and the crowd were done out of their winning bets. When one cheetah went into the lead the other stopped and refused to compete. When they tried betting on the speed of a single cheetah running alone, the sixty-m.p.h. supercat would only run about half the course. Then he'd sit down and wait for the hare to come round again!

THE CHEETAHS CHEETED THEM

Diarist Samuel Pepys died on this day in 1703. He wrote, 'Dying is the very last thing I wish to do.'

King Cheops ended his 4854-year cruise on this day in 1954 . . . when archaeologists dug up his ship in Egypt, the craft intended to carry his soul to heaven. He must have thought his mummy would enjoy the cruise.

'The Human Fly' climbed the New York World Trade Center – 110 storeys in 3½ hours! George Willig made his historic climb today in 1977. The climb was not only historic – it was illegal! 'The Human Fly' was fined one dollar and ten cents.

26 MAY

'BANG!' – and the cod war started today in 1973, as an Icelandic gunboat shelled a British trawler. The start of the cod war was an awful strain. The opening of the cod peace should bring some relief.

The Noah Project . . . to escape from earth . . . was launched today in 1980! Ex-marine Ray Hansen, aged twenty-five, announced his campaign to raise £5000 million and enlist the support of 20,000 technicians to build a spaceship to take man away from a polluted planet 'whose days are numbered'. Robert Orben says, 'If I were an astronaut, I'd be one of the backup pilots. The minute they tried to put me on a spaceship, I would back up!'

'Wild Bill' Hickok was born today in 1837; when he was shot to death in 1876, Wild Bill was packing a rifle, two .38s, two .44s, a .32 and two derringers. Didn't do him any good. Someone shot him in the back while playing poker in Deadwood, Dakota Territory. The cards he was holding included two pairs, eights and aces – a hand that's been known ever since as 'the dead man's hand'.

27 MAY

Duncan Goodhew, the champion swimmer with the built-in bathing cap, does not shave his head. His hair started to drop out after he fell from a tree when he was ten. Born today in 1957, Duncan told me, 'With care, your body should last a lifetime.' A pretty bald statement if you ask me.

On this day in 1947 the great conductor Bruno Walter conducted the Royal Philharmonic Orchestra in a concert in Glasgow. Next day he received the following note from a well-meaning member of the audience: 'I think it is only fair to inform you that the man in your orchestra who blows the instrument that pulls in and out only played during the brief periods when you were looking at him.'

HE GAVE A SERMON TO A PILE OF STONES!

Today in the year 735 St Bede died . . . the only man who ever got a heap of pebbles to sing 'Rock of Ages'.

Four fishermen set out from a bay near Dassen Island, South Africa, on this day in 1978 – to be rescued by their prey! Lost in impenetrable fog and quite unable to navigate, the men, who had hoped to catch a dolphin, suddenly felt their helpless boat pushed and propelled. Four dolphins drew them off a collision course towards dangerous rocks and then shoved the boat for another hour. As the fog dispersed and the dolphins departed, the men found they were safely back in the same bay from which they had started out.

Anne Brönte died on this day in 1849, aged only twenty-nine. Youngest of the three sisters in Thornton, Yorkshire, her first and best-known novel is *Agnes Grey*. You'll find it in the public library under Vintage Fiction, next to the British Rail timetable.

On one foot for thirty-one and three-quarter hours! That's how long Anton Christy balanced on one foot without support or rest until today in 1977 (he started yesterday) in Jaffna, Sri Lanka. He said, 'I would have done it for a lot longer but I started off on the wrong foot.'

THE DUKE OF WINDSOR DIED IN THE EARLY HOURS OF THIS DAY IN 1972. HE TREATED THE DUCHESS AS IF SHE WERE MORE ROYAL THAN HE WAS, NEVER LETTING HER HANDLE USED MONEY. EVERY DAY HE GAVE HER A WAD OF NEWLY MINTED FRENCH NOTES.

I TOLD MY WIFE ABOUT IT. I SAID, "HE was right! Germs live on money!" SHE SAID, "They couldn't afford to live on what I get from you."

MUST BE THAT NEW BUG THAT'S GOING AROUND –

bigMonkhouse...

For shame, ladies! Fifteen brazen hussies on the staff of the *Ladies Home Journal* had to be sacked today in 1912 for their wicked behaviour in the lunch hour! I hate to dredge up the disgusting details but the dirty deed must be exposed. They danced the Turkey Trot!

Manchester United won the European Cup today in 1968. News of their victory made the front pages. News of Fulham's results usually makes the 'Help Wanted' column.

29 MAY

King Charles II was born today in 1630. Nell Gwynn was the comely wench who was loved by Charles II. Well, she told him he was only the second Charlie but nobody believed it. Every time she said it there were quite a few Laughing Cavaliers. (All the lads used to pop round to Covent Garden for a quick Gwynn and orange.)

The first lighted beacon on the Pacific Coast was the Spanish lighthouse, erected and lit tonight in 1855 at Ballast Point on Point Loma, San Diego, California. The ad for a resident keeper was answered by a sixty-year-old cleaning woman. Puzzled, the clerk asked, 'But what attracts a woman like you to lighthouse work?' 'Listen, sonny,' said the woman, 'I'm just too damn old for heavy housework.'

Six million four hundred thousand dollars for a single work of art! That was a world record when it was paid for a painting by Turner at today's auction by Sotheby Parke Bernet in New York in 1980. Mind you, I once paid £500 for a genuine drawing by Michelangelo. The dealer said it was one of the very few he ever did in ballpoint.

A future US president fought a duel today in 1806 – and killed his opponent! It was at Harrison's Mills by the Red River in Logan County, Kentucky, that Andrew Jackson survived a bullet in the ribs – then shot Charles Dickinson to death at twenty-four paces. It was one of a dozen or more duels to the death for young Jackson, destined to become Prez on 4 March 1829. A born survivor, Jackson wrote, 'I leap out of bed the moment the first ray of sunshine enters my window. Thank God my window faces West.'

30 MAY

Britain's greatest jail escape happened today in 1973 when twenty prisoners got out of Brixton Prison. The wall had been breached by a rubbish lorry. My uncle Stan is still in that prison for something he didn't do. He didn't run fast enough today in 1973.

Let's set the record straight for poet Alexander Pope – who died on this day in 1744, aged fifty-six. He did *not* say, 'A little knowledge is a dangerous thing.' This is one of the most widespread misquotations in all literature. Here, from part two of his magnificent *An Essay on Criticism*, are the lines which the twenty-one-year-old Pope wrote:

A little learning is a dang'rous thing;
Drink deep, or taste not the Pierian spring:
There shallow draughts intoxicate the brain,
And drinking largely sobers us again.

There! I'll bet you're a better person for knowing that.

Today in 1918 a black cloth lying on the Khartoum sand of the Sudan in North Africa measured a sunshine heat of 194° F (that's 94° C) – while the heat in the shade was recorded at a comfy 109° C (42.8° C). It was so hot the Sudanese farmers fed their chickens ice cubes to keep 'em from laying hard-boiled eggs.

31 MAY

The Russians revealed to the world that they had television – way back in 1907. That was the claim the USSR issued today in 1951. Subsequently they've seen me on 'The Golden Shot', 'Celebrity Squares' and 'Family Fortunes' – and now they're putting all the blame on Britain.

The first wedding performed in an airplane took place today in 1919, in a Handley-Page bomber 2000 feet over Houston, Texas, at the 'Flying Frolic' air show, when Marjorie Dumont wed Lieutenant R. W. Meade. Well, they do say that marriages are made in heaven . . . and, like most, I expect it came down to earth with a bump. But this wedding in a bomber coincides quite uncannily with . . .

A wedding that went like a bomb . . . today in 1906 for King Alfonso XIII of Spain. As he left the church with his bride, the assassin chucked an explosive device. I guess I was luckier. All I had at my wedding was her father's shotgun.

It was the first great action of the French revolutionary war which gave this day in 1794 the title 'the glorious first of June'. France was starving. Admiral Villaret-Joyeuse had to get a huge grain convoy through at all costs. Robespierre himself had told him that if he failed his head would drop into the guillotine basket but Robespierre's own nut landed in there before he was able to execute either the order or the admiral. Villaret-Joyeuse was to say, 'I saved my convoy and my head' because the precious grain got through safely – but his own fleet was broken and his ships captured – by 'Lord Howe's Manoeuvre'. Chucking aside the *Permanent Fighting Instructions* of the British Navy, Lord Howe had sailed his fleet straight into the French ships in an entirely new strategy – he broke the fixed enemy line. It was an amazing new tactic. Admiral Hudson went so far as to say it wasn't 'acceptable warfare'. Lord Howe suggested that he take a deep breath and hold it. Forever.

Ernie drew the first Premium Bond prize in Britain today in 1968. ERNIE is *meant* to stand for 'Electronic Random Number Indicating Equipment'. Actually it means, 'Easy Revenue and No Interest Expected'.

SUPERMAN WAS BORN TODAY – and so was the *Daily Planet*'s mild-mannered reporter Clark Kent. The world's first costumed superhero in comic books was created by two seventeen-year-olds, writer Jerry Siegel and artist Joe Shuster. The comic strip was rejected by every major newspaper syndicate in the USA! Then publisher Harry Donnenfield bought it for $130 and put it on newsstands as a thirteen-page comic book. By 1941, Superman was being advertised as 'The World's Greatest Adventure Strip Character'.

Leslie Howard was killed – but no one knows where. Today in 1943 the press reported the famous actor's death in a civilian transport plane en route from Lisbon to London. Attacking German planes are said to have believed that Winston Churchill was on board. The bodies and wreckage were never found. He once wrote, 'This damned "Gone with the Wind" has made me appear as Ashley in everyone's eyes. But Hollywood is not a place where people look very deeply. Here, an intellectual is someone who can read street signs without moving his lips.'

2 JUNE

Abdicated King Edward VIII wed Mrs Wallis Simpson today in 1937. The British fascist leader Sir Oswald Mosley insisted that if Edward had been allowed to keep his throne and marry Mrs Simpson, it would have prevented World War II! Instead of anti-appeasers like Churchill and Duff Cooper taking charge, the king would have been advised by Mosley and Lloyd George to follow his own antiwar leanings and tell Hitler to 'do what he liked in the East but not touch France or move against the West. If he wanted the Ukraine as far as we were concerned he could have it!'

3 JUNE

THE WORLD'S LARGEST BABY WAS BORN IN 1961

– weighing twenty-four pounds and four ounces! John Fultz commented, 'When you burp that kid, you'd better wear ear plugs.'

Today in 1978 *The Guinness Book of Records* went into *The Guinness Book of Records* . . . as the Most Stolen Book from British Libraries.

THE FIRST WALK IN SPACE WAS TAKEN TODAY IN 1965

The spacehiker was Ed White, his route – around *Gemini 4*. Of course, a Russian dog was a few years ahead of him – Laika in *Sputnik 2*. He was the first to go for space walkies.

The world's first supermarket trolleys trundled down the grocery aisles today in 1937. Oklahoma City's Sylvan Goldman constructed his push-baskets by fixing baskets and wheels to kiddie chairs. Even then, three wheels went north while one wheel went south. I once asked a lady shopper, 'Do you know the real origin of that little basket you have there?' I noticed her small child just before she knocked me unconscious with a frozen leg of lamb.

4 JUNE

John Profumo resigned from Parliament on this day in 1963, admitting he had misled the House of Commons on 22 March. Another indiscreet lover, Casanova, died on this same day in 1768. He was arrested in 1755 for having sexual relations with underage girls but pleaded insanity. He said he was crazy about it.

King George III (monarch from 1760 to 1820) was born today in 1738; few historians note old George's love of wordplay. When he created the earldom for the earl of Onslow, he punned his name by changing the family's motto from *semper fidelis* – always faithful – to *festina lente* – make haste slowly! That's a pretty funny joke. Well, it is when a king makes it.

TODAY IS OLD MAID'S DAY

That's a lady who reckons no man is good enough for her. She may be right. And she may be left.

Forty-two-year-old Robert Kennedy was shot to death by Sirhan Sirhan. The Palestinian-born clerk from Pasadena planned to assassinate Senator Kennedy on the anniversary of the Arab–Israeli Six Day War – and five other people were wounded as his .22 calibre revolver fired eight bullets into the group of Democratic supporters in Los Angeles on this day in 1968. Robert Kennedy's dexterity with words was intriguing. In a debate with a senior senator he was corrected on a mistake in a point of law. He told him, 'The honourable senator is right and I am wrong, as the honourable senator usually is.' The honourable senator didn't know whether to smile or smoulder.

5 JUNE

Two condemned murderers were reprieved today . . . by a collapsing scaffold. In 1797 at Newgate the two convicted killers were flanked by the hangman, his assistants and two clergymen. The weight was too much for the scaffold. It caved in. This was seen as an 'act of God' and the men were saved from execution, giving thanks to the Lord for creating wood-worms.

The Arab–Israeli Six Day War began on this day in 1967. The Arabs claimed the war wasn't fair, that Israel had two million Jews on their side and the Arabs had none. As a result, Israel won the war in six days. They had to. They'd hired the equipment.

The British Blue Streak rocket made its first test flight from Woomera, Australia, today in 1964. It was immediately christened 'The Civil Servant' . . . 'It won't work and you can't fire it.'

His memorial statue is – his own body! One of England's greatest reformers, philosophers and economists, Jeremy Bentham, died on this day in 1832, aged eighty-four. When Bentham died, in accordance with his directions, his body was dissected in the presence of friends (he had a lot) and the skeleton carefully reassembled. A wax head, made to look like his own, was stuck on top. (His own head was mummified.) Padded out, the figure was dressed in Bentham's best clothes and set upright in a glass case. The effigy (and the head) are preserved in University College, London. Some people just never know when to leave, do they?

6 JUNE

Happy birthday to tennis world champ Bjorn Borg, today in 1956. In the 1979 French championships he broke the strings on sixty rackets in two weeks – it's a highly strung game. In 1975 in São Paulo he went through twenty-eight in six days. His rackets are strung at eighty pounds pressure and weigh fourteen and a half ounces, each turned to the pitch of a violin in Stockholm. He's also one of the best customers world airlines ever had. His £1,800,000 a year isn't made sitting in Monte Carlo, is it?

D-DAY TODAY!

And it was on this day in 1944 that the Irish Commandos dug in the beaches of Normandy . . . and Sergeant Sean O'Donegan won the prize for the most unusual sand castle.

The world's first drive-in cinema opened in Camden, New Jersey, USA, today in 1933. An Irish vandal was seen slashing his seat.

Sixteen-year-old Mary Pickford made her screen debut today – with the release in 1909 of Biograph Pictures' 'The Violin Maker of Cremona'. Her mother urged her to go into film acting 'to tide us over'. Mary became the wealthiest female movie star in the world. She was to say, 'Some tide! It didn't exactly leave us washed up!'

7 JUNE

The first zeppelin destroyed in combat was bombed by Lieutenant Warneford today in 1915. The 520-foot LZ-37 airship was on reconnaisance, passing coded radio messages back to German HQ. Its last message described Warneford's plane above them as 'friendly'.

MILLER, THE TROPIC SHOCKER, DIED AT 88

On this day in 1980 Henry Miller passed away peacefully in Pacific Palisades, California, leaving to literature an amazing legacy of explicit sexual memoirs, quasi-philosophical speculation and a Greek travel book. When his allegedly obscene *Tropic of Cancer* first appeared in Paris in 1934, poet Ezra Pound declared, 'At last – an unprintable book that is fit to read!'

King George VI became the first British monarch to step onto US soil today in 1939. As he went to his eighth banquet in eight days, he remarked to Lord Beaverbrook, 'Nothing makes travelling so broadening as the meals.'

George had the phone engineers losing by a neck – until this day in 1964. The telephone system at Chester Zoo had been totally haywire for six months. All day and

every day calls became crossed, lines suddenly went dead and phones rang for no reason. Today they traced the cause – George, the tallest giraffe ever held in captivity! In 1970 George stood a record twenty feet tall and had discovered a delicious secret. The telephone wires which ran past the Giraffe House tasted terrific! He loved to lick their fifty-volt tingle and salty flavour. Much to his displeasure the wires were raised three feet higher where even the Kenyan skyscraper couldn't reach. Chester Zoo compensated George by obtaining a female giraffe to occupy his time but they never mated. He wouldn't even neck with her.

Last night in 1958 Cambridge students went on the tiles in an Austin Seven . . . and left it there! This morning the sun rose on the incredible sight of the Senate House with a car on its roof.

Germany's Otto Voss patented his ride-on golf cart today in 1938. It went, 'Putt . . . putt . . . putt . . .'

President Lyndon B. Johnson authorized US forces to go into combat against the Viet Cong in South Vietnam on this day in 1965. I'm very much against war. So much so I don't even talk to my wife.

Marilyn Monroe was fired from her last film job today in 1962. The movie had a prophetic title: 'Something's Got to Give'. (It was later made starring Doris Day and had a surprise ending. Just when I thought it would never end, it did.)

Composer Cole Porter was born today in 1893. The Adlai Stevenson of songwriters, he lived in an era of flourish, inherited money and loved it, made more by himself and loved that as well. Elegant, witty, painfully crippled by a horse, he had a billion dollars and a wife so sophisticated she didn't know how to open a door.

9 JUNE

West Germany agreed to pay compensation for British victims of Nazi persecution. The final figure was fixed today in 1964 – at £1 million! Of course, it wasn't the Germans who started World War II. It was Vera Lynn's agent.

NERO DIED ON THIS DAY IN AD 68.

He had decreed that the new calendar should begin with his death but the calendar just didn't catch on. Everyone knew its days were numbered.

At Hong Kong's Happy Valley race course on this day in 1972 a cleaner found £8350 in a Kleenex box. Hardly to be sneezed at, was it? I'm never lucky on the race course. Every time I bet on a horse, I always hear the same thing: 'They're off! All except one . . .'

Today in 1915 the British troops in France were first issued with oval and grooved grenades. The nickname for them was 'pineapples' . . . because if you didn't chuck them fast, you were in chunks.

Australian inventor Paul Defrater flew his solar-powered plane for 11 minutes 15 seconds this morning in 1976. Can you imagine a solar-powered airline? Their slogan would be, 'Come rain or shine, we go or we don't.

10 JUNE

The first Oxford and Cambridge boat race took place on the Thames today in 1829. Establishing the great tradition, they began as they meant to go on . . . by colliding! The shambles sorted out, the race had to be restarted. Last year I stood on a bridge watching the boat race and heard a very old lady say to her companion in a suspicious tone, 'How is it the same two teams always manage to get into the final?'

James Earl Ray escaped and was recaptured on this day in 1977 Bob Orben said, 'It's time we stopped coddling criminals. We've had nothing but trouble since we took the electric chair out and put the wind-up one in.'

THE BALLPOINT PEN WAS PATENTED IN THE US TODAY IN 1943.

As the triumphant patent holder left the Patent Office with a victorious air, a clerk returning from lunch commented to the registrar, 'Get a load of His Nibs!' 'No,' said the registrar, proffering the diagrams, 'get a load of his balls.'

The worst calamity in the history of motor racing occurred at Le Mans on this day in 1955. More than eighty spectators were killed and another hundred injured seriously. A collision was caused accidentally by Britain's Mike Hawthorn as he braked to pull into the pits for refuelling. A Mercedes driven by Frenchman Pierre Levegh exploded, killing him outright, while large pieces of the car and engine were flung into the crowd. Mike Hawthorn drove on to an empty victory. By an ironic coincidence in racing history, today's the birthday of three-times world champion Jackie Stewart. Jackie's also been British and European clay pigeon shooting champion. I asked him if he liked a small bore better than a large bore and he said, 'Why? Have you lost weight?'

11 JUNE

James III, King of Scotland, was assassinated on this day in 1488, after his defeat at the Battle of Sauchieburn. He wore the tartan of the McDougalls. That explains why the girls said his kilt was self-raising.

Adding machines were first used by HM tax officials today in 1882. They were so successful they began to multiply.

The first oil was pumped ashore from Britain's North Sea oilfields today in 1975, helping to solve our energy crisis. Till then I thought an energy crisis was something that happened on a honeymoon.

ACROSS THE ENGLISH CHANNEL ...ON A BIKE!

That was the amazing achievement of Bryan Allen on this day in 1979. Together with a dedicated team and generous RAF assistance, the toothy athlete from Pasadena, California, made the world's first manpowered flight between England and France, pedalling all the way. His flimsy craft was the *Gossamer Albatross* . . . and Bryan made the trip encased in plastic to preserve his body moisture. The builders of the *Gossamer Condor* and the *Gossamer Albatross*, both people-powered planes, have gone on to develop their solar-powered model, the *Gossamer Penguin*. They've given up on a sand-hopping model for the Arab market when it kept burying its head in the desert. It was the *Gossamer Ostrich*.

12 JUNE

Sir Billy Butlin, MBE, died on this day in 1980. He was eighty. Born in South Africa on 29 September 1899, a teenager in Canada, three times married, he virtually invented holiday camps for 'the perfect holiday'. The perfect holiday! That's when you stay at home and send the kids.

And today's the birthday of Charles Kingsley, 1819, the poet and novelist best remembered for *The Water Babies* and *Westward Ho!* He was rector of Eversley in Hampshire most of his life and once told his churchwarden, 'I thoroughly enjoy truly horrendous jokes if they be of me!' Okay – in 1848 he wrote a novel called *Yeast* – but only did it for the dough. Horrendous enough?

Today in 1952 Paul Anderson set a world record when he lifted 6270 pounds. I tried weight lifting once. Gave myself a hernia putting the leather belt on.

Thirty-nine would-be escapers, twenty-six recaptured, seven shot, three drowned! That is the Alcatraz escape score. Spanish explorers named it 'The Island of Pelicans' 200 years ago. Its existence as the most infamous prison in the world lasted only twenty-nine years – from 1934 to 1963. It's a ten-minute ferryboat ride across San Francisco Bay to the rock, quite the most awesome and depressing place I've ever visited. Did any of 'America's worst criminals' ever really escape? Well, maybe. Today in 1962 Frank Morris, bank robber, disappeared from the 'escape-proof' prison, accompanied by two brothers named Anglin. There's never been sight or sound of them since.

13 JUNE

England paid a humiliating penalty today in 1980. European soccer bosses fined the Football Association $8000 following the savage riot by England fans in Turin. Soccer violence inspired the 'Two Ronnies' to announce: 'Fighting between Rovers and United fans was interrupted for ninety minutes when the pitch was invaded by twenty-two players.'

Writer William Butler Yeats was born today in 1865 (Dublin) – 28 January 1939; leader of the Irish literary renaissance (Nobel prize, 1923), founder of the Abbey Theatre; he observed, 'Married men make very poor husbands.'

BURIED ALIVE FOR 134 DAYS!

That's the world record set today in 1978 by Bill White of New Bedford, Massachusetts, interred with radio and TV in his coffin. He said, 'People procrastinate too much these days and that includes funerals. Why wait till the last moment?'

Battling Yorkshire and England cricketer Geoff Boycott batted his way into the Queen's birthday honours list this morning in 1980 – with an OBE. My father was a cricketer. He told me that if rain hadn't stopped play I'd never have been here.

14 JUNE

The European Space Research Organization was established in Paris today in 1962. I saw a scary sign on a wall. Some passing intellectual had written, ''Is there intelligent life on earth?' And underneath someone or something had added, 'Yes – but I'm only visiting.'

The first conviction made in Britain on fingerprint evidence was obtained today against Harry Jackson. He had stolen billiard balls! I once had an affair with the wife of a finger-print expert. She had to be handled with kid gloves.

Whisky distilled from maize was first produced on this day in 1789 – by a church minister! He was the Reverend Elijah Craig who called the liquor 'bourbon' because he lived in Bourbon County, Kentucky, USA. People often ask me what makes me drink whisky. Nothing makes me drink whisky. I volunteer!

Londoners can watch a total eclipse of the sun today . . . in 2051. Can't you picture the occasion? All the typical Londoners of the year 2051, cele-brating the event in their colourful cockney costume – turbans, flow-ing white robes, riding camels . . .

Japanese students staged a gigantic riot on this day in 1960 – a protest against the Mutual Co-operation and Security Treaty with the USA. Eisenhower cancelled his visit at once. (But on 19 June Japan ratified the treaty.) Puzzling country, Japan. Where else can a girl win a beauty contest and measure 16-16-16?

15 JUNE

The Russian spacecraft *Soyuz 29* was launched today in 1978 and arrived safely back on earth 140 days later – a new space endurance record. Spike Milligan reported, 'The Russian Soyuz spacecraft has docked with the American rocket *Saturn 8*. The punchup is still going on.'

The first greenhouse in Britain was erected in Oxford today in 1621 – in preparation for a predicted severe autumn and winter. It had no heating and, during the winter nights, a gardener had to wheel round a charcoal fire to keep the temperature up. Asked what he was growing he replied, 'Tired.'

IVORY WAS HARD TO GET SO BILLIARD BALL MAKERS OFFERED $10,000 FOR A CHEMICAL SUBSTITUTE....

ARE YOU DEVELOPING SOMETHING TO MAKE OUR LIVES BETTER---OR JUST TO MAKE THEM SEEM BETTER?

BOB MONKHOUSE

SO TODAY IN 1869 JOHN AND ISAIAH HYATT DISSOLVED PYROXYLINE & CAMPHOR IN ALCOHOL AND CAME UP WITH---- 'CELLULOID!' THEY MADE MILLIONS WITH THEIR BALLS.

The Duke of Wellington and Napoleon looked at each other at 1.15 p.m. today – through their telescopes! Napoleon's 68,000 infantry and 12,500 cavalry confronted 84,000 Prussians on this day in 1815 . . . and the Battle of Ligny was waged. It's a little-known fact that the Iron Duke had a very small vestigial tail and had to have a special hole made in his saddle to accommodate it! (This has nothing to do with his reputation as a wag.)

16 JUNE

Soviet ballet dancer Rudolf Nureyev defected at Paris airport on this day in 1961. Despite his disenchantment with Communism it is obvious to observers that he still tends to swing to the Left.

The Russians put the first woman in space today in 1963. Wally Malston observed, 'She'll be able to look down on everybody – just like Margaret Thatcher.'

The first atomic bomb blast sent up its mushroom cloud today in 1945. Bob Orben said, 'From that moment you couldn't even take refuge in religion. How can you gather at the river when it's no longer there?'

'AWAY IN A MANGER'

first appeared in print today in 1885. Jeremy Beadle reports, 'Although thought to have been written by Martin Luther, it is now known the real composer was an unknown American.' Christmas has become so commercialized since then. These days the only time you hear someone mention Jesus Christ is when they hear the price of the turkey.

It's 'Peanuts Day' in San Diego, California . . . where creator Schulz got the key to the city in 1971. Quite an achievement for the St Paul's (Minnesota) Central High School student who failed Latin, English, algebra and physics, had his cartoons rejected by the yearbook editors and was turned down as a cartoonist by Walt Disney. Charles Schulz's nickname is 'Sparky', after the horse Sparkplug in the 'Barney Google' strip cartoon. '"Famous" is a relative term,' he told Joey Adams, 'The final test of fame is to have a madman believe he's you.'

17 JUNE

THE SURGEONS DUG UP A FORTUNE IN DIAMONDS

– from a patient's stomach – today in 1952. Smuggler Joseph Baskin had swallowed £18,000 worth of gems but was taken ill at London's Heathrow Airport and rushed to nearby Uxbridge for examination. X-rays revealed the cause of his agony and the contraband was quickly removed. The customs men were laughing. Baskin was in stitches.

The first round-the-world airline service was opened today in 1947 – by Pan-American Airways. Now Pan-Am is developing a plane that'll seat 630 people. And that's just in the toilet.

Mack Sennett introduced his bathing beauties to the silent movie screen on this day in 1915. Now nothing can replace the modern swim-suit – and it almost has.

NAPOLEON MET HIS WATERLOO TODAY IN 1815

It was maintained that he should have won the battle but was preoccupied with his haemorrhoids. Who really won the Battle of Waterloo? Wellington refused to discuss it. When pinned down, he said impatiently, 'There was glory enough for all.' Hours after he called it, 'The nearest run thing you ever saw in your life!' The Congress of Vienna was held immediately afterwards to deliberate on the outcome. The only uncontested resolution passed by the Allies was that Brie deserved the title of the 'King of Cheeses'.

Question of the day: Why could the Duke of Wellington never have said his famous remark that 'the Battle of Waterloo was won on the playing fields of Eton'?

Three answers: It was written by the French political philosopher Montalembert in 1855 (forty years after the battle). In 1815 there were no organized games at all at Eton. And, thirdly, Eton had no playing fields anyway.

On this day in 1972 a BEA Trident crashed on takeoff from Heathrow. All 118 passengers and all the crew were killed. Michael Flanders said, 'The airline people have calculated that it's safer to fly than it is to cross the road. And they've employed men to drive the airline buses with instructions to keep the statistics favourable.

Egypt was proclaimed a republic today in 1953. Egypt and Israel may have buried the hatchet since then . . . but they've kept a map of where.

19 JUNE

The longest kidnapping on record ended today in 1978. An Italian film producer, Niccolo de Noro, was released after 524 days on the payment of a £3.3 million ransom. Criminals are so brazen these days. Bob Orben says he was in a department store and saw a guy trying on nylons over his head.

THE WORLD'S 1st ALL-MOTION-PICTURE THEATRE OPENED TODAY IN 1905 IN PITTSBURGH, PENNSYLVANIA, USA. FOR 10c. ADMISSION YOU COULD SEE 'POOR But Honest' AND 'THE BAFFLED BURGLAR'.... ACCOMPANIED BY 'Melodies on the Harp by Madame Durocher.'

BobMonkhouse

Julius and Ethel Rosenberg were the first US citizens to be executed for espionage – on this day in 1953. Mort Sahl said, 'Let the Russian agents come to the USA to spy and steal our secrets. Then they'll be six years behind like us.'

The Loch Ness monster may have a distant cousin – 6500 miles away in Tibet! On this day in 1980 Chinese scientists announced that they were investigating reports that a monster as big as a house had eaten one person and a cow. Farmers and Communist Party officials swore they'd seen the gigantic beast in the 400-square-mile Lake Wembu. Les Dawson says his mother-in-law went swimming in Loch Ness once. The monster got out and picketed the lake.

Today in 1815 Colonel Robert Ellison survived the Battle of Waterloo – and then fought the Battle of Loo Water! With only a lavatory pail of cold, brackish water and a sword, he faced the death of a thousand cuts. Well, a British officer never refuses a daring wager, and every man in every regiment under Wellington knew of Ellison's boast: 'Once we've cut off Napoleon, I'll cut off my beard in less than a minute!' Sure enough, the week-old beard was whisked off in under sixty seconds and, Jeremy Beadle records, that's how Robert Ellison earned his nickname of 'Black Bob'. Of course, it's my close shaves with the TV censors that have earned me the nickname of 'Blue Bob'.

20 JUNE

Princess Victoria was awoken in her bed at 5 a.m. today in 1837 to find the archbishop of Canterbury there! For a moment she thought she'd got lucky but, no, he was only coming to tell her she was queen of England.

Eight thousand miles of pipeline opened in 1977 – carrying oil across Alaska. Remember when 'one-armed bandits' were slot machines? Now they're petrol pumps.

SIXTY MILLION DOLLARS

– history's biggest kidnap ransom – was paid today in 1975. A guerilla gang in Buenos Aires collected the bumper bundle in exchange for two businessmen, Jorge and Juan Born. That's a tough city for crime. They've got 'watch your coat' signs in the police stations.

THIS IS THE BIRTHDAY OF JEAN-PAUL SARTRE, 1905.

The great existentialist wrote *Nausea* (1938), *Being and Nothingness* (1943), *No Exit* (1944); resisted the Nazis in Paris during World War II; told Malcolm Muggeridge, 'You can believe that nothing is without value. Cancer cures smoking.'

Today in 1777, the first volume of the *Encyclopedia Britannica* was published, in its second edition. In their latest edition they've made an embarrassing mistake. Volume twelve is 'Raspberries to Thatcher'.

After 301 days at sea, travelling 37,500 miles, Bernard Moitessier landed at Tahiti today in 1969, completing the longest single-handed yachting trip ever! Imagine what he could have done if he'd used *both* hands. (Have some respect for that joke. It's older than either of us.)

Brazil beat Italy 4-1 to win the World Cup for the third time – today in 1970. Italian fans nicknamed their goalkeeper 'Cinderella' because he kept missing the ball.

Elvis Aaron Presley revealed his upper torso for the first time on Ed Sullivan's famous US TV show, tonight in 1958. Elvis had a twin brother named Jesse who died at birth on 8 January 1935. He claimed to have made contact with his spirit and told the *National Enquirer*, 'Many singers are mediums.' Except for Tom Jones, of course. He's a large.

22 JUNE

Eighteen-year-olds got the vote in US elections when President Nixon signed the bill into law today in 1970. He made very few jokes but in a rare moment of honest humour he did say, 'Whenever anyone in the White House tells a lie, Nixon gets a royalty!'

NAZI TROOPS INVADED RUSSIA ON THIS DAY IN 1941

Now everyone's trying to get *out* of there. With all those Russian defectors, I'll lay three to one Lenin's Tomb is empty.

This was yet another of Lana Turner's wedding days. She wed her sixth husband, Robert Eaton, in 1965. Robert Orben said, 'I won't say how the honeymoon went, but when they came down to the breakfast room she asked for separate checks.

Roman Emperor Vespasian died on this day in AD 79. Son of an equestrian tax collector, he distinguished himself as a commander when Claudius invaded Britain. Nero nearly executed him for falling asleep while the emperor was singing! But Legion Commander Vespasian waited while Nero died, Galba was murdered and Otho did himself in before having his legions proclaim him as emperor. When his own last illness came he said, 'Vae, puto deus fino!' ('Wow, I'm turning into a god!') Lots of people thought they'd become gods in those days. Now there's only Brian Clough.

23 JUNE

The typewriter was patented today in 1868. (Me, I'm a touch typist. If I'm your type, you may touch!)

The bull horned in on matador José Candida's act today in 1771. The pioneer bull-fighter introduced many of his own ideas to the bullring, including the classic stance and the killing plunge and, finally, the loud scream.

William Penn, the Englishman who founded Pennsylvania, signed a peace treaty with the American Indians today in 1683. Indian chiefs organized a great celebration. According to Ronnie Corbett, Running Deer arranged the banquet, Running Bear arranged the cabaret and guess who arranged the catering? Wait for it . . . Running Buffet! (The toilet arrangements were by Running Water and his son, Little Drip.)

The British army's mightiest field marshal was born in County Kerry, Ireland, today in 1850. The 1st Earl Kitchener of Khartoum won the Battle of Omdurman and occupied Khartoum in 1898. I dreamed I saw the famous image of Lord Kitchener pointing straight at me and saying 'I . . . WANT . . . YOU!' I wouldn't have minded but he was winking!

24 JUNE

The Battle of Bannockburn took place today in 1314. Sir Harry Lauder said, 'The British dispersed the Scottish army with an underhand trick. They passed the hat round.'

Today in 1751 Benjamin Franklin published his pamphlet concerning watch- and clock-making. Everyone said it was about time.

ROBERT FORD WAS GUNNED DOWN ON THIS DAY 1892.

As a new recruit to the James gang, Ford shot and killed Jesse James on 3 April 1882, earning $10,000 reward. Drifting through the West, Ford opened a saloon in Creede, Colorado, where a customer plugged him. Asked why he'd shot Ford, the Red Indian chief replied, 'He wouldn't stop calling me his "fine feathered friend".'

Samuel Beckett's play *Breath* was first performed tonight in 1970. It had no actors, no dialogue, and lasted a total of thirty seconds. As an added attraction, it had no audience – and no second performance.

The first massage parlour opened in London today . . . in 1801! The self-styled 'Doctor' Edward Fell was a believer in hot baths. Me, I can't afford massage parlours. I just strip at the car wash.

The United Nations Organization was founded on this day in 1945. Would you call the UN the Tower of Babble? Joey Adams says, 'The United Nations is made up of states that cannot tolerate injustice or oppression – except at home.'

25 JUNE

BARBED WIRE WAS PATENTED TODAY IN 1867

(It was used for de fence). I've always admired inventors. My favourite inventor is Pat Pending. His name's on nearly everything, except army lorries. They were invented by Max Speed when he was forty.

The first colour TV transmissions began in the USA today in 1951. Early colour pictures were inclined to blur and mix. Bob Hope said, 'I saw a new kind of Western on TV last night. The Indians stood still and the colours ran.'

Happy birthday too to ballerina Doreen Wells, born in 1937 and less well known as marchioness of Londonderry. Of disco dancing she said, 'The only person dancing cheek to cheek these days is Rudolf Nureyev.'

The heroine of the film 'Carve Her Name with Pride' was born today in 1921. Violette Szabo's legendary courage as a French resistance fighter against the Nazis never failed her. After her death aged twenty-three in a German prison camp she was posthumously awarded the George Cross and the Croix de Guerre. Her father was English, her mother a French writer who wrote, 'The truth never hurts unless it ought to.'

26 JUNE

King George IV died on this day in 1830. Before he was seventeen he confessed to being 'rather too fond of women and wine'. From Drury Lane actress Perdita to the merry widow Mrs Fitzherbert, his sex life was in fits and starts. The ladies agreed, 'If it fits, he starts.'

Britain's first cafeteria opened today at Bristol Market in 1864. James Ludaire, the proprietor, displayed a sign: 'Courteous and efficient self service'.

Happy birthday to *Punch* Editor, Alan Coren, 1938. Fantastically funny writer, he educated at Oxford, Yale and Berkeley – which helps to explain why his appeal is transatlantic. In an 'Explanation' of his 1980 book *Tissues for Men*, he wrote, '5 years ago, I produced a book entitled *Golfing for Cats*, which sported on its dustjacket a fetchingly irrelevant swastika. Since I had gleaned from W. H. Smith and other major outlets that golf, cats and Third Reich books were the 3 best-selling categories, it seemed only a matter of time before I should unload some 2 million copies.' He admitted it was an unwise trick, 'added to which, in the 5 years since then the bottom has dropped even further out of the book market: what the crowds besieging Smith's are *really* after these days is paper handkerchiefs.' He felt that *Tissues for Men* would become a runaway best-seller, and would also redeem his reputation at the fair trading offices – 'there are 80 good wet-proof blasts' in the book. 'The law is on my side.'

27 JUNE

The Central London Electric Railway was opened today in 1900. My wife won't ride in the rush hour any more since she came home one night and found something inside her tights . . . a glove!

Cherbourg was taken by the Allies as the war in Europe reached a decisive stage today in 1944. Ted Rogers says, 'Britain was never greater than in World War II. Hitler gave us the V-1 . . . Churchill gave him the V-2.'

The starting pistol was fired for World War I on this day in 1914 – when the Serbian assassin Gavrilo Princip shot the Archduke Franz Ferdinand and his wife as they drove through the Bosnian town of Sarajevo. Austria–Hungary held Serbia to blame (Ferdy was heir to their throne, you see) and before you knew it Russia jumped in to support Serbia, France supported Russia, Germany declared war on Russia and Britain joined in the fight on 3 August 1914. My father said his uniform fitted him like a glove . . . it covered his hands.

28 JUNE

The Home Office appointed Sir Francis Marking as Britain's first film censor today in 1905. He held the post for nearly two years before he was invited to watch a film of the Folies-Bergère. He declined the invitation, pointing out that he was totally blind.

Today in 1919 they signed the Treaty of Versailles in France, ending World War I. French Premier Georges Clemenceau observed, 'War is too important to be left to the Generals.' The first Battle of the Marne remained controversial. A reporter tried to pin down Marshal Joffre: 'When the battle was won, did you win it?' Joffre side-stepped, 'I can't answer that – but if the battle had been lost, I would have lost it.' He should have been a politician.

EARLY BIRD CHIRPED FOR THE FIRST TIME TODAY

– the first satellite to relay trans-atlantic phone calls. That was back in 1965. Last week I tried to call New York and I had to try seven satellites before I found one that was working.

Today is the birthday of the *Daily Telegraph*, born in 1855, price twopence. They haven't missed much, from 'Dr Livingstone, I presume?' (the paper sponsored Stanley) to exploits they deplored. When Blondin crossed Niagara on a tightrope, stopping to cook an omelette in midstream, they reported, 'These foolhardy exhibitions drew some 10,000 people to witness the result. The facts appear to be so well attested, that they deserve mention as record of extraordinary folly, leading to an inevitable fatality.' Blondin's folly took place tomorrow, 30 June, in 1859, in the first of his many Niagara crossings. In 1861 he packed London's Crystal Palace, walking on stilts on a 170-foot-high rope without a net – and did somersaults! He died in bed aged seventy-three. Well, the *Daily Telegraph* warned him it'd kill him, didn't they?

The trade unions were legalized by Act of Parliament on this day in 1871. The Scottish convener of shop stewards was told by a Harley Street specialist, 'You've only got a week to live.' Jock said, 'How can this happen to me, Britain's greatest campaigner for the workers?' – and the specialist said, 'In that case, we'll make it a five-day week.'

29 JUNE

The first mass-produced chocolate bars in North America began churning out of Arthur Ganong's factory in New Brunswick, New Jersey, today in 1910. We eat more chocolate in Britain per person than the average consumption of seven Americans. Then there's the Irish lorrydriver who heard that all the blokes in his line of work ate Yorkies . . . so he called at Battersea Dogs' Home and asked for one barbecued with chips.

Sixty-two miles an hour . . . on a bicycle! Cycling on a wooden runway, Charles Murphy became the world's fastest self-propelled person today in 1899! The runway was constructed behind a railway engine which set the pace for Murphy to pedal a mile in 57.8 seconds. He was riding a bike with a shortened frame because he was only five feet tall. When he was born, his mother said, 'We must be grateful for small Murphies.'

30 JUNE

On this day in 1908 a giant fireball devastated Tunguska in Russia – and nobody knows why. There are dozens of theories about the fantastic explosion which dis-integrated a valley the size of a large city, turning trees to powder and burning the skin of observers over thirty-two miles away. Least likely cause is a meteorite – no crater. Some say a comet, others believe it was an atom-sized black hole – but Russian author Alexander Kazantsev believes it was a nuclear explosion in a space ship! In 1908? 'Ah!' says Kazantsev, 'It wasn't one of ours!'

'Here lies the sixpenny piece, born 1515 in the reign of Henry VIII. Executed on this day, 1980, aged 429 years, another victim of decimalisation and raging and inflation. RIP.' That's how Colin Reid mourned the passing of the tanner, the sprazi, the lord of the manor. Well, there are bigger things in life than your money. Your bills, for instance.

Margaret Mitchell's *Gone with the Wind* was published this morning in 1936. A copy was placed in the first-ever Time Capsule, buried in 1938 under Flushing Meadows on the site of the New York World's Fair, along with the Bible, the Lord's Prayer in 300 languages and a rhinestone clip from Woolworth's . . . all for posterity. To hell with it. What has posterity ever done for me?

This is the first day of Quintilis Well, it would have been but for Mark Antony who suggested the month should be named after Julius Caesar. So in 44 BC this became the first of Julius. At first, the month had thirty-six days. This was probably because July is the hottest month of the year and you know how heat expands things.

1 JULY

It was seven-thirty on a perfect morning . . . 1 July 1916. For the past ten minutes, the birds had swooped and sung between the lines of the trenches. The British guns and mortars – one for every seventeen yards of the sixteen-mile front along the River Somme – had stopped firing. In the trenches, young officers glanced at their watches. Zero hour. Whistles blew. Thousands of men went over the top. The first day of the Battle of the Somme – the bloodiest day in the history of the British Army – had begun. My father told me that he was there that morning and very nervous. His captain reassured him, 'Buck up! Not one of those shells is going to get you unless it's got your name on it!' Just then a German popped his head over the edge of the trench and said, 'Pardon me, gentlemen, but how do you spell "Monkhouse"?'

The jolly, jolly sixpence that has seen Britons through 429 years, 21 monarchs and a good few singsongs went out of circulation at midnight last night in 1980. Very few sixpences are worth much. Those minted in 1952 have a rarity value and may bring up to £25 –and pre-1920 coins are almost entirely silver. My grandfather preserved the first pound note he ever earned in a sixpenny frame. Now the frame's worth £1 and the pound note's worth 6p.

Jack Dempsey k.o.'d Georges Carpentier in four rounds today in 1921. The battle attracted boxing's first million dollar gate. Asked by Edward R. Murrow, 'Were you ever afraid of an opponent?', Jack

hesitated, then blurted out, 'No I was too dumb!' (In fact, Jack's shrewd intelligence in the ring matched his amazing courage.) On Gypsy Rose Lee's TV chat show, she asked him what he did before the start of a big fight. 'I pray everything will come off all right,' said Jack. The striptease queen smiled: 'Me too.'

Amelia Earhart and her co-pilot vanished over the Pacific on this day in 1937. They were on a round-the-world flight. The way air travel is accelerating, soon it will take only five hours to go around the world. One hour for the flying and four hours to get to the airport.

TODAY COULD BE THE DAY

. . . if you play your cards right! In the year 969 the first playing cards appear in the history books . . . and on this day in 1395 a Bologna woodcut printer named Calva

The famous French astrologer Michel de Nostradamus died on this day in 1556 – just as he'd predicted!

produced his first deck of cards on triangles of parchment stiffened with starch. The rarest pack is the Bowles family's 'Lives of the Saints', made in the seventeenth century and worth about £2000. My favourite card game is patience. That way I meet a better class of people.

In Lyons, France, a man charged with stealing a horse today in 1958 told the court that the higher altitude on top of the horse was good for his asthma.

On this day in 1862 John Speke and James Grant joined at Lake Victoria to mark the Nile's exit — and on July 28 they named the spot 'The Ripon Falls'. Theirs was 'a perfect partnership'...

GIN

TONIC

Forty-six thousand miles around the world in the first solo circumnavigation – and the sailor couldn't swim! Captain Joshua Slocum sailed his 36¾ foot gaff-yawl into Newport, Rhode Island, USA, today in 1868. He'd left the same harbour over three years earlier – on 24 April 1895. Travelling via the Magellan Strait, he's become the first man to sail around the world. He was fifty-one years old and never learned to swim. I've never learned to swim either – and I'm fifty-two so I'm not keen to start. David Wilkie, Scotland's gold medal water baby, once offered to teach me! He said, 'At least you'll be able to float alone.' I can go to my bank manager to do that – and at the bank's rate of interest, I'll get just as soaked.

3 JULY

Hetty Green died on this day in 1916, aged eighty. She was the richest woman in the US at her death, with assets of $100 million. Her eccentric habits – wearing rags and living in flea-bag hotels – earned her the name 'The Witch of Wall Street'! But money *does* bring happinss. Send me some and watch me smile!

4 JULY

So it's the fourth of July – the day on which the American Declaration of Independence was *not* signed! On, yes, the historic document is *dated* 4 July 1776, and most people think that this is the anniversary of its signing and adoption by Congress . . . but it just isn't so. A tersely worded resolution was adopted by Congress on 2 July. But a final draft, beautifully developed by Thomas Jefferson to express the true spirit of the declaration, was *not even approved* unanimously by 4 July! New York, for example, didn't vote on it until five days after that. And as for the signing by the 'fify-six original members', most of the signatures were not attached until 6 August and one as late as 1781! England more or less ignored the whole thing. It received only a mere half-dozen lines of casual mention in the *London Morning Post* – squeezed in under a theatrical announcement. King George III noted in his diary, 'Nothing of importance happened today.'!

BUT I'M NOT A POLE-- I'M A HUNGARIAN!

Frank Perkins sat on a pole for 399 days! The Pole said, 'For the first 390 days I quite enjoyed it. Then it got itchy.' Frank (of San Jose, California) completed his world record on top of that pole today in 1976. When asked what he was doing up there, he said (are you ready?), 'My firm ordered one hundred flag poles . . . and we received one hundred and one . . . and I'm the fella who asked the boss what to do with the extra one.'

The stinking corpse lily got a new name . . . and smelled just as bad. Like Juliet's rose which would have smelled as sweet by any other name, the world's largest flower retained its ghastly pong even though it changed its nomenclature . . . to the rafflesia. The name change was in honour of Sir Thomas Stamford Raffles, who died one day before his forty-fourth birthday on this day in 1826.

Raffles founded Singapore and was the first president of the London Zoological Society. When he was dying at his country house near Barnet, he wrote to a friend, 'The best time to give advice to your children is while they are still young enough to believe that you know what you are talking about.'

5 JULY

Thomas Cook launched his first 'Cook's Tour' on this day in 1841. Tom arranged a special train from Leicester to Loughborough for anyone who wanted to attend a temperance meeting. The advertisement invited everyone to come along 'who has learned that alcohol is a great magician that can make a monkey out of an ass.'

SHOWMAN P.T. BARNUM WAS BORN TODAY IN 1810

He was the mayor of Bridgeport, Connecticut, in 1875, but failed to endear himself to the town's aldermen when he later referred to his circus monkeys as 'the Bridgeport Council'. He once said, 'There are two things that never live up to their advertising . . . the circus and sin.'

The bikini was revealed today in 1946 – just four days after the USA tested its earliest atomic bomb on an insignificant atoll in the Pacific called . . . Bikini. A Paris showgirl named Micheline Barnard modelled the skimpy beachware and the press nicknamed it unanimously. Probably because of its 20 per cent fall-out.

6 JULY

The last battle on English soil was fought through this night in 1685 – when Monmouth attacked the royalists at Sedgemoor. And this is the very month when we still have bloody battles in England but now they're called the July sales. Last year I went to Selfridge's and for two hours hundreds of women squashed me and climbed over me and pushed themselves against me. Well, roll on next July!

Satchmo died today in 1971. Louis Armstrong got that nickname when the editor of our very own *Melody Maker* described him as 'Satchelmouth' – and Louis abbreviated it saying, 'It's too long for the marquee!' He advised Jimmy Corrigan at the Batley Variety Club, 'Don't try to understand females. By the time you learn to read women like a book – your library card has expired!'

At Cardiff, George Thornton was summoned for driving a motorcar 'at a greater speed than reasonable'. Police claimed the car was propelled at a rate of ten miles an hour which the stipendiary 'held with great confidence to be a dangerous if not insane' velocity. Today in 1901 he imposed a fine of £5. What would he think of today's speeds? Driving's getting so bad, St Christopher's thinking of calling in all the badges.

The first rock-'n'-roll biggie Bill Haley was born today in 1927 in Highfield Park, Michigan. Bill himself is vague about his birthdate but remembers 1955 better, the year he recorded 'Rock Around the Clock'. Bob Orben says, 'Rock isn't dead. It always smelled like that.'

Pierre Cardin was born today in 1922 in Venice, Italy. From 1957 creator of elegantly cut fashions for women and the first collection of men's clothes by a top designer. Asked if women dressed to please men, Cardin said, 'If they did, they'd do it faster – and in last year's clothes.'

Pinocchio was born today in 1883 . . . in print, that is. Carlo Lorenzini, under his pen name of Collodi, wrote the children's cautionary tale ten years before he died in 1890 and was paid only twelve weeks' rent for the rights to what was to become one of the world's most popular kids' classics. I expect you remember the story from Walt Disney's 1940 animated cartoon feature. Every time the puppet boy Pinocchio told a lie his nose got longer and longer. Last I heard, he was starring in Eskimo stag movies.

7 JULY

Today in 1979 Bjorn Borg beat Roscoe Tanner to win Wimbledon for the fourth consecutive year. He beat John McEnroe for his fifth consecutive victory on 5 July 1980. I'm such a sporting misfit I get tennis elbow playing golf. I have nightmares about playing in a charity tennis match and being drawn to play Borg. In the dream, my first foot fault is stepping on to the court.

You couldn't get stuffed until this day in 1517 . . . when the first taxidermy was recorded. According to the British Association of Taxidermists, the most difficult animal to stuff is a cat. The process tends to give it a cynical expression.

America's greatest quack isn't Donald Duck. He was John Romulus Brinkley, born today in 1885 in Jackson County, North Carolina, a marvellous medical faker who made millions of dollars promising to make hundreds of bucks. His restoration of sexual prowess to impotent gents was 'guaranteed by God's most virile creatures'! In short, old J.R. transplanted goat gonads into the senile but solvent senior citizens and, until the FCC chucked him out of the USA, he pushed mail order drugs through his own radio station in Kansas. Exiled, he carried on broadcasting from Mexico. His radio station's call sign: K.O.K.K.

8 JULY

They read the US declaration of Independence in public for the first time today in 1776 . . . then rang the Liberty Bell. Ironically, this giant symbol of the American Revolution was cast and finished in England. And for extra irony, this is also the day when . . .

Havelock Ellis died in 1939. I saw a second-hand book catalogue with this entry: '*Studies in the Psychology of Sex and Unconventional Sex Practices* by H. Ellis, spine broken and appendix torn.'

"THE RICHEST MAN IN THE WORLD"

That's what they called financier John D. Rockefeller born today in 1839. The US capitalist gave away a total of $750 million in his lifetime. When he was a baby he was wetnursed by a caterer. And when he grew old, his hearing aid had an answering service.

Seven-year-old Roger Woodward became the first person to go over Niagara Falls *without* a barrel – and survive! Roger fell into the river above the falls today in 1960. When they pulled him out below the falls he was crying – because he'd lost his new shoes. TV quizmaster Lennie Bennett took his wife to Niagara Falls for their honeymoon. They were still brushing confetti off their clothes as they got on to the plane. The pilot stopped at their seats and said, 'What a beautiful bride!' Lennie said, 'With eyesight like you've got, you shouldn't be flying planes.'

IS TODAY YOUR BIRTHDAY?

In 1970, a seven-storey office block was built in Hamburg, West Germany, in a total time of 65 hours, 41 minutes 23 seconds! It was Jerry built.

Congratulations! You share it with the first rhinoceros to be born in Ireland! The zoo officials were thrilled in 1969 when the horny little beast came into the world. They fed the rhinos on nearly a ton of vegetables per day and reported that mother and daughter were both doing a lot. All the zoo staff were pleased too – except for the bloke who had to clean out the rhino's enclosure whose wife made him give up the job. She said he kept bringing his work home with him.

One queen of England never lived or visited here! She was Berengaria, who married Richard I, the Lion-Hearted, today in 1191. And was she ugly! Vultures used to fly past her with one wing over their eyes.

10 JULY

'As he crouched – like an animal – she turned the pistol and put it to his face – and to her horror the thing went off!' With these words – and equally histrionic gestures – that giant of the English bar Sir Edward Marshall Hall told the jury of the events that took place on this day in 1923. Marie Marguerite Fahmy, a twenty-three-year-old Parisian beauty was on trial for the murder of her playboy husband, Prince Ali Kamel Fahmy Bey. The millionaire Egyptian was shot dead in London's Savoy Hotel. Due to her husband's 'unnatural desires', the appealing Marie had to undergo an operation for a complaint which the decorum of a 1923 court required her to write down – 'piles'. She was acquitted but had to fight again in the Egyptian courts to be found innocent – and so be entitled to a sixth of her victim's vast fortune!

Telstar was launched today in 1962 – the first US communications satellite, enabling us to get much quicker transatlantic wrong numbers. I don't want to spread bad news but I heard that the first seats on the US space shuttle have been reserved by dedicated phone vandals.

TODAY'S THE BIRTHDAY OF H.J. HEINZ, BORN 1908, CHAIRMAN OF THE FAMILY FOOD TINNING FIRM WHO ADMITS HE PREFERS FRESH VEGETABLES!

HEINZ MEANZ GREENZ!

BOB M...

The Flying Dutchman was seen today in 1881! Old records show that, in 1680, Captain Hendrik van der Decken sailed a Dutch Eastindiaman out of Amsterdam for Batavia, a settlement in the Dutch East Indies. Unable to round the Cape of Good Hope in unceasing gales, van der Decken is said to have heeded Satan's advice in his attempts to defy God's will – and got himself condemned by an Angel of the Lord to roam the seas forever 'until the trump of God shall rend the sky'. God hadn't trumped by this day in 1881 . . . the phantom ship was 'clearly observed' and a figure in ancient clothes identified on her poop by a midshipman on HMS *Bacchante* and others, sailing fifty miles off the cape. Before you write him off as a liar or a fool, here's the punchline . . . the midshipman was the future King George V of England.

11 JULY

I wrote my first script for Lew Grade's new ATV company today in 1955 – a comedy play I later performed for him, live in 1956. I saw him only last week and though he's Lord Grade now, he not only remembered that first show I'd done for him over twenty-five years ago, but he told me the cheque is in the post.

The first tick-tock clocked in today in 1088 . . . this day marking the first recorded example of a clock in any real way similar to the tickers we use now. Everyone agreed the new clock was better than those rotten old sundials. As soon as it gets dark, they stop working.

Two totally blind soccer teams played to a 2—2 tie in Lima, Peru, today in 1973 . . . using a sonic ball containing a handful of dried peas. In Britain we use footballers who can see. Only our referees are blind.

The Michelin Brothers made car racing history in 1865 – they set off to win the Paris–Bordeaux race in a Peugeot car named *L'Eclair*. It was the world's first four-wheeled petrol car to run on pneumatic tyres! Well, the boys had a puncture. They had a lot of punctures. Then they had a hell of a lot of punctures. Before long they'd fitted on their entire supply of twenty-two spare inner tubes, patching and plugging holes like a pair of inexperienced tinkers mending a colander. After ninety hours they packed it in. The race was won by Levassor in under forty-nine hours and whose place in the motoring hall of fame is assured by his confident declaration that 'the airfilled tyre will obviously never be of the slightest use for motor cars.' Levassor was about as good a judge of the future as I am. I put my life savings into a 20,000 chicken farm. It turned out the cockerel was gay.

12 JULY

King Henry VIII married his sixth and last wife today in 1543. She was Catherine Parr. Unfit for sexual athletics, his performance in bed was definitely below Parr.

Dolly Madison died on this day in 1849, aged seventy-seven. As wife to US President James Madison, she was the most famous Washington hostess of them all. The most exotic foods were brought in from every corner of the world to her White House kitchens every day and turned into hamburgers.

Today's issue of the *Advocate* newspaper in Barbados, 1977, has the headline, 'NEW HOME FOR OLD FOLKS IN THE PIPELINE'

Six days ago in 1930 Sir Arthur Conan Doyle died . . . and today he tried to make a comeback! Ten thousand hopeful believers and unhopeful sceptics attended a mass seance at London's Albert Hall, expecting something from him. They got it. It's called dead silence.

13 JULY

'Three-Finger Brown' – a.k.a. Gaetano Lucchese – died on this day in 1967. The US mobster had been boss of the five families in New York City. He was sixty-seven, a native Sicilian, and once asked Walter Winchell, 'How do you know honesty is the best policy until you've tried some of the others?'

'WHAT A BEAUTIFUL PUSSY YOU ARE!'

sang a soprano . . . as the first cat show was judged in 1871. As one lady tabby wrote to her girlfriend, 'Having a wonderful Tom . . . wish you were here.'

Four students kept the bagpipe playing for 100 hours today in 1976, a new world record set, of all places, in Salisbury, Rhodesia. Isn't it ironic? In Rhodesia at that time you could get killed for doing nothing – but these blokes got away with 100 hours of playing bagpipes. There's no justice.

Billy the Kid was shot and killed in Fort Sumner, New Mexico, USA, in 1881. He wasn't born in the West but in New York City. At the age of 12 he shot his first victim. Nine years later he'd killed twenty more. Then Sheriff Pat Garrett plugged him. Garrett was pretty tough. The homesteaders were being terrorized by a gang of cowpokes, but Garrett stopped them. He told them to go and poke someone their own size.

14 JULY

Dr Benjamin Spock said it all today in 1946 – and took it all back tomorrow in 1974. His famous baby bible was published this morning – *Baby and Child Care* – to become a thirty-year best-seller. Even though Spock announced on 15 July, twenty-eight years later, that he no longer supported his own theories on upbringing and training. I'm not surprised. Have you read the chapter on 'How to stop a teething baby from crying'? It says, 'The first thing to do is throw the baby over your shoulder. Pick up off the floor and repeat till satisfied.'

'TODAY IS BASTILLE DAY' . . . and French school children have a holiday to celebrate that day in 1789 when the people of Paris captured the grim stone prison with its hundred-foot moat, eight big grey towers and seventy or more foul cells, where some prisoners spent their lives in utter darkness. On the brink of their Great Revolution, the first fierce gesture the people wanted to make was the storming of the evil Bastille and the freeing of its suffering mass of unjustly convicted victims – but the mob found only seven prisoners in it! By some penitential coincidence . . .

The first tape measure was patented today in 1868 . . . by Alvin J. Fellows. It was coiled in a round tin with a spring lock to fix it in any position. A tape measure is a device used to measure the acting talent of the stars of 'Charlie's Angels'.

In the USA on this day in 1852 San Quentin became a penal institution. One hundred and thirty years later the prison is so overcrowded, solitary confinement is four to a cell.

When was the first game of cricket played? Well, drawings exist from around 1250 which show men playing with bats and balls . . . but it seems that basic rules were observed in a game played at Sevenoaks, Kent, on this day in 1552! In those days it was a leisurely game. Today our bowlers work up such a sweat they have to use overarm deodorant.

Margarine was patented today in 1869 by Hippolyte Mege-Mouries of France. His wife swore she couldn't tell it from butter.

15 JULY

Many happy returns to Sir Larry Lamb, born 1929, the editor who raised the price of the *Sun* to 12p! That's 6p each!

MARINER 4 sent back the first close-up pictures of another planet – Mars – today in 1965. It turned out to be bleak, lifeless and empty. They might just as well have snapped some photos of Swindon on a Sunday.

The battle of Smolensk was fought today in 1941. Germans surrounded 300,000 Russians in the Smolensk–Orsha pocket. A Russian Air Force doctor told Air Marshal Vorkov, 'I have six cases of *la grippe* on my hands – what am I to do?' Vorkov radioed back, 'Give it to the infantry. They'll drink anything.'

Seventy-two years old, Chairman Mao swam nine miles of the River Yangtse in sixty-five minutes today in 1966 – or so they say. That made him faster than any Olympic gold medallist! Mao's timekeeper was that famous Chinese political commentator, Wot Wen Wong.

16 JULY

Apollo 11 began its voyage to man's first moon landing today in 1969. The first thing the astronauts did when they reached the moon was to pray. From there it was only a local call.

The first atomic bomb was tested today in 1945 at Alamogordo, New Mexico. Since then at least 500,000 nuclear warheads have been prepared all around the world. If they're ever used, it'll be the first time in history a planet was ever mugged!

The world's first parking meter was installed this morning in 1935 – in Oklahoma City. I once asked an Irish traffic warden, 'What does the yellow line mean?' He said, 'It means you can't park there at all.' I said, 'Then what does the *double* yellow line mean?' He said, 'That, sir, means you can't park there at all, at all!'

KISSING WAS MADE ILLEGAL IN ENGLAND IN 1439...

. . . in an attempt to stop the spread of diseases through contact. Women run after some men's kisses. After mine, they limp.

Just after midnight this morning in 1918 a commandant named Yurovsky awakened the family. He told them that Czech forces threatened the area and that they should rise, dress and come to the lower floor of the big merchant's house in which they were staying. He said it was for their own safety. There had been alarms of this kind before, and the father and mother were not unduly upset. Quietly they did as they were asked and soon they were sitting in a basement room with their ailing son, four pretty daughters and their pet Japanese dog. Suddenly Yurovsky and eleven armed men burst into the room and opened fire, each having been allotted his own target in advance. The parents and daughters died at once but the son needed two more bullets from Yurovsky to finish him off. The corpses were carted off to an abandoned mine called the Four Brothers, chopped up, burned, drenched with acid and the ashes scattered so effectively that only odd bits of bone were ever found So ended the lives of the most powerful royal family of the past hundred years – the Romanovs. Tsar Nicholas II, his beloved Alexandra, Tsarevich Alexis and the four grand duchesses had been slaughtered in the name of revolution. Not the first nor, God knows, the last. Personally, I've never understood why the Russians are so violent and cruel. Three vodkas and I like *everybody*!

Disneyland was opened today in 1955 . . . the first time a mouse ever built a trap for people.

James Abbott McNeill Whistler died on this day in 1903, seven days after his sixty-ninth birthday. 'My God, mother!' cried Whistler when he saw the old lady scrubbing the floor. 'Have you gone off your rocker?'

THEY ROLLER COASTERED FOR FIVE DAYS

James Bruse and Richard Rodriguez wanted to get their names into *The Guinness Book of Records*. So on this day in 1978 they completed a roller coaster ride of 1805 miles. They were riding high . . . until 4 September, less than seven weeks later, when Jim King set a new endurance record by riding a roller coaster at Panama City, Florida, USA for 168 hours, travelling a distance of 1946 miles! Well, that's the roller coaster endurance game for you. It has its ups and downs.

18 JULY

Happy birthday to John Glenn, 1921. The astronaut who originated that famous line, 'I wasn't nervous until I was fifty miles up and it suddenly struck me – everything that makes this ship go was supplied by the lowest bidder.'

The second death of Petrarch took place on this day in 1374. Jeremy Beadle reports, 'Thirty years earlier Petrarch had been declared dead but, when only four hours from burial, he awoke and scolded his servants for leaving the door open, demanding: "Do you want me to catch my death?"'

'ROME WASN'T BURNED IN A DAY'...

. . . but today's the day the fire 'broke out' in the year AD 64. Two Roman malcontents planned to burn down the city despite a rumour that Nero himself planned its destruction. They argued, 'Why wait for Nero to do it? If we burn it ourselves, we can eliminate the fiddle man.'

KING GEORGE IV WAS CROWNED ON THIS DAY IN 1821

19 JULY

Before he was seventeen he confessed to being 'rather too fond of women and wine'. After giving the royal elbow to the Drury Lane actress Perdita, he fell like a ton of fun for Mrs Fitzherbert and paid a young curate £500 to marry them in secret. The marriage was illegal, of course, but they had one son. Though George was forced into a loveless marriage with his ghastly cousin Caroline (she was so vicious, when lightning struck her it was in self-defence), he never stopped loving Maria Anne Fitzherbert and died with her miniature portrait round his neck in 1830. Bit sad, isn't it? It's like Benjamin Franklin said, 'Where there's marriage without love, there will be love without marriage.'

Dry cleaning was invented by accident – when a Parisian spilled oil and spirit on a table cloth in 1849 and found that the stains disappeared. True! Lucky he spotted it, wasn't it?

Sacco and Vanzetti were declared innocent of a 1920 robbery and 1921 shooting today *in 1977*. It was a shade tardy. The two Italian workers were executed for crimes in 1927, fifty years before. That's a little late, isn't it? Like getting a refund on your ticket for the maiden voyage of the *Titanic*.

The creator of the immortal Peter Pan died on this day in 1937. The Scottish dramatist J. M. Barrie was made a baronet for his most famous play. Some people have described me as a Peter Pan. I have to be revived every Boxing Day.

20 JULY

Making an outer space treble with the US astronauts 1969 landing on the moon today (they were the first three men to go to the airport on a business trip without their wives pleading, 'Take me along.'), this is also the day when . . . NASA launched its first ion rocket in 1964 . . . and the US Viking rocket sent back the first view of Mars in 1976. 'If you think the space programme's expensive now,' gagged Joey Adams, 'just wait till the astronauts' union is organized – and they start charging by the mile.'

'ONE SMALL STEP FOR A MAN. ONE GIANT LEAP FOR MANKIND,'

adlibbed the first men on the moon, Armstrong and Aldrin. Ted Rogers exclaimed, 'What courage those men had! They filmed unknown areas of the moon, they mapped dangerous craters – and what a thrill when Neil Armstrong went behind that boulder and created another unique moon first!' Today is Ted's birthday since 1935, but nowadays Ted counts his age the same way he counts the name of his popular TV quiz, '3-2-1' – backwards!

Sir Edmund Hillary was born today in 1919. Asked why he'd climbed Mount Everest, he gave the classic answer, 'Because it was there.' Asked why he divorced his mermaid wife immediately after the wedding night, Sinbad the sailor replied, 'Because it wasn't there.'

On this day in 1935 Mrs Klarius Mikkelsen became the first woman to reach the South Pole. Her husband was the Danish seaman and explorer Ejnar Mikkelsen who led the famous 1906–08 Anglo-American North Pole expedition. She went south and he went north. No wonder the marriage broke up. They were poles apart.

History's strangest picnic was held today in 1861 – to watch the first major battle of the American Civil War! Promoters in Washington sold tickets and charged three times the normal prices for hampers of food, beer, champagne – and even specially made Union flags 'to wave on the victorious army of the United States as they adminster punishment and defeat to the Rebels'. The spectacle was guaranteed to 'amuse, instruct and instil in all observers the pride of patriotism'. The organizers forgot to explain the plot to the Rebel army of the South. For this was the historic Battle of Bull Run – and the Confederates thrashed the Union Army and scattered them all the way back to Washington.

21 JULY

Chosen to be king when he was five months old – and the Lion of Swaziland celebrated his golden birthday today in 1980. King Sobhuza

THE WORLD BEGAN ON THIS DAY

– or so the ancient Egyptians believed. They also believed the world would end after 6000 years. According to my calculator, that's next Monday, so don't start any serial stories.

II, born in 1899, has ruled his tiny kingdom for sixty years. He has one hundred wives and has fathered about five hundred children (one in a thousand of his half-million population) but advises his subjects to practise family planning. 'The Inexplicable' (a favourite title of his) lives in a mud hut without plumbing or electricity, preferring it to his £6 million palace. For his party today eighty-one cattle were ritually slaughtered, his sons formed a platoon as his military guard of honour and a fly past was given by his air force – both planes. As usual, King Sobhuza delivered a speech full of wise practical advice to his people. He urged them, 'Drive safely and don't catch the flu.'

Question of the day: An astonishing character died today in 1903. He came from a slave-owning family in Kentucky – but published a passionately abolitionist paper called the *True American*. That was a pretty brave thing to do in the 1840s down South! His enemies physically ran his press out of town – to Cincinnati. He just carried on publishing where they put it. He stormed off to the Mexican War as a captain, killed four of the nine soldiers who captured him, then created such a furore among his fellow prisoners that his jailers allowed the troublemaker to escape. On his way out, he killed them. At eighty-four he married a fifteen-year-old girl. On his death-bed, he sent for his guns and shot flies off the walls.

Here's the question: What baby born a century after the crusader's anti-slavery campaign began, was named after him?

Clue: Like the man whose name he bore for much of his life, the baby grew up to be loud of voice, fearless in combat and a champion of black and oppressed people. Got it?

Here's the answer: US mobster John Dillinger was shot dead by FBI agents today in 1934. He was outside Chicago's Biograph Theatre where he'd gone to see Clark Gable and Myrna Loy in 'Manhattan Melodrama' – a film about a US mobster who dies in the electric chair. For Dillinger it should have been called 'The Last Picture Show'.

If you were born under the zodiacal lion, you consider yourself a born leader. Other people just think you're pushy. You are vain but insecure so you loathe honest criticism. Most Leo people are bullies. My wife Jackie is Leo. She told me I haven't enough social life. She's made me join a bridge club. I jump next Wednesday.

LEO IS YOUR BIRTH SIGN FOR THE NEXT 4 WEEKS

The first Olympic Games were held –
776 years before the birth of Christ.
Today in 1980 Duncan Goodhew
won Britain's first gold medal at the
Moscow Olympics by winning the
100 metres backstroke.

23 JULY

The first ice cream cone was
created today in 1904 by Charles
Menches in St
Louis, Missouri,
USA. When it
was shown at a
press confer-
ence, newsmen
got a big scoop.

Haile Selassie
was born today
in 1892. His
mother was
Haile Relieved.

'EXILED SOVIET GRANDMASTER OF CHESS PLAYS FOR SWITZERLAND'

That was the headline, as a BBC
commentator on Radio 4's 'PM'
recalled, 'I watched him as he
mated with a bishop and two
rooks.' Well, whatever turns you
on. And the man himself, Viktor
Korchnoi was born today in 1931.

It was on this
day in 1965 that
my first wife
said to a poll
interviewer at
the front door:
'Just a minute –
I'll get my husband. He's the
opinionated one.'

This notice
appeared in
tonight's edition
of the London
Evening Star in
1953: FOR SALE,
100 YEAR-OLD BRASS
BED, PERFECT FOR
ANTIQUE LOVER

Stars fell in south-west France on this day in 1790 . . . and made holes in the landscape! Over three hundred honest French folk observed this amazing rain of meteorites, collected the hot rocks and sent them to the Academy of France together with their written statements. The academicians scoffed and called the incident 'a physically impossible phenomenon'. They reckoned all those people must have been stoned out of their minds.

I missed an important trans-atlantic phone call this morning in 1979 because my wife, Jackie, still in bed while I was shaving, wouldn't get up to answer the phone. Are you ready for her excuse? She said it *sounded* like a wrong number.

24 JULY

'A FREE QUEBEC'

– that's what de Gaulle demanded in his historic speech at Montreal on this day in 1967. I once talked to a Frenchman who had listened to every one of de Gaulle's speeches. I asked him, 'Are you a patriot?' He said, 'No a masochist.' Which brings me to that well-remembered Super Masochist . . .

St Simeon Stylites died on this day in the year 459 – and no wonder! His entire life of religious dedication had been spent trying to do himself in with nonstop torture. Most of what the poor blighter did to himself is too yucky awful to tell you in a jolly almanac like this. Even his own crowd of self-punishing monks kicked him out for going too far with the masochism. He spent the rest of his ghastly life sitting on top of a sixty-foot pillar, waiting to die of exposure. He was still alive up there thirty-six years later! It recalls the tale of the masochist who begged the sadist, 'Beat me!' – and the sadist said, 'No.'

Bleriot became the first person to enter England other than by sea. The French aviator flew across the Channel from France to Dover on this day in 1909 . . . in a little plane he designed himself. The engine was a tiny 25 hp and the plane only had one wing (on each side, of course). He won £1000

25 JULY

from the *Daily Mail* . . . but Louis Bleriot was already enormously rich as the inventor of automobile lights and accessories. I flew in a plane in Kenya last year and I think it was one of Bleriot's rejects. You could tell it was old because it had two pilots, a navigator and a stoker. We had to refuel every twenty miles. Stopped to take on wood.

This is the birthday of the world's first test-tube baby! Louise Brown was born in Bristol, in 1978. In the old days you only had to worry about your daughter dating some stud with a motorbike. Now you've got to watch out for the guys with chemistry sets.

Mussolini resigned and was arrested on the orders of King Victor Emmanuel today in 1943. He was an able aviator, an amateur violinist and was known to the women of Italy as 'The Mechanical Man' – because he was always trying to screw his head off. Me, I never have any luck with women. Once I picked up a girl who was a bisexual nypho-maniac and she told me I wasn't her type.

A Paris judge refused to allow singer-impressionist Jacques-Yves Rostand permission to change his name legally on this day in 1935. Rostand wanted to change his name to Maurice Chevalier! The judge said that, since there was already an international entertainer of that name, two of them might cause confusion in the minds of the theatre-going public. Gosh, I wish there were two Bob Monkhouses. We could form a fan club for each other.

'There's no money in poetry, but there's no poetry in money either!' So said Robert Graves, born today in 1895, author of *I, Claudius*, retired to Majorca. He also said, 'If I were a girl, I'd despair: the supply of good women far exceeds that of the men who deserve them.'

Mick Jagger was born today in 1943 in Dartford Kent. His epitaph should be, 'Here lies Mick Jagger . . . gathering moss.'

26 JULY

SOCRATES LEFT NO WRITINGS !

The great Greek philosopher is known chiefly through the works of his pupil, Plato. Today is celebrated as Socrates' Memorial Day in Greece. His last words were, 'A good hemlock, but not a great hemlock.'

The FBI was established today in 1908. The Alcatraz Prison newspaper acknowledged its help once when they announced a change of staff: 'The former editor of this newspaper has reluctantly resigned. He was paroled. However, we are fortunate to have back with us the previous editor who, thanks to the FBI, has just become available for the next fifteen years.'

ONE HUNDRED AND SIXTY-THREE MILES PER HOUR !

That was the world record set for speed on water by a woman today in 1978 on Lake Washington, Seattle, USA, by twenty-eight-year-old Sue Williams. Her advice to would-be record breakers: 'Speed on water is dangerous.' Speed on whisky is fatal.

Ian Michael Miles of Corsham, Wiltshire, made a perfect diving front somersault over thirty-three men at Harrogate, North Yorkshire, today in 1977. Our drill sergeant in the RAF made us practice diving front somersaults in the gym for two hours once. Then he asked, 'What does this exercise develop?' 'Hatred', boomed a voice from the rear.

On this day in 1956 my late partner Denis Goodwin and I posed for a joke wedding photo with our new secretary named Jacqueline Harding and seventeen years later she married me. She used to tell our clients, 'Bob says I'm the most attractive spanner that ever got into the organization.'

27 JULY

WHAT A FLIGHT!

One hour, one minute, forty seconds – and no toilets! Orville Wright set this flight duration record, carrying one passenger on this day in 1909. I flew about the same distance in Kenya for about the same duration in what may have been the same plane. We flew so low we passed signs saying: 'Beware of falling rocks.'

The world's most wedded couple married for the first time today in 1937. Since then Jack and Edna Moran of Seattle, Washington, USA, have taken their place in *The Guinness Book of Records* by repeating the full ceremony forty times! 'It's not that we love each other . . . it's just that we're both crazy about wedding cake!'

28 JULY

A nuclear disaster was narrowly averted in Britain on this day in 1956 – the day after the beginning of the Suez crisis – but it was hushed up for twenty-three years! An American B47 bomber crashed at Lakenheath Air Base, Suffolk, and it damaged three atom bombs. A retired USAF general has admitted, 'It is possible that a part of Eastern England would have become a desert.' But the Lakenheath fire chief ordered his men to ignore the burning plane and the four trapped men – and put out the blaze that threatened the bomb store. No one was allowed to reveal the nature of the bombs secretly stored there. Evan Esar observed 'Tired as I am of discussing the bomb, I hope the subject will never be dropped . . .'

After two gruelling days, the duke of Wellington's Battle of Talavera ended on this day in 1808. Victory was plucked from the French grasp by his heroic British Guards and the King's German legion. 'Never was there such a murderous battle!' said Wellesley, later to become the Iron Duke. He'd been outnumbered two to one, lost over 5000 men; the French more than 7000. As a result, he was made a peer but why 'Wellington'? His brother chose it under pressure. 'No time to consult Arthur,' said William, 'Wellington is a Somerset town not far from Wellesley.' Kitty, the new 'Lady Wellington', hated the title. 'It recalls nothing,' she sniffed. 'It is readily forgotten.' How was she to know that her new name would grace the boots of a million Irish labourers?

Is this the day on which Noah sent a dove and a raven from the ark in search of dry land? Many biblical scholars have adopted this as the day in that unknown year of the Great Flood. Noah's Ark was, of course, the only cruise ship that's ever had enough males to go round.

THE HEAVIEST PERCH EVER---422 LBS---WAS CAUGHT IN UGANDA TODAY IN 1980--- BY A MR. HOOK!

BOB MONKHOUSE

29 JULY

This is the birthday of two of Hollywood's most famous sex queens: the 'It' girl, Clara Bow, born today in 1905 on exactly the same day and year as the beautiful, tragic Thelma Todd. One of Hollywood's strangest mysteries surrounds the death of this dazzling comedy star of Marx Brothers and Bing Crosby movies. She left Ida Lupino's party one Saturday night with a mock solemn 'Goodbye' – and was never seen alive again. On the following Monday morning in 1935 her maid found her body slumped in her car, blood on her face, dead from carbon monoxide poisoning. The police called it suicide. But her lawyer and closest friends knew of her romances with the most violent of underworld villains. They believed Thelma had been knocked out, dumped in her car with the motor running – and murdered. Much of the evidence indicated the murder theory – but the power of the studios was opposed to scandal. The truth, so swiftly obscured, will never be known.

The poet who composed 'Elegy written in a Country Churchyard' died on this day in 1771, aged 54. London's Thomas Gray, noted for his charming neoclassical light verse, is mostly recalled only for his famous 'Elegy' which was cherished by everyone who read it, even Dr Johnson who generally disliked Gray – yet Gray himself hated the poem and despised the fame it brought him! Gray was deeply embarrassed by his homosexuality and went to great lengths to keep it secret. I suppose he felt that if God had meant us to be gay, he would have made the Garden of Eden with Adam and Bruce.

30 JULY

When the *Chicago Sun* called him an ignoramus, he sued them for a million dollars – but was awarded only six cents! Born today in 1863 in Wayne County, Michigan, USA, Henry Ford had changed the world – before his death on 7 April 1947. Father of the mass-produced car, he said, 'It is not the employer who pays wages – he only handles the money. It is the product that pays wages.'

The first interlocking jigsaw puzzle in a box went on sale at Merriman's Bookshop in Liverpool today in 1832. It caused a national craze as the whole country went to pieces.

England won the World Cup today in 1966 – when we beat West Germany 4–2 in the final. Mind you I know absolutely nothing about football. In fact, the only difference between me and Malcolm Allison is – I admit it.

The Iron Chancellor died on this day in 1898. The mighty German statesman Otto von Bismarck was utterly frank. He said, 'There is never so much lying done as before an election, during a war and after a hunt.'

America mislaid the ex-president of the Teamsters' Union today in 1975 – when Jimmy Hoffa vanished so mysteriously. Why the gang/syndicate bosses whom Hoffa served so faithfully had him rubbed out – and what became of his corpse – has never become wholly clear. But the takeover of the largest and most important union in America is one of the Mafia's supreme accomplishments. Everyone talks about today's fashion for acupuncture to end pain but the Mafia's used it for years. Only instead of a needle they use an icepick.

31 JULY

Melchor and Victoria Javier of Manila ordered a $1000 bank draft from the Mellon bank in Pittsburgh, Pennsylvania, USA, this morning in 1977 – but the bank accidentally sent them a cheque for $1 million! Just to show there were no hard feelings, the Javiers spent $750,000 immediately. The case is still tied up. So is the bank manager – in the asylum.

On this day in 1952 a member of Winston Churchill's Tory government crossed the floor of the House of Commons to sit on the left with the Labour Party.

Winston's observation: 'This, gentlemen, is the first time I have ever seen a rat swimming *toward* a sinking ship.'

A national fly-catching day in Japan in 1933 produced a total of 11,530,000 flies killed in Tokyo alone. When in Japan, I never eat their Garibaldis.

Surrey bowler Jim Laker took nineteen wickets between 26 July and today in 1956 – the most ever taken in a single cricket match. After which he ordered a pint of ale, found it flat and short-measured, and poured it over the publican's head. He was appealing against the light.

1 AUG

The Warsaw rising began on this day in 1944 . . . as the Polish Home Army began its heroic sixty-three-day struggle against the Nazi German garrison. Three German soldiers were killed by the first bomb of the uprising. Their names were Montag, Oktober and Zweite, all SS officers. Their three names put together form 'Monday, 2 October' – the exact date in 1944 when the Warsaw rising ended!

Fashion designer Yves St Laurent was born on this day in 1936 in Oran, Algeria. Guided by Christian Dior, he introduced the 'chic beatnik' look using fur and leather. Beatniks were an earlier form of hippies. They looked like Tarzan, walked like Jane and smelled like Cheeta.

King Louis IV of France died of dysentery on this day in 1137. He never left the throne for a moment.

Thanks to Johannes Estermeier of Althegnenberg, Germany, this is the day of history's first flasher – in 1930. The first photographic flash bulb was popped on this date. And an Irishman tried to start a business in trading second-hand ones.

GOOD HEALTH, GOOD NUTRITION AND HAPPY POPPIES!

Those are some of August's adopted blessings today. 'Health foods' offer their special benefits in this late summer push, so be sure to drink only 'health food' wines. These are wines made exclusively from grapes crushed by a man wearing orthopaedic shoes.

Hannibal and his elephants thrashed the Romans at Cannae on this day in 216 BC. When his jumbos saw the Alps for the first time, they were terrified by the mountains in front of them . . . and consequently left a few mountains behind them.

'DORO I CAN'T GET MY BREATH!'

gasped the owner of the most powerful lungs in operatic history – then Enrico Caruso died on this day in 1921. His recording of 'Vesti la giubba' from 'I Pagliacci' in 1902 was the world's first 'gold record', selling over a million copies. Full of vigorous good humour, Caruso was an incurable practical joker. He had the habit of dropping cigar ash in his hand and then dumping it in his pocket. One day he sent his suit to be cleaned, and you know how in dry cleaning shops, the cleaners always go through your pockets? That's how they get to open more shops. Well, this cleaner phoned Caruso and said, 'You know sir, I found a lot of ashes in your jacket pocket.' And Caruso said, 'Yes, please to be careful with that. My uncle Giuseppe, he die last month – and I want to keep him near me!'

The US Air Corps was established in 1909. Right away they established the tradition of military tailoring which has been maintained ever since – too big, too small and out of stock.

The composer of 'Cavalleria Rusticana' died on this day in 1945. Pietro Mascagni was eighty-one. At the age of twenty-seven he wrote his brilliant one-act opera in competition for a prize – and never produced anything else as successful. Many men of great creative genius produce their finest work while they're young and fresh. I may do the same thing myself.

Christopher Columbus set sail from Spain today in 1492 to prove the world was round. And Joe Hickman says, 'I'm glad. Can you imagine what it would cost to launch satellites into a *square* orbit?'

The four Marx Brothers screened their first movie – 'Coconuts' – in 1929. Groucho, comedy's greatest anarchist, was intolerant of emotional frankness (he wouldn't speak to his daughter Melinda for a year because she kissed her husband on the mouth in public) and rejected his hero Somerset Maugham when he learned he was gay. Of his brother Zeppo, he said, 'We've been through some tough times but I'll always remember him as a tower of weakness.'

3 AUG

On this history-making day in 1907, Kaiser William II and Tsar Nicholas II met at Swinemunde to discuss the Baghdad Railway. They went home in a rotten mood. The Tsar complained of William's stinginess and the Kaiser said Nicholas had no royal charisma. How'd ya like that? One was a miser Kaiser . . . and the other lacked Tsar quality.

The play *Halfway to Hell* opened in the West End tonight in 1926 . . . and closed at the first interval! The audience had left the theatre. James Agate wrote, 'The author of *Halfway to Hell* underestimates the distance.'

And so to the heroine of 'I Dismember Mama' . . . 'Lizzie Borden took an axe and gave her parents forty whacks!' (Elizabeth Borden, cleared of crime, should sue the berk who wrote that rhyme!) But it was on this day in 1892 that the young lady was arrested for the murder of her parents at Fall River, Massachusetts. She was acquitted in spite of strong circumstantial evidence, partly because nobody could find the axe with which the slaying was done. Years after Lizzie's death an axe was found concealed in the wall of her house!

4 AUG

Roy Plomley's fifteen hundredth 'Desert Island Discs' was broadcast today in 1979. Those seagulls have been over his head since 1942. No wonder his hair's gone white.

HANS CHRISTIAN ANDERSEN WAS A STUFFED SHIRT!

The great Danish storyteller who died on this day in 1875 was so self-conscious about his 'sunken chest' that he used to stuff paper under his shirt. Small wonder that he was eccentric: his grandfather was insane, his grandmother was a pathological liar and his mother was a superstitious illiterate. His father, a poor shoemaker, volunteered for the Napoleonic Wars, came back a broken man and died when Hans was only eleven. Although Hans became world famous for his fairy tales, he remained a lonely bachelor to the end.

They buried Alexander Graham Bell in Baddeck, Nova Scotia, today in 1922. To prevent the harsh Nova Scotian winds from blowing down the tall memorial, it was secured to the ground by wires. A passing drunk saw them and observed, 'I see he's got the phone put in already.'

Sir Humphrey Gilbert founded the first English colony in North America today in 1583 – he called it St Johns, Newfoundland, and declared that its great fisheries were under British law. It was an act of Cod.

Newfoundland also featured in an historic flop – the first cable across the Atlantic Ocean was completed today in 1856 – after two previous unsuccessful tries. They spliced it together in mid-ocean and four ships paid out the cable as they made for home, two of them heading for Valentia, Ireland and the other two for Trinity Bay, Newfoundland. By the time the ships had reached their terminals, the cable was 1950 miles long and over two-thirds of it was laid more than two miles deep. Everyone was thrilled with it – even Queen Victoria. She exchanged self-satisfied messages over it with US President James Buchanan tomorrow in 1858. That's when they noticed something was wrong. Her message said, 'bands across the tea' instead of 'hands across the sea' and Buchanan's name was spelled with an embarrassing capital 'F'! The electrical current was too feeble. On the following 1 September the service was suspended.

5 AUG

The first traffic light in North America was installed on this day in 1914 – at the junction of Cleveland's Euclid Avenue and East 105th Street. An astonished woman driver pulled up and stared as the lights changed – red, amber, green, green and amber, red – until a traffic cop strolled over and asked, 'Whatsa matter, lady? Haven't we got a colour you like?'

Nixon admitted – but only just – his complicity in the Watergate affair today in 1974. The air was full of his denials. And vice versa.

Seventy-four years old . . . and she bailed out at 3000 feet! Ardath Evitt of Paris, Illinois, USA, set a world record today in 1978. She was the oldest woman ever to make her *first* parachute jump. Bernie Clifton advises any first-time parachutist, 'If your 'chute fails to open, cross your right leg over your left leg . . . so they can screw you out of the ground when they find you.'

The electric chair was used for the first time in the USA in 1890. A greengrocer named William Kemmler from Buffalo axed his missus and got the hot seat at New York's Auburn State Prison. Evan Esar pointed out that there's no capital punishment in primitive society: 'Otherwise for his last meal a cannibal might want to eat the warden.'

6 AUG

BRITAIN'S 1st DRIVING SCHOOL OPENED IN BRISTOL TODAY IN 1929. IT OWNED TWO CARS --- AND THEY RAN INTO EACH OTHER ON THE FOLLOWING DAY!

PLEASE PASS

BOB MONKHOUSE
(AFTER GEORGE WOLFE)

Today in 480 BC Leonidas got it wrong at Thermopylae. He tried to cut 'em off at the pass – but the entire Persian army took a lot of cutting off. Mind you, Ephialtes didn't help. He was the Greek traitor

7 AUG

who led the pick of the Persian infantry along a mountain path so they could attack Leonidas and the Greek army from the rear. The suicide squad was called the 'Immortals' but that didn't fool anyone, especially them. Anyway, Leonidas and his Spartan lads were wiped out in this pincer movement. So were the 'Immortals', but Xerxes, the Persian leader, insisted they were still alive to keep up morale. I expect he just listed them at the Bureau of Missing Persians.

The revolving door was patented today in 1888. The swinging idea came from Theophilus van Kannel of Philadelphia who also unwittingly gave birth to the subject of 1001 jokes . . . including the one about Raquel Welch having a morbid fear of revolving doors. She reckons they're booby traps.

Roger Bannister became the first person to run a four-minute mile today in 1954. The Russian theory was that he'd cheated and used a short cut.

Ranger Roy Sullivan was struck by lightning today in 1973 as he drove through Shenandoah Park in Virginia, USA. It blew him ten feet out of his jeep, shot down both legs – whacking one shoe off – and set his hair on fire. But then if it weren't for accidents there wouldn't be so many people in this world.

The Peace Bridge – linking Niagara Falls in Ontario, Canada, with Niagara Falls in New York, USA – was dedicated today in 1927. 'When a bride goes to Niagara for her honeymoon,' said Oscar Wilde, 'seeing the Falls is her second disappointment.'

It became possible to purchase stock in the Ewing Land, Oil and Cattle Company: the 1000 stock certificates costing £3, issued and dated today in 1980. The novelty firm printing them added the slogan: 'Pardner, you've been ripped off by J. R.'

In Goissevain, Manitoba, they hold the Canadian Turtle Derby to establish the title of world champion racing turtle. The contest is sometimes delayed . . . waiting for last year's winner to complete his lap of honour.

The Spanish Armada went after a Drake and were out for a duck today in 1588.

The Battle of Savo was fought tonight in 1942 – as Japanese naval forces in the Pacific destroyed three US cruisers and HMAS *Canberra*. After the war the two opposing naval commanders corresponded and refought the battle many times with diagrams and two chessboards! When Admiral Keeley wrote in ornate style, '. . . and may Heaven preserve you always', Commander Kuromigusha ended his reply with, '. . . and may Heaven pickle you too.'

The Great Train Robbery of 1963 took place this morning. Remember 1963. When we thought two-and-a-half million quid was a lot of money? And by an unhappy coincidence . . .

INCOME TAX WAS IMPOSED IN THE USA TODAY IN 1861...

. . . 3 per cent on incomes exceeding $800! The way taxes are now, I figure that if I continue to save at my present rate, I could retire owing £250,000.

Louis Philippe was crowned king of the French today in 1830. He was called the 'Citizen King' but turned out to be a ghastly snob so they made him abdicate in 1848. He was argumentative too. The only way you could get him to change his mind was to agree with him.

And today's a big day for reigning monarchs (or those who would like to be!) . . . Richard M. Nixon resigns! The president of the USA surrendered his post on this day in 1974. Ted Rogers describes him as, 'The only US President ever to lie in state while still in office.' When President Ford was inaugurated, Nixon added, 'What'll you give me?' Ford said, 'Pardon?' Nixon said, 'I'll take it.''

A landslide destroyed 69 houses in a suburb in Dunedin, New Zealand, on this day in 1979 . . . making more than 170 people homeless. One resident was caught looting his neighbours' houses. He pleaded for leniency on the grounds that he came from a broken home.

And Edward VII was crowned on this day in 1902. He was known as 'Edward the Peacemaker'. Arthur Askey added, 'The piece he made was Lily Langtry.'

RAF fighter pilot Douglas Bader was shot down and seized by German troops on this day in 1941. His captors were surprised and impressed when they discovered that Doug's apparently 'fractured' legs were both artificial. Realizing they had caught Britain's legendary legless pilot, the Germans provided new false limbs. 'They wanted to have the old ones mended,' Bader told Ted Ray, 'but I wouldn't stand for it!'

10 AUG

Magellan set sail from Spain to become the first to circle the world in a single round trip on this day in 1519 . . . and failed! Most people remember Ferdinand Magellan as the first to circumnavigate this globe in one historic voyage. What he did was two voyages – each over halfway round in opposite directions. And no one can convince me that doing something in two goes is the same as doing it in one go. If that's true, then I can run a four-minute mile. In twenty-four ten-second bursts.

Tonight at 8 p.m. in 1895, the proms began. Henry Wood and an orchestra of eighty opened the first series of Queen's Hall Promenade Concerts. Admission: 1s. (5p) to stand; 2s. a balcony seat. Cigars 3d. Inflation has certainly hit the 'Land of Hope and Glory'. I'm suffering from inflation lips. They're chapped from kissing my money goodbye.

Today in 1959 Henry Cutri's car was a deadly weapon, threatening the lives of crowds shopping in the centre of Funchal, Madeira. Henri was driving down the steep hill from Reid's Hotel when his brakes failed. As the car gathered speed, he knew a crash would probably kill him and his helpless victims. To save lives other than his own, Henri twisted the wheel and deliberately drove into what appeared to be a vacant shop. The premises were a temporary store for thousands of soft cushions and bedding! Heroic Henri came to a comparatively gentle stop and his only injuries were a bruised forehead and broken glasses!

John Farlane was taken ill with food poisoning today in 1959 after eating German sausage . . . at the West German Food Hygiene Exhibition in Hamburg! Doctors feared the wurst.

The start of the longest open sea voyage took place on this day in 1977. Thankfully, the intrepid quartet (one was replaced halfway) made the journey of over 2000 miles in their two kayaks, paddling three-quarters of the way. By 29 April the following year, travelling from Venezuela, through the West Indies, they reached Miami, Florida, USA. Their night-time solar-powered blankets failed, proving the truth of the old proverb: 'You can't have your kayak and heat it too.' Learn to put up with that pun if you can. It may crop up again.

11 AUG

The next total eclipse of the sun visible from the UK will happen today in 1999 on the Cornish coast. 'It's only during an eclipse,' observed Evan Esar, 'that the man in the moon has a place in the sun.'

Fourteen Polish women climbed the 26,000-foot Gasherbrum mountain today in 1975. 'And they say they're the weaker sex,' laughs Ted Rogers. 'Ever tried to pull the bedclothes back when she's got 'em all? It takes stronger tugs than it does to get the QE2 in dock.'

Andrew Carnegie died on this day in 1919. Between 1901 and his death he gave away 350 million dollars' worth of cash and goods . . . including 7689 church organs. He was so rich, he once wrote a cheque and the bank bounced.

The first satellite of the planet Mars was discovered in 1877. A leading British astronomer said we were being watched by people from outer space. Yes, and I believe they're going to contact the responsible leaders of earth . . . just as soon as they can find one.

'Desquamation can be a positive danger,' warns *The Guinness Book of Records*. It leaves it up to would-be challengers in the 'longest shower bath' stakes to look it up. 'Desquamation', of course, means skin flaking off (you knew that) – and Arron Marshall of Rockingham Park, Western Australia, must have looked pretty flaky today in 1978. Since the previous 29 July, Arron had spent a nonstop 336 hours under the shower. I know how that feels. I live with a cleanliness fanatic. My wife even washes the windows on envelopes. Some people walk in their sleep. She vacuums.

It was seventy-three degrees Fahrenheit . . . below zero . . . in Canada in 1852. Today's issue of the London *Times* in 1853 announced it and it still stands as Canada's lowest-ever screen temperature, clocked at Floeberg Bay, Ellesmere Island. It was so cold a mounted policeman and his horse took turns wearing his uniform.

The last US combat troops left Vietnam today in 1972. At a protest parade demanding US withdrawal, comedian Charlie Fleischer was clubbed by a cop who called him a 'goddam Communist'. 'But I'm an anti-Communist!' argued Charlie. 'I don't care what *kind* of a goddam Communist you are!' yelled the cop. 'Get outa here!'

'Jealousy,' sang the night club chanteuse Elina Diaz, 'Hearts were broken . . . angry words were spoken' – and no wonder! She was so possessive of her fiancé Fernando, she figured out a way to scare off rivals. Today in 1934 Elina was fined £680 and jailed for four weeks in Paramaribo, Dutch Guiana (now Surinam) – for drugging Fernando and having her name tattooed on his forehead while he slept! A month later, they got married.

The world's strangest suicide? In protest against Dr Caetano's visit to Portuguese Guinea on his African tour in 1969, Osami Kamaga, a Japanese student in Via Salazar, Timor, poured the contents of a petrol can over himself, squatted in the main street and set a flame to his clothes. It went out. The can had been refilled with detergent. Kamaga came back an hour later and said he would shoot himself. The gun jammed. Two hours later he reappeared with sticks of explosive strapped all round his body and announced he would blow himself up. But the stolen sticks were not dynamite. They were smoke signals used by the coastguard. As Kamaga vanished in a dense cloud of smoke, a timber truck came round the corner and ran over him. Coroner's verdict: Kamaga took his own life through 'non-observation of normal safety precautions'.

13 AUG

The first two-way telephone conversation was held via satellite on this day in 1960. By an odd telephonic coincidence . . .

The Berlin Wall was sealed today in 1961. 'The Russians are so hospitable,' said Elsie to Doris Walters (the famous 'Gert and Daisy' of BBC Radio fame), 'they're always taking in boarders.' 'Yes,' agreed Doris. 'So far they've taken in the Hungarian border, the Rumanian border, the Czechoslovakian border . . .'

The coin-operated phone was patented in the USA on this same day in 1889 – by William Gray of Hartford, Connecticut. I can remember when it only cost two old pence to make a phone box call . . . that was less than one new pence. Now it's getting so expensive, obscene phone callers are taking shorter breaths.

Today the ballpoint pen was invented in 1944 by Laslo Biro, a Hungarian refugee in Argentine. A famous pen manufacturer asked him, 'I heard a ridiculous tale that you'd found something to replace pen-nibs . . .?' 'Balls!' cried Biro. 'Quite,' said the manufacturer, 'I knew it couldn't be true.'

Tunnellers from France and Italy met under Mont Blanc today in 1962. They christened themselves the 'Moles'. That's what I call making a molehill out of a mountain.

The huge cathedral in Cologne, Germany, was completed today in 1880. It was *started* in 873! Did you say, 'What was a British building firm doing in Germany?' Well, the cathedral *was* burned up a bit in 1248 – so the rebuilding really only took 632 years. In 1946 a prominent citizen of Cologne donated a loudspeaker to the cathedral – 'in memory of his wife'!

'SAVE OUR WILDLIFE' may be a dolphin slogan. The Soviet news agency TASS reported a fantastic incident observed by Russian sailors on the fishing ship *Nevelskoi* on this day in 1978. A sea lion was crying for help, attacked by a murderous ring of killer whales. Suddenly a herd of dolphins arrived, like the US Cavalry coming to the rescue of the stagecoach. The killer whales dispersed but, as soon as the dolphins had moved on, they returned to finish off the sea lion. At once the dolphins rushed back, leaped up and over the whales, formed a protective circle all round the sea lion and so saved its life.

THE PANAMA CANAL OPENED TO TRAFFIC TODAY IN 1914, THANKS TO A POSTAGE STAMP

In 1882 the French had secured the right to construct a canal across Panama but the project failed. A young French engineer named Bunau-Varilla tried to interest the USA; but the Americans said 'No' to a canal across Panama: they wanted it to go across Nicaragua. As the US government moved to raise funds for the Nicaraguan canal, Varilla moved faster. The resourceful Frenchman wrote to every Congressman – and enclosed a dramatic stamp in each envelope. The stamp was from Nicaragua and depicted one of the

local volcanoes in spectacular eruption. Congress got the message. It would be crazy for the US to build a canal through a land full of volcanoes, all boiling over! So in 1904 they switched to Panama, bought the rights from France, and the first ship passed through the canal ten years later – thanks to a little picture on an almost forgotten stamp.

Today in 1978, thirty-three years to the day after V-J day, China and Japan signed a 'Peace and Friendship' treaty, formally ending their part of World War II. But World War II isn't really over. There has never been a formal peace treaty between Germany and the Soviet Union!

The eccentric Irish philosopher Edwyn Kerrygan wrote in his diary today in 1782, 'My diet is perfect, blending water, air and heat in most life-sustaining proportions.' He died the next day after nearly a year of eating only hot, wet moss. His last words, 'It is a phase, this dizziness. After it is passed off, I shall live forever!' I'm sure my wife will live forever. She has nothing but dresses she wouldn't be seen dead in.

This was the day of the Makin Raid in 1942. US marines known as Carlson's Raiders landed from submarines on Makin Island in the Gilbert group in a daring attempt to divert Japanese attention from operations on Guadalcanal. Nine marines were captured and beheaded, as the Japanese immediately began to convert nearby Tarawa Island into a virtually impregnable fortress. Fifteen months later, it took 18,600 US infantry men to seize Makin and Tarawa. Harvey Stone said, 'I went through the entire battle without a scratch. No kidding, that DDT is great!'

The *Mayflower* set sail from Plymouth today in 1620 – taking pilgrims to religious freedom in the New World of America. When I was a young man I called my sports car 'Mayflower' . . . on account of all the puritans who came across in it.

16 AUG

'ELVIS LIVES' – but the King of Rock dies on this day in 1977. He was pronounced dead at 3.30 p.m. in the emergency room of Baptist Hospital, Memphis, Tennessee, ending the most aston-ishing career in American pop music and beginning a posthumous in-dustry of incredible proportions. Elvis occupied a British charts position for more consecutive years than anyone else – twenty-three years from 1956 to 1978. He had the highest number of Top Ten hits – 54, compared with Cliff's 41 and the Beatles' 23. Altogether, Elvis appeared on the UK record charts for a world-beating 1057 weeks!

According to legend, today's the day Robin Hood won the archery contest at Nottingham Fair. But only by an arrow margin.

'GROCER WULLY MAKES THE BIG TIME'

17 AUG

was the headline . . . but the curse of Penkill Castle struck him down. The locals christened him the 'Milk Laird'. For years he had carried everything from milk to paraffin in his old blue van. When he began calling on the seat of the Boyd family, Penkill Castle, he saw his chance of striking it rich. The ancient walls, built in 1420 to guard Ayrshire's valley from predators, couldn't keep Wully Hume out. He and his wife befriended the frail old spinster who lived alone in the great building, the last survivor of the Boyd family. They moved into the gatehouse and told visitors that old Miss Boyd was 'indisposed'. Then the art treasures housed in Penkill Castle began to appear in local antique shops, courtesy of Grocer Wully. Wully Hume then made his big move. He induced the eighty-two-year-old owner to sell him her castle, lands, building and contents . . . for £5,000! Wully's triumph was shortlived. Asked about the castle's legendary curse, he scoffed, 'Dead Boyds cannot harm me.' On this day in 1977, Wully was trying to sell a valuable portrait to a dealer. When he took it down from the wall, both men saw this inscription: MOVE NOT THIS PICTURE. LET IT BE, FOR LOVE OF THOSE ON HIGH. The dealer knew of the Penkill curse, said to disturb the castle. He backed out of the deal. Wully Hume said, 'Bugger off then!' – and promptly died of a massive heart attack!

Renee Richards refused a sex test on this day in 1976. I don't know why people make such a fuss about sex change surgery. There's nothing to it. A snip here, a snip there – and Bob's your auntie!

"WHO REALLY DISCOVERED GOLD IN THE YUKON TODAY IN 1896? SOME SAY THE WHITE PROSPECTOR CARMACK. OTHERS CLAIM IT WAS THE INDIANS SNOOKUM JIM AND TAGISH CHARLIE. ODDEST GOLD STRIKE: JACK SMALT DISCOVERED A 9 LB.5 OZ. NUGGEST ON THIS SAME DAY IN 1927 ON A SOUTH AFRICAN GOLF COURSE, WHEN HE HIT IT WITH HIS CLUB!

SO YOU CAN GET LUCKY ON A GOLF COURSE....

The first English child was born in America in 1587 today. She was Virginia Dare and – as John Fultz comments – giving birth in those days wasn't easy. They used to 'induce labour' by telling the expectant mother that the Indians were about to attack!

The earliest successful appendix operation was performed in 1736! The surgeon was sergeant surgeon to King George II, Claudius Amyand. George III hated the royal doctors and acquired a full range of medical books so that he could ignore their advice and treat his own illnesses. That's dangerous. You could die of a misprint.

18
AUG

Condensed milk was patented today in 1856 – by Gail Borden. The secret was in getting the cows to concentrate.

Able Seaman Harry Middinham was nineteen today in 1902 . . . so he celebrated with his first shore leave in Colombo, his first pint of the local brew, his first kiss – and his first naval prison sentence! The high-spirited kiss together with an escape-proof embrace and a bit of waltzing thrown in, had been given, unasked, to the first European woman young Harry had seen in the streets of Ceylon . . . a spinster named Flora Danbrugh, who also chanced to be the nervous daughter of the British naval attaché. Harry got twenty-eight days in the jug and lost six months' pay. Eighteen years later in 1920, Harry was approached by a private detective who had traced him to the Shrewsbury draper's shop where he worked. Miss Danbrugh had died, still unmarried, in 1919. And she had left £31,500 in her will – her entire fortune – to the man who had given her the only kiss she had ever had in her lonely life. What is love? 'Love,' says Ken Dodd, 'is Harry Corbett tenderly warming his hand before he slips it into Sooty.'

Mitch Malone, an Australian tourist in Rome, was knocked unconscious in the Colosseum today in 1962. The bolt from the blue that hit his head was just that – a bolt! Malone had worked as an aircraft construction worker. He was able to identify the bolt that connected with his nut as coming from a plane flying on schedule for Alitalia. The airline paid him £8400 damages. What you might call a 'lump sum'.

Sixty-year-old Leon Trotsky fed his pet rabbits today in 1940, then went into his study to read an article written by a young admirer . . . and that's when the young admirer pierced his skull with a mountaineer's ice axe! Ramon Mercader's assassination of the exiled Bolshevik giant in Mexico was ordered by Stalin. Trotsky was writing anti-Stalin articles. Stalin figured, 'Better dead than read.'

20 AUG

We lost Groucho today in 1977, aged eighty-seven. When Chico Marx asked him, 'How would you like one gala day before you died?' Groucho leered, 'One gal a day is all I can handle.'

' NEVER IN THE FIELD OF HUMAN CONFLICT WAS SO MUCH OWED BY SO MANY TO SO FEW !

– the words of tribute to the RAF fighter squadrons from Winston Churchill on this day in 1940. Even in his last years Churchill liked to drop in at the House of Commons. Once, as he was helped down the aisle to his seat by two aides, a couple of young MPs looked on disapprovingly. One said, 'He really shouldn't come in these days. I'm told he's almost lost his memory.' The other whispered, 'Yes – and I understand he can barely see where he is.' Churchill turned slowly in his seat and rumbled, 'They also say he's going deaf.'

Soviet troops invaded Czechoslovakia on this day in 1968. Alexander Dubček was the first Czech to be bounced.

The 'Mona Lisa' was stolen from the Louvre today in 1911. Its creator, the legendary Leonardo da Vinci, was the illegitimate son of a Florentine notary and at the age of twenty-four was accused of 'frequenting a notorious boy prostitute'. The real title of his 'Mona Lisa' is La Gioconda and although it's meant to be a 'portrait of the duchess of Milan in 1503', lots of scholars believe it's a reject! They say Leonardo actually painted Madonna Lisa Gherardini, but her old man refused to pay for it. King Francis I of France probably bought it for 492 ounces of gold in 1513 – and in 1962 its value was assessed at $100 million!

Twelve women arrived in Virginia, today in 1691 to be sold as wives – for 120 pounds of tobacco each! They came directly from British jails. 'Why a man would want such a wife is a mystery,' wrote the Irish dramatist Slattery Devane, who was later imprisoned for having married two sisters simultaneously! Why a man would want two wives is a bigamystery.

Princess Margaret was born today in 1930 during a storm of thunder and lightning at Glamis Castle. I admire her. And I liked Roddy Llewelyn. In fact, we called our dog 'Roddy' because he loved his Pedigree Chum as well.

Hawaii became the fiftieth state of the USA on this day in 1959. Hawaii – that's the place where men make passes at girls who wear grasses.

Today in 1864 Jean Henri Dunant proposed an international Red Cross organization, agreed to at a convention of sixteen nations at Geneva, Switzerland. To cut down on road accidents, the British Red Cross backed a campaign of adverts that advised 'Show Something White At Night'. My uncle did and the magistrate fined him £100 with a month's suspended sentence.

22 AUG

BBC TELEVISION WAS BORN TODAY IN 1932 –

– as the first regular service began. No need to wonder what they showed. They're sure to repeat it.

King Richard III was killed on Bosworth Field on this day in 1485. He stood in the bog yelling, 'A horse! A horse! My kingdom for a horse!' Percy Thrower once looked around his flagging rose garden and said the same thing.

Today's issue of Argentina's *Fiesta* magazine in 1974 carried this ad in its personal column: 'Alcoholic now completely reformed is intending to write autobiography and would like to contact anyone who knew what he was doing between 1956 and 1972.'

'THE WORLD WILL END ON OCTOBER 13TH, 1736!'

predicted the English mathematician William Whiston. Wrong! For William, however, it *did* end today in 1752. I hope he was grateful for the extra sixteen years.

23 AUG

Four hundred and forty-five thousand pounds for a wedding! That's how much the sixty-four-year-old multi-millionaire Antonio Helmut Varboza forked out to wed his bride, twenty-five-year-old model Rita de Recife on his huge coffee plantation near São Paulo, Brazil, today in 1970. Eight hundred guests drank over four hundred quarts of champagne and thirty-seven wedding cakes were eaten. Three years later they divorced! Remember US TV's 'Laugh-In'? Ruth Buzzi asked Goldie Hawn, 'Do you like big weddings or little ones?' Goldie said, 'BIG weddings! Without big weddings you can't have little ones.'

'SUPER KERMIT'

surfaced today in 1960 in Equatorial Guinea. Scientists snatched a rare Goliath frog from its marshy warmth and found it measured a record thirty-two inches in length! I feel sorry for frogs. They have a worse life than I do. They just hop on, hop off and croak.

The Great Lover died today in 1926 – and over 100,000 mobbed the funeral. Rudolph Valentino was thirty-one years old when his appendicitis proved unnecessarily fatal. His sexy look supposedly came from a dead nerve in one eyelid. I think a dead nerve is what's ruining my sex life. Every time I make a pass at a girl, she says, 'You've got a dead nerve!'

Christopher Columbus was arrested in Haiti for mistreating the natives. Today in 1500 it was ordered that he be chained and returned to Spain. Some people say Columbus did *not* discover America. I asked a Red Indian. I said, 'Who do *you* think discovered America?' And the Indian said, 'What makes you think it was lost?'

On this day in 1974 a Swiss scientist named Maurice Stonckelbann invented a machine for milking mice. I have no idea why. For baby orphan mice maybe? Anyway, he did it, greatly to the relief of whoever had been milking them by hand up until then, I dare say. You'd need tweezers and a very low stool for that.

24 AUG

WASHINGTON BURNED TODAY IN 1814...

... the British set it afire ... and we couldn't even claim the insurance. US presidents have had streets, dams, hotels, schools and even cars named after them but George Washington is the only president to have both a city and a state named after him. If he never told a lie, how come he got so far in politics?

The motion picture camera was first patented early today in 1891 – by Thomas Edison. Little did he dream what sort of industry he was founding. Today almost all the new motion pictures are for adults only. If you're not an adult when you go in, you sure are when you come out.

YOU MIGHT NOT THINK MUCH OF TODAY

– but the folks in Pompeii got a big bang out of it. Yes, this is Vesuvius Day, in the year AD 79, when the volcano blew its top. John Fultz says, 'The biggest eruption in Italy since then was when Sophia Loren reached puberty!'

The first couple ever married during 'a parachute jump' were Ann Hayward and Arno Rudolphi. Together with a minister, best man and a four-piece band, the New York City couple were wed while

dangling from parachutes at the New York World's Fair, today in 1940. Odd . . . most couples don't fall out until *after* the wedding.

The seventeenth Olympic Games opened in Rome on this day in 1960 – and the light-heavy-weight boxing gold medal was won by a youth named Cassius Clay. One of his opponents said, 'He hit me so hard, I was still in the air when they counted me out.'

The world's first scheduled civil airline began its regular service between London and Paris today in 1919. I remember my first flight. Before take-off the stewardess told all the passengers to fasten their belts. I called her over and whispered, 'What do I do? I wear braces.'

The Free French Second Armoured Division marched into Paris today in 1944 to receive the surrender of General von Choltitz. The Nazi commander of the Paris garrison had defied Hitler's order to defend the city – thus saving the lives of his hapless soldiers and preventing the destructive shelling of the French capital. The first evening I went out to dine there, some bloke jumped on a table and yelled, 'Vive wine, men and song!' – and I thought to myself, 'So they don't call it "Gay Paree" for nothing.'

A hovering host of angels saved British troops on this day in 1914. The German soldiers in pursuit of retreating tommies during the Battle of Mons were halted by the petrifying spectacle of winged messengers from heaven, suspended above the battlefield and glowing brightly! An aura of mystique surrounds this opening British engagement of World War I. General Joffre, the French commander in chief, was an unflappable bloke but even he wrote of 'angelic voices whose advice and encouragement sustained me'.

26 AUG

THIS IS WOMEN'S EQUALITY DAY!

It marks the date in 1920 when American women gained the right to vote through the ratification of the nineteenth amendment to the US constitution. A women's libber, demonstrating outside Liverpool's Adelphi Hotel, cried out, 'Free women! Free women!' – and a male chauvinist pig drunk paused and yelled back, 'Terrific! Send two to room 204!'

The cost of guard dogs in New York hit $200 a month today in 1976. A Seventh Avenue jewellery shop reacted in desperation with a sign: 'Warning! This area is patrolled by tarantulas.'

KRAKATAU KRAKKED TODAY IN 1883!

The eruption could be heard 3000 miles away as the volcano chucked 5 cubic miles of this poor old planet 50 miles into the sky. Tidal waves over 200 feet tall swept outwards from the explosion. If you're keen on volcanoes, try reading Arthur Holme's *Principles of Physical Geology*. If you're interested in the world's biggest bangs, try Britt Ekland's memoirs.

Earl Louis Mountbatten was killed by an IRA bomb on this day in 1979. Three others of his party were also killed by the blast on board his fishing boat during his holiday in Ireland. But the sea knew triumph as well as tragedy, for . . .

On this day in 1966 Francis Chichester sailed from Plymouth on his epic voyage around the world, alone in *Gypsy Moth IV* . . . a voyage which he said 'began because I was terrified of Cape Horn. If anything terrifies me, I must try to conquer it.' I agree. I'm so brave I once dreamed I was being chased by two huge man-eating tigers but I wouldn't wake up. I didn't want those damn tigers to think I was yellow.

27
AUG

And today is the traditional birthday in 551 BC of the great sage Confucius, to whom many absurd but merry proverbs have been good-naturedly attributed – among them: 'When the cat is away, house smell better' – 'Love with wrong woman maybe fun – but on nestee is best policy' – and even, 'Man who wash face in vinegar go round all day with sour puss'.

TARZAN IS BORN

. . . the first hero in fiction with a monkey on his back! On this day in 1912, the magazine serial entitled *Tarzan of the Apes* by the great Edgar Rice Burroughs went into print. By 1924 the jungle hero's tigerskin garment was so popular, comedian Leon Errol cracked, 'America's changing its anthem to the "Tarzan Stripes"!'

The world's first Wild West show was presented today in 1872. Showman Sid Barnett – 'Honest Sid' to strangers – offered a curious bunch of attractions including, '*Real* Injun scalpin's, dry-gulchin' the lawmen, bison stampeding over sheep – and the great "Wild Bill" Hickok rasslin' a buffalo!' What price pioneering? Sid's cowboy circus idea continues to pull crowds to this day but he was through before you could spot a fake scalp, a stuffed sheep or a doped buffalo. 'Honest Sid' wound up in the back streets of Latin America, peddling books to people who couldn't read.

Great at monkey business – that was mathematically minded Sally, the famous African chimpanzee who died at London Zoo on this day in 1891. She could give visitors exactly the number of straws they asked for, up to twenty! I once adopted a chimp at Regent's Park Zoo. When I posed for publicity photos with the ape, some zoo official shouted, 'What are you doing with that ugly baboon?' I said, 'It's not an ugly baboon, it's a chimpanzee!' He yelled back, 'I'm talking to the chimpanzee!'

29 AUG

The last live performance by the Beatles was played in San Francisco on this day in 1966. The setting was Candlestick Park and the final appearance of the famous four occurred eight years to the day after George Harrison first performed with the Quarrymen, led by John Lennon and Paul McCartney. 'We had pretty crude equipment in those early days,' says George. 'Our microphone had a rope starter.'

Fred and Ginger danced 'Cheek to Cheek' for the first time when 'Top Hat' opened today in 1935. They had introduced 'The Continental' on 11 October the previous year, and it was the first song to win an academy award. Astaire told US TV host Dick Cavett, 'Hollywood hasn't changed as much as you think. It's still like it was in the thirties . . . the place where you spend more than you earn, on things you don't need, to impress people you don't like.' We're a bit like that in Leighton Buzzard too.

The last Inca ruler was put to death on this day in 1533; his name, Atahualpa. The Incas mourned his murder by the Spanish conqueror Pizarro with a thirty-day wake, remaining pickled on alcohol for a month. A sort of Inca-drinker-do?

TODAY IN 1842 BRIGHAM YOUNG PROCLAIMED HIS APPROVAL OF POLYGAMY

Since he already had seventeen wives, the declaration seemed a bit superfluous. Every man should have at least one wife. Because there are some things that go wrong you can't blame on the government.

John Camden Nield died on this day in 1852 in London. Dan O'Day reports, 'Even though he was rich, Nield was famous for being stingy. For instance, he wore the same set of clothes for his entire adult life and he refused to have them cleaned. He said cleaning might wear them out. Legend has it he died on his feet; even though he had passed away, his clothes remained standing!' Odd to the very end, Nield bequeathed his £250,000 fortune to Queen Victoria.

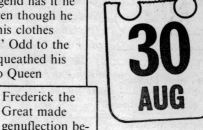

30 AUG

Thirty-nine-year-old Cleopatra made her exit in 30 BC today. She held a poisonous snake to her sumptuous bosom. It took three hours to get the snake to coil again.

Frederick the Great made genuflection before him illegal today in 1783, and I for one can understand it. It must be nerve-wracking to have everyone on their knees all around you. Their heads would only come up to your groin. If one of them bit you, you'd be in terrible trouble.

Today in 1941 Winston Churchill gave orders that commandos sent on dangerous missions should be told the ultimate purpose of their endeavours. General Sir Thomas Vale advised against it, commenting, 'Familiarity breeds contempt.' Winnie replied, 'Dear Thomas, without a certain amount of familiarity, it is impossible to breed anything at all.'

The demure twenty-one-year-old who created *Frankenstein*, wife of the great English poet, Mary Wollstonecraft Shelley, was born today in 1797. (Shelley's first wife Harriet drowned herself in the Serpentine.) It was Baron Frankenstein who said, 'That monster is worse than five of my greedy relatives put together . . . and he *is* five of my greedy relatives put together!'

WELCOME TO THE FIRST OF SEPTEMBER!

Well, it *would* have been but for that greedy old Roman Emperor Augustus Caesar. According to Uncle Claudius, Augustus wanted a month named after him, just as his leaky predecessor had. (You remember Julius Caesar . . . big conk, wife above suspicion, nooky with Cleopatra, July named after him and a full set of Senate cutlery buried about his person.) Well, in 27 BC, Augustus became the noblest Roman of them all and wanted everyone to know it. That's when he grabbed the month of Sextilis for himself – but as it only had thirty days, he pinched a day from September and called it – that's right – the thirty-first of August.

This is a big day in Canada. The first woman ran all the way across it today in 1976 . . . a matter of 3,841 miles! Carallyn Bowes lost 15 pounds in weight as she cantered from Halifax to Burnaby for 133 days, wearing out 13 pairs of shoes. She said she only took on such a challenge in order to give up smoking! An easier way is to carry wet matches.

John Bunyan died on this day in 1688, aged fifty. The greatest literary genius produced by the Puritan movement, Bunyan was born at Elstow near Bedford, the poor son of a travelling tinker. He became an inspired preacher and was frequently chucked into prison for offending authority. He once complained to the richest member of his congregation, 'I hesitate to bring this up but since I constantly risk my liberty to preach my sermons, why do you always fall asleep during each one?' 'Dear Sir,' was the consoling reply, 'would I sleep if I didn't trust you?'

1 SEPT

Hollywood actor William Bendix made live TV history on this day in 1958 when he appeared for ATV on 'The Bob Monkhouse Hour' as a guest star in a comedy sketch based on his prison drama 'Crashout'. About eight million viewers heard this exchange of dialogue between Bill and the warder played by singer Dickie Valentine.

Dickie: 'How come they threw you in jail, Rocky?'

Bill: 'Some lousy squeal pigeon stooled on me!'

The first triangular Cape of Good Hope stamp was issued in 1853. Ken Dodd says he has Britain's largest collection of foreign stamps. Now all he needs is some foreigners to write to.

Chop Suey was created today in 1896 – but not in China! A chef of the Chinese Ambassador Li Hung-Chang in the USA, weary of seeing his finest oriental cuisine left uneaten by unappreciative guests, dreamed up chop suey to 'look Chinese and taste New York'. It is never served in China. I've been suspicious about their food ever since a Chinese chef I know told me he was going home 'to wok the dog'.

RUSSIA PUT A TAX ON BEARDS TODAY IN 1689

And in those days, the Russian people didn't dare to criticize their leaders. Today in Russia a citizen can say anything he likes about the government and still get a decent burial.

Engelbert Humperdinck was born in 1854. Yes, this was the German classical composer whose amusing name was adopted by singing idol Gerry Dorsey. In 1893 he wrote the opera 'Hansel and Gretl' based on the charming German children's tale about two youngsters who push an old lady into an oven and bake her. Ex-President Amin used it as a recipe book.

China opened its first TV station at Peking today in 1958. Transmissions began with a programme about the necessity of observing traffic laws! I believe they're very strict. I heard of some poor old rickshaw man who lost his licence for having no tread on his running shoes.

Japan surrendered formally to the Allies on the US battleship *Missouri* on this day in 1945. It was obvious to the whole world that Japan faced economic and political ruin for the remainder of the twentieth century. I heard that next year they're going to buy Pearl Harbour.

2 SEPT

In 31 BC the Battle of Actium was fought all day today. Caesar's adopted son, Octavian, staged a successful showdown with his rival Mark Antony and so became the first Roman emperor. Today Actium welcomes tourists in every way. I recall standing there once looking at an old ruin and she winked at me.

'LONDON'S BURNING!' was the cry that went up on this day in 1666 as the Great Fire began in a baker's shop in Pudding Lane. It ended at Pie Corner. Dinner was ruined.

The American Communist Party was formed in the USA today in 1919. A Communist, of course, is a person who is willing to share everything you've got.

Yes, I remember it well! I was an eleven-year-old schoolboy breathlessly listening to an HMV radio in West Worthing, Sussex, as Prime Minister Neville Chamberlain told us all, 'a state of war now exists' . . . and both Britain and France were off with World War II against Nazi Germany. Me, I just went off to the Rivoli Cinema and saw a film called 'Behold Delilah' in which Samson reversed the events of the day by using the jawbone of an ass to *end* a war.

This is a bad day for trusting in air ships! The first zeppelin was destroyed in England on this day in 1916 . . . and nine years later, the US dirigible *Shenandoah* broke apart at Caldwell, Ohio . . . at the same hour of the same day! I say that if God had meant us to fly He'd have given us more parking spaces at Heathrow.

3 SEPT

Here's another fateful coincidence . . . Oliver Cromwell died today in 1658 – seven years to the day after the Battle of Worcester! He was a very strict Puritan and refused to sleep with his wife on the grounds that she was a married woman.

Today's question: Where would you find a character with no courage, a character with no heart and a character with no brain?
Answer: In the yellow pages under 'cabinet ministers'.
Or . . . In the pages of Frank L. Baum's *Wizard of Oz* books. Yes, that's 'books' in the plural. He wrote fourteen of them, all about Oz. And the most famous one, upon which the MGM film is based, was published on this day 1900.
Birthday: Engineer Matthew Boulton, 1728, Birmingham, who said, 'People are steam mill mad!' and proved it by running James Watt's new steam engines into millions of pounds. He put them to work in the Royal Mint. Sterling chap!

4 SEPT

The world's worst spectacle took place in 1827 when the entire circus went over Niagara Falls! Eight thousand thrill-seekers paid fifty cents each to watch bankrupt owners release all their tents, caravans and livestock into the plunging waters, consigning caged animals to certain death. The *New York Evening Post* commented, 'Better to have set the tigers and lions upon the proprietors, thus affording a bloodier spectacle, a greater justice and a final settling of accounts.' To me, the story underlines the ruthlessness of all displays in which men debase animals for paying spectators. I knew a tattooed lady who married an india-rubber man and, on the wedding night, he rubbed out all the pictures.

SIR GARY SOBERS WAS CAUGHT OUT... BY PLASTIC GRASS

– today in 1977. The setting was the baseball stadium of the New York Giants and, with his Caribbean All-Stars, Sir Gary seemed certain to thrash the inexperienced US eleven. Instead the reverse happened . . . and Sobers put some blame on the artificial grass wicket made of 'Gaylon'! Was someone trying to queer his pitch?

The first Boy Scout Rally was held today at Crystal Palace in 1909. I used to get lost a lot when I was camping. I was always looking in vain for an easy guide.

The world's first cafeteria opened in New York City on this day in 1885. Cafeterias are rather like a marriage. When you see what the other fellow's got, you wish you'd taken that instead.

Question: Which indian chief led the ambush at the Little Bighorn in which General Custer was killed? Answer: Did you say Sitting Bull? Wrong! Sitting Bull wasn't even present. He stayed up in the hills, making powerful medicine. What's more, it was not an ambush. The Indians knew the site as 'Greasy Grass River', a camp which Custer attacked, only to die in his fight with warriors led by Crazy Horse! And today – in 1877 – old Crazy Horse finally bit the dust. (Some of them pesky Indians bit the dust so often, they had to hoover their dentures.)

Today is the birthday of Raquel Welch, 1940, whose publicity for her film 'Fathom' said, 'She sets the oceans ablaze!' Well, I suppose, if you've got the bellows for it . . .

The world's first petrol pump was manufactured on this day in 1885 by Sylvanus F. Bowser of Fort Wayne, Indiana. It offered gasoline for sixteen cents a gallon. Now the prices are so criminal, pump attendants fill your tank and then wipe their fingerprints off the nozzle.

5
SEPT

My favourite unintended humour of the month: today in 1969 the *Morning Star* ran the headline,

'CANNABIS SMUGGLING BY TROOPS. INVESTIGATION BY JOINT CHIEFS'

6 SEPT

There was a crafty old pirate named Wilson in the Scilly Isles – no, this isn't another tasteless reference to Sir Harold – this was in 1591, when privateers used the Scillies to pounce on French traders. Wilson Scarlet was the buccaneer who seized the good ship *Bonaventure* on this day and was hanged for that and other crimes including 'devious deceptions'. Gosh, it *does* sound like Sir Harold, doesn't it?

Today the *Mayflower* set sail from Plymouth in 1620 – but contrary to nearly everyone's belief, the pilgrims did *not* land first at Plymouth Rock! The ship first touched land at the tip of Cape Cod on 11 November 1620, and didn't reach Plymouth Rock until the following 21 December. Of course, if you thought Plymouth Rock was just souvenir candy you brought back from Devon, this is no big deal.

McKINLEY ASSASSINATED!

On this day in 1901, just a year into his second term as US president, William McKinley was shot and the world was shocked . . . even though his assassination had been threatened for twelve months by the same terrorists who then murdered King Umberto of Italy to prove their intentions. Despite elaborate security precautions and 150 intelligence men surrounding McKinley, no one even suspected that the bulky scarf wrapped around Leon Czolgosz's proffered handshake concealed the lethal revolver. Then his doctors decided the wound wasn't serious. So although President McKinley died on 14 September, it was a comfort for him to know that it wasn't from anything serious.

THE WORLD'S 1st CAR RACE ON A TRACK WAS RUN TODAY IN 1896, AT CRANSTON, RHODE, ISLAND, USA, WHEN A·H·WHITING CAME FIRST AT A SPEED OF 24 MPH! AT THAT SPEED, MY POOR OLD CAR SHAKES SO MUCH, EVERYBODY ON THE CAR RADIO SOUNDS NERVOUS. ITS ONLY HAD ONE PREVIOUS OWNER. I THINK IT WAS SOMEONE CALLED A·H·WHITING OF CRANSTON, RHODE ISLAND, USA...

STILL, IT'S BETTER THAN BEING MARRIED TO A *BACK-SEAT DRIVER*...

SUGGESTION BOX

Bob Monkhouse

This is the birthday of Queen Elizabeth I of England, 1533; she once told her loyal subjects that she had 'the heart and stomach of a king'. According to her boyfriends, everything else she had of any importance belonged to a queen.

And Buddy Holly, innovative pop legend, was born today in 1936: called 'the main man' by Stevie Wonder. I like Stevie Wonder. I always buy his crisps.

7 SEPT

Jesse James robbed his last train today in 1881. The takings: $840. The place: Blue Cut, Missouri. His rule: 'Shoot first and ask questions afterwards'. Of course, he didn't get many answers that way.

NIXON PARDONED, 1974!

President Gerald Ford made this gracious gesture and simultaneously knocked over a vase. Nixon responded by vowing, 'From now on, I swear nothing I say will be taped, be taped, be taped, be taped . . .'

Today saw the world's first air collision in 1910 over Austria. It was 'brother against brother' as the pioneer aviators were sibling rivals. They had argued over who should hand-crank the other's engine! After that it seems they flew off the handle.

8 SEPT

Harry Secombe and Peter Sellers were born today in 1921 and 1925. Two superb comedians who combined gloriously with Spike Milligan for nine years of 'The Goon Show' from which I quote the Great Eccles:

'WHEN I DIE, PEOPLE WILL LOOK UP TO ME! I'M GOING TO BE BURIED IN A TREE.'

Today's the birthday of King Richard I of England, 1157, who neglected his country for the Crusades. While he was overseas they started calling him 'Richard the Lionheart', evidence of the world's first transplant operation.

Three hundred and fourteen years ago today Samuel Pepys recorded the story of a prisoner who threw a stone at the judge, missed . . . and was hanged for it! The judge, who had been leaning forward on his elbow, remarked, 'If I had been an upright judge, I had been slain!' That was a pretty funny joke 314 years ago.

Cardinal Richelieu was born today in 1585. Crafty chief minister to Louis XIII of France, he was once suspected of plotting the king's death but later explained that he'd only said he fancied a stiff Bourbon. . . . And today in 1737, Italian anatomist Luigi Galvani was born in Bologna; he discovered galvanism by making an electric current cause a frog's muscles to twitch. Luigi died in 1798. The frog croaked too.

9 SEPT

WILLIAM THE CONQUEROR DIED TODAY IN 1087.

Towards the end of his life he would sit on the throne all day and night. Thus it came to be named after his initials . . . WC.

The Allies landed at Salerno in 1943. The Italian troops were remarkable for being the first in military history to have reversing lights on their tanks.

THEY LET THE DOG SEE THE RABBIT TODAY!

Well, the greyhounds saw the first hare which was made of rabbit fur, doused in the scent of a romantically inclined bitch, shaped like a rat and hand-winched for 400 yards. That was in 1876 and Britain has been going to the dogs ever since.

'Ta-ra-ra-boom-de-e!' sang the British Empire . . . but the biggest song hit of the gay 1890s was a rip off! Yes, Henry Sayers pinched the phenomenally successful song from an original singalong piece already published in middle European countries many years earlier. On this day in 1891, the Canadian opportunist took out his US copyright – even though he had first heard the magical song in the States . . . played by a pianist in a brothel! It's hard to imagine how enormous the popularity of one simple ditty could be in the days so long before radio and 'Top of the Pops'. Comedian Dan Leno be-came the first major comedian to suffer the censor when the palace officials ordered Dan to cut from a 'Royal Amusement', attended by various regal persons, the cheeky parody of the song: 'Ta-ra-ra-boom-de-e! Did you have yours today? I had mine yesterday! That's why I walk this way!'

10 SEPT

Two to one against . . . but England beat Scotland at Pinkie. Sounds such a pretty place, doesn't it? It wasn't, on this day in 1547. Ten thousand Scots soldiers were left dead on the fields of Midlothian whilst the English loss was barely two hundred, despite the Scots outnumbering the English two to one. Football's such a violent game, isn't it?

ICE BULLETS TO IRRIGATE CROPS...

. . . that's what the Ice Machine-gun offered farmers when it was patented today in 1918. Must have been invented by the same genius who crossbred glow-worms with fleas so you could see dogs at night.

Japanese premier Tojo attempted suicide by swallowing his chopsticks today in 1945. Can you think of a better way to go? Apart from throwing yourself headfirst into a heap of manure and dying of loneliness, I mean.

11 SEPT

Nikita Kruschev died today in 1971. He invented the slogan for the Russian tourist industry: 'Come and visit Russia . . . before Russia visits you!'

The marvellously crazy Roger Crab died today in 1680. One of the great English eccentrics, old Roger lived as a hermit eating only grass and leaves. He was also partial to issuing Crab's laws from time to time, one of which was, 'Henceforth no man shall be allowed to marry his widow's sister.'

' PENNY THE HEN '

set the world egg-laying record . . . and was laid out! The busy Black Orpington died today in 1930 in Taranaki, New Zealand, after laying 361 eggs in 364 days. During the winter the ground was so cold she had to lay them from a standing position.

On this night in 1909 they first observed Halley's comet at Heidelberg. For a while they thought they'd observed the first Black Hole but then someone took the lens cap off the telescope.

12 SEPT

Five boys found a priceless treasure on this day in 1940 . . . they stumbled upon the painted caves at Lascaux. Here in Dordogne, South West France, breathtaking examples of palaeolithic art were discovered, drawn on the walls by primitive man. Unfortunately the caves had to be closed to the public in 1963. Primitive men kept drawing on the walls.

Today the Hudson River was discovered by, of all people, Mr Hudson. The year was 1609 and Henry Hudson went on to locate and name Hudson Bay, before being set adrift by mutineers to die in 1611. He was very English and very brave and if he were alive today he would probably refuse his pension and take a job as a Lolipop Man on the M1.

JACKIE WEDS JACK!

This was the 1953 wedding day of JFK and Jacqueline Bouvier, when minister said, 'And Jackie, do you take this man for richer or even richer?' Winnie weds Clem! This was the 1908 wedding day of Winston Churchill and Clementine Hozier. She wrote, 'He wanted to hire a brass band.' Well, it's cheaper than buying a gold ring.

THE WORLD'S FIRST BURLESQUE SHOW EXPOSED ITSELF IN 1866

The local police immediately booked the leading stripper for obscene behaviour but unfortunately she was too busy.

It's Maurice Chevalier's birthday today, in 1893. After a lifetime of love affairs and romantic successes, he sang, 'I'm Glad I'm Not Young Any More'. At a Variety Club lunch in London he added, 'It's true I'm not as good as I once was. But I'm as good as once I ever was.'

The first space craft ever to land on another heavenly body did so today in 1959! *Luna 2's* moonfall was 'like hitting the eye of a fly at a hundred yards,' said Russian scientists. Now the Soviet space programme is speeding up its effort to put men on the moon. They have no choice. Siberia is full.

On this day in 1922 it was too hot to think. And in Parliament, nobody noticed. The highest natural weather temperature ever recorded was reached on this day at Azizia in North Africa. It was 136 degrees Fahrenheit. Dogs were lifting their legs and steaming on trees.

Louis XVI took his oath today in 1791 – as constitutional monarch of France . . . but it didn't save him from the guillotine. There's no truth in the tale that just as the blade was about to fall, a messenger arrived with a letter for the king – and he said, 'Drop it in the basket, I'll read it later!'

13 SEPT

WORLD'S WIERDEST LYNCHING? THEY HANGED AN ELEPHANT!

On this day in 1916 in Erwin, Tennessee, mob justice caught up with a rogue female elephant named Mary who ran amok and killed a man at a circus. Down Tennessee way you can't tell 'em that capital punishment doesn't work – they've never had an elephant murder anyone since. (I met a rogue elephant once. The ivory he sold me turned out to be plastic.)

A different form of 'happy days' took shape in Britain from 14 September 1752. We adopted the Gregorian calendar. Which means that today used to be 3 September. So the next time your boss complains that you're a week behind in your work, tell him you're actually four days ahead.

The great soldier and statesman, the duke of Wellington, died on this day in 1852. His last words: 'Thank God, I shall be spared from seeing the consummation of ruin that is gathering about us.' He must have felt like death.

14 SEPT

The first football penalty was awarded in Britain today in 1891. Before then a broken rule resulted only in a free kick for the other side. Of course, in those days football was football. The smell of sweat and leather in the changing room . . . today, that's only the manager's wallet.

The typewriter ribbon was patented today in 1886 by George Anderson of Memphis, Tennessee, USA, thus making it possible for my secretary to type as fast as seventy-five mistakes per minute.

Napoleon entered a frozen Moscow today in 1812 . . . and started that habit of keeping one hand under his coat. It was holding a hot water bottle. Meanwhile, his new wife, Marie Louise, was back in Paris tucked up in bed and covered in chaps.

15 SEPT

ISAMBARD KINGDOM BRUNEL, FAREWELL!

On this day in 1859, the great son of a great father died in Westminster of worry and overwork, aged only fifty-three. But during the previous fifty years, just look what he and his dad gave the world: Sir Marc built the world's first underwater tunnel (between Rotherhithe and Wapping), the Ile de Bourbon suspension bridge, the floating landing stage at Liverpool, invented the timber sawing and bending machine, the bootmaking machine and the stocking knitting machine. Then came young Isambard's turn. He designed the Clifton suspension bridge over the Avon Gorge, built the new broad-gauge railway from Paddington to Bristol . . . plus a thousand miles more main line railways, creating historic landmarks as he went along like the Box tunnel, the Maidenhead and Chepstow-and-Saltash bridges. Then he designed and built the three largest ships in the world, *Great Western, Great Britain* and the *Great Eastern*, which laid the first successful transatlantic cable. Among countless other marvels, he designed a complete prefabricated hospital building which was shipped in parts to the Crimea in 1855. Today we're all used to hospital buildings which come apart. But they're not supposed to.

THIS IS OLD PEOPLE'S DAY IN JAPAN

To old Japanese people, 'Lust' is just something which is eroding the bodywork of their Datsuns.

The Manchester–Liverpool Railway opened today in 1830. That trip once took me three hours. A fellow passenger said, 'Well, that's the worst part of the journey over.' I said, 'Where are you going?' He said, 'I'm leading the next Everest expedition.'

'Forty years difference in our ages means nothing!' protested the sixty-four-year-old showman Phineas T. Barnum when he wed twenty-four-year-old Nancy Fish today in 1874. 'She will soon feel old age creeping up on her.'

16 SEPT

TODAY'S BIRTHDAYS

Actor Peter Falk, best known as TV's 'Colombo', 1927, was born today in New York City. When starring on Broadway in the Neil Simon comedy *The Prisoner of 2nd Avenue*, he was so overjoyed at the opening night reception, he collared the producer and demanded, 'I want a star on my door – and I don't care who she is.' He shares the birthday with . . .

Lauren Bacall, New York City, 1924; onscreen from 1944, told Bogey, 'Whistle if you want me.' . . . He whistled.

WAS THIS REALLY THE OK DAY?

Many deranged researchers have invested thousands of hours in the task of identifying the origin of the expression 'OK'. You could read one zany theory on your average bottle of 'OK Sauce'. Some insist it stands for the illiterate indication of 'Orl Korrect' on an approved consignment of goods. But there is an equally goofy body of opinion to support this day in 1840 as the birth of the term. It's the anniversary of the foundation of a Democratic Party group in New York City, taking its title – the OK Club – from the birthplace of President Martin Van Buren in New York. And where was he born? Old Kinderhook. Like it? Keep it.

Thirty-three and a third rpm records were first used today – in 1933! LPs – or albums – are generally regarded as a post World War II development but the slow revolution took place in recordings fifteen years before the microgroove process became commercially successful. I'll never forget the first long-playing disc I made, singing the score of Cole Porter's 'Aladdin'. The company released me and kept the record.

17 SEPT

It was on this day in 1960 that I passed with honours from my correspondence course in 'Building a Perfect Memory'! Or was it on this day in 1957? Or tomorrow in 1975? Or . . .

Still on the subject of America the beautiful, on this day in 1911 the first transcontinental airplane flight left New York for Pasadena, only eight years after the historic three-minute hop by the Wright Brothers. I'd have made a lousy flying pioneer, with my weak stomach. With me, 'Up – up – and away!' is my lunch.

TODAY IS CITIZENSHIP DAY IN THE USA, celebrating the constitution of 1787, which ensures that every American citizen has a chance of becoming president. That's just a risk he has to take!

18 SEPT

Eight hundred million Chinese stood still and silent for three minutes today in 1976 . . . as a memorial tribute to Mao Tse Tung. That's how many Chinese there are – at least 800 million – some say 900 million and that's just in China, not counting the ones over here running chip shops. That represents about 20 per cent of all mankind! If the population continues to grow at its present rate, by 1999 there will be standing room only in China. That should slow it down a bit.

THE NEW YORK TIMES WAS FIRST PUBLISHED THIS MORNING IN 1815.

Their correspondent in the Congo was scooped by the *Herald* correspondent. The *Times* editor telegraphed him, 'Demand explanation why *Herald* outscoop?' The weary *Times* correspondent wired back, 'I am 59 years old and temperature is 120 in the shade.' Immediately came another wire from the editor, 'Why in shade?'

It was on this surprising day in the History of Political Strategy, 1790, that President George Washington tried to blame the country's economic troubles on the previous administration.

Dr Samuel Johnson was born today in 1709. He said of adversity, 'It is the state in which a man most easily becomes acquainted with himself – being especially free from admirers then.'

HAPPY BIRTHDAY MICKEY MOUSE!

But – contrary to belief – Disney's rudimentary rodent did *not* make his true movie debut in 'Steamboat Willie'. That oft-screened piece of primitive mousework was Mickey's first *sound* film, yes, but countless reference books perpetuate the false idea that this was his first-ever starring film. In fact, it was his *third*! Two silent, black and white cartoons were made earlier . . . 'Plane Crazy', concocted on a cross-country train trip by Walt and Lillian Disney . . . and 'Gallopin' Gaucho', unreleased until the success of 'Steamboat Willie' made it possible to add a soundtrack to Mickey's swash-buckling rescue of Minnie Mouse. The *Picture Show*, Britain's leading film magazine (twopence weekly), stuck its neck right out. 'I think it is always a pity,' wrote the editor, 'when cinema cartoonists can animate pretty creatures but choose to give screen life to vermin. One thing is sure – the British picturegoer could never come to enjoy the capering of a rodent.' Whatever became of the *Picture Show*?

19 SEPT

False teeth were first advertised for sale in America today in 1768 by a goldsmith named Paul Revere, born – are you ready for this? – in Massachusetts! It seems that Destiny enjoys a pun sometimes.

THE SIEGE OF PARIS

– by the Germans – began in 1870 and carried on according to precise instructions written by Prussian generals eight years earlier! Comedian Roy Hudd once ob-served, 'Germans believe in doing everything by the book – which is why their newlyweds leave the light on.'

Ferdinand Magellan set off to sail round the world on this day in 1519, accompanied by 270 men on five ships – but he was *not* the first to circumnavigate the earth in one voyage. This common misconception is

20 SEPT

given continued life by many textbooks but the fact is that Ferdy did it in two separate voyages. Each trip went more than halfway around the earth, going east and then west . . . but he was killed before completing the second. No, the first appointed expedition commander to get all the way round in one go was good old Sir Francis Drake. But wait! There was Juan Sebastian del Cano. He took over as chief when Magellan died and completed the round trip.

So let's hear it for the first: . . . Juan! (Alas, he was eventually lost at sea under slightly mysterious circumstances. Apparently he'd climbed up the mast to the crow's nest to see if he could sight land and when he came down the ship had gone.)

Today's question: Crippled by financial panic, the New York Stock Market closed for the first time on this day and stayed closed for twelve days . . . but in which year? Answer: As you'd expect, most people guess at the year of the most recent Wall Street slump, 1929. In fact, it happened in 1873 . . . and the US Treasury had to issue an extra $26 million in legal tender before normal business could resume.

Sterling came off the Gold Standard today in 1931. Things are just as grim today which is why we urge our athletes to do well in the Olympic Games. One gold medal doubles our reserves.

The first gasoline-powered automobile was demonstrated in the USA on this day in 1893 by Frank Duryea of Springfield, Massachusetts. With its one-cylinder engine, the Duryea got eighty miles to the gallon. Duryea also designed a car that ran on turpentine. Only problem with that was, it removed all the white lines down the middle of the road.

Midnight marks the beginning of the era of the French Republic and the French Revolutionary calendar in 1792. Robespierre ruled that aristocrats should not be beheaded until they had confessed to their crimes in cowardice and shame . . . thus coining the deathless phrase, 'Don't hatchet your counts before they chicken!'

WHAT PRICE NOVA SCOTIA? ONE SCOTTISH PENNY!

On this day in 1621 that was the price King James I demanded from Sir William Alexander . . . not bad value for 21,425 square miles! Bill named the peninsula with the Latin for 'New Scotland' . . . until then it was known as Arcadie. Before *that*, the native Indians called it 'Farta-bot'. That was Micmac Indian talk for 'Land of moose'. Not a pretty language, that Micmac.

'WANT TO BUY A HOT MIG?'

Yes, US General Mark Clark did – for $100,000. After broadcasting his interest in purchasing the top-secret Soviet fighter plane, a North Korean pilot named Noh Keun Suk did a little pilfering and landed the stolen plane in South Korea . . . on this day in 1952. With the reward money he bought an automobile repair shop and garage. Well, once a thief, always a thief.

I gave thanks for this day in 1955! Commercial TV began in Britain. Remember those innocent early days – when Hughie really was Green, Jimmy really was Young, Hope was still Keen and the Bachelors were actually bachelors? Back in those experimental ITV times, before Johnny Craddock had shown us his Fanny, everyone

22 SEPT

was glued to their sets. The only night you went out was when Rosalina Neri was on. Such memories! There was Sabrina . . . remember them? Back when 'Macmillan and Wife' were still living at 10 Downing Street, before Sir Harold Wilson sold his old raincoat to 'Columbo' . . . and I was brashly cramming half-baked jokes into my patter as I hosted some primitive quiz show. Yes, well, some things never seem to change.

BOBMOURHOUSE. THE WORLD'S FISHIEST FISH TALE? MICHAEL FARADAY WAS BORN TODAY IN 1791 AT NEWINGTON BUTTS. THE ELECTRICAL GENIUS WAS A KEEN FISHERMAN. HE ONCE DROPPED HIS RING IN A LAKE – AND SWORE HE FOUND IT 3 YEARS LATER IN THE BELLY OF A FISH PULLED FROM THE SAME LAKE!

'That wicked, wicked witchcraft' was nothing to sing about on this day in 1692 around Salem, Massachusetts, when two women were hanged as witches. My home town was superstitious too. Everyone believed in witches except me. And then, one dark night, I rubbed this girl on the knee and she turned into a motel.

Today is Bruce Springsteen's birthday, 1949. Arguably the greatest rock-'n'-roll performer of his time, his marathon stage performance with the E-street Band establish him as the living boss. I like 'Spirit in the Night' but it's playing hell with my liver.

Chewing gum was manufactured for the first time today in 1848 by John B. Curtis of Bangor, Maine, who said, 'I've got a good idea and I stuck to it!'

23 SEPT

The planet Neptune was discovered today in 1846 by Johann Galle. I hope the new space probe doesn't find any life on Neptune. That's all we need . . . one more foreign aid policy.

SIGMUND FREUD DIED TODAY IN 1939

A genius, Freud discovered how to train people to pay £10 an hour to talk to ceilings.

24 SEPT

Actor Paul Michael Glaser – Starsky in the hit TV series – was recovering today in 1980 after collapsing with stomach trouble in a snowstorm on a mountain in Wyoming. He was trapped for four days. Rangers who found him said he had been unable to eat and could have died. The next day I interviewed his TV partner David Soul (Hutch) for Thames TV in NBC's Burbank studios in Los Angeles and, despite his obvious concern, he was still able to quip, 'Of all people for this to happen to! He's such a hypochondriac he wouldn't visit the Dead Sea till he found out what it died of.'

The birth of the forty-hour week in the USA – the midwife: Henry Ford! Today in 1926 the industrial and engineering giant introduced the popular new work pattern in his car factories. And the irony of that was: Ford would have nothing to do with unions!

Enter the Libra person 24 September to 23 October, cultured, diplomatic, reasonable, easy to get on with but too easily influenced by others. This month's advice: never eat in an Indian restaurant where the waiters and chefs all wear gasmasks.

Today in 1536 King Henry VIII said to his lawyer,

'FORGET THE ALIMONY I'VE A BETTER IDEA!'

One hundred and eighty-three degrees Fahrenheit (that's 84 degrees Centigrade) was measured today in 1960, in sand on the plain north of Port Sudan in North Africa, one of the highest land temperatures ever recorded. Remember that heat wave we had in 1976? You weren't allowed to use the garden hose because of the drought. I sprinkled the garden with my bath water. We had the only lawn in the country with a ring round it.

The great English footballer who began by playing against England! Stan Mortensen broke plenty of soccer records in his historical career – but his international debut on this day in 1943 wasn't exactly the best way to kick off. He was an England reserve but replaced an injured Welsh player to play against his own country in an eight to three victory for England. I once played on the same team as Stan in a charity match at Blackpool. I failed to pick up three passes and then headed the ball into our own goal. 'I could kick myself!' I moaned. 'You'd only miss,' said Stan reasonably.

25 SEPT

Vasco Balboa crossed Panama, sighted the Pacific Ocean and *took possession of it* today in 1513. How do you take possession of an ocean? Well, first you have to evict the tenants . . .

Philip the Handsome died today in 1506. He was King of Spain and so good looking he wouldn't take a hot shower in case it clouded the mirror.

The first recorded cremation took place today in London, 1769. Honoretta Pratt believed that 'vapours arising from graves' damaged the health of the city's residents, so ordered her own disposal by fire. There's one advantage in running a crematorium. You very rarely have to worry about shoplifters.

They began to relieve Lucknow today in 1857. The ancient Indian city's residency had been besieged from the previous 1 July in the Indian Mutiny. That's a curious city. They play a game there called 'Indian Roulette'. You get six cobras in a room, you play a flute . . . and one of the cobras is deaf.

The *Queen Mary* was launched on this day in 1934 (and tomorrow, 27 September, the *Queen Elizabeth* was launched in 1938). They were floating hotels with the slogan, 'Going Cunard is a State of Grace'. I sailed to New York on the QE1 the year before she went out of service and she was gigantic. A person could be lost for days and never be missed. But, of course, I wasn't worried. I always carried identification with me. A card that says, 'My name is Robert Monkhouse. I live in Leighton Buzzard, Bedfordshire, England. If lost please return me to Britt Ekland.' But the trip was fine except the captain told everyone I was Bob Monkhouse. I said, 'You shouldn't have done that.' He said, 'I know. From now on, sleep with this life belt on.'

26 SEPT

The world's greatest feat of endurance took place in Liverpool, today, according to Ken Dodd. The night receptionist at the Adelphi Hotel put the cat out 3000 times through the revolving door.

Sir Freddie Laker's Skytrains began regular service today in 1977 flying between Gatwick and New York. On BBC Radio 4's 'Week Ending' they announced, 'Skytrain is going to operate on the Tokyo–London route, which will make it a sort of Nippon–Nipoff service.'

GOODBYE, DIVINE DEGAS!

On this day in 1917 the great French painter of nudes, ballet and horseraces died, aged eighty-three. I tried to copy Degas at Art School. Then I went through my Post-Impressionist period. And it's very awkward, doing an impression of a post. Dogs keep befriending you. And the soles of your shoes rot off.

Captive of pirates, Tunisian slave, this stammering French priest was a true saint. Vincent de Paul died on this day in 1660. His wild adventures had brought him to the court of French King Henry IV as a humble chaplain. He changed France. Founding organized charity, seminaries, reforms of every kind, he postponed the French Revolution by his enlightened work and was made a saint in 1737. St Vincent de Paul coined the phrase 'the power of prayer'. He might have approved of that Post Office service for people with faith . . . you dial a number and they say a prayer. And now there's another service for atheists. You dial a number and someone crosses their fingers for you.

27 SEPT

JUST WHAT THE WORLD NEEDS - CHEAPER CAVIARE!

Today in 1978 scientists announced the first successful breeding of sturgeon in laboratory tanks, though admitting the fish roe had a plastic quality. Imagine, everyone will soon be able to afford their own plastic sturgeon.

On this day in 1800, the frankfurter originated in the German city of Hot Dog.

We had the world's first public railway on this day in 1825! Admittedly it only ran between Stockton and Darlington, and to this day BR say it's hard to find people who want to go to either.

28 SEPT

Louis Pasteur died today in 1895. Incredibly, the French genius did most of his historic work in immunology, creating vaccines for anthrax, chicken cholera and rabies, after a massive stroke in 1868 which left him paralysed on his left side.

Marks & Sparks sold their first item on this day in 1894 . . . from a market stall in Manchester. Tom Spencer teamed with Michael Marks to sell 'all pieces for one penny' in . . . of all places . . . 'Cheetham' Hill! That's a bad pun that never rang a till more than once. Jerry Stevens says he saw a woman in the food section of his local Marks & Spencers. She was surreptitiously grabbing tins of salmon and stuffing them down her panties. The manager got hold of her and said, 'Why do you have to do that?' She said, 'Me bra's full of frozen pork chops.'

The first edition of the *Radio Times* went on sale today in 1923, with a print order of 200,000 copies. That, in BBC talk, is one origination and 199,999 repeats.

NAPOLEON WAS FORTY-SECOND IN A CLASS OF FIFTY-ONE!

Low marks as he scraped through military school today in 1785 did not depress France's future emperor. Among the possessions of the Empress Josephine after her death was a note: 'Dear Jo, It's very cold in Moscow and I'm short of one glove. Look in my drawers and see if I left it there. If you find it, send it by courier. I'm having to keep one hand tucked in my coat and people are beginning to laugh. Your loving hubby – Nappy.'

This is Michaelmas Day. The custom of eating goose today is popularly based on the story of Queen Elizabeth I's famous journey to Tilbury on 29 September 1588. She dined at the home of Sir Neville Umfreyville along the route. After eating goose she gave a toast: 'Death to the Spanish Armada!' At once the messenger ran in and announced the destruction of the enemy fleet by a storm. The queen demanded a second bumper of Burgundy and proclaimed, 'Henceforth shall a goose commemorate this great victory'. That's the story and it's been told and written thousands of times. But the Spanish fleet was dispersed by the storm in July . . . and the thanksgiving sermon for the victory was preached at St Paul's on 20 August!

29 SEPT

Britain's first official police force was mobilized on this day in 1829 and the men named 'Bobbies' after 'Bobby' Peel, the home secretary who founded them. His real first name was Robert . . . but they couldn't very well name the men 'Robbers', now, could they?

The Battle of Marathon was fought in 490 BC. On this same date it's said that 'Upon the field of battle Laknes built a marble building'. It's not there now. I suppose it just rolled away.

In 1650 the world's first marriage bureau opened in London. Robert Orben says, 'Back in those days people took marriage seriously, but not today. You can tell. There's a department store downtown that carries its wedding gowns in the sporting goods section.'

Alas, poor James Dean, I knew him . . . he died today in 1955. Brilliant, eccentric young star of 'Giant', 'East of Eden' (both of which won him best actor nominations), his first professional job was in a Coca-Cola commercial in the early 1950s. James had no front teeth and wore a special bridge to fill the gap. When he wanted to shock people he would slip the bridge out and grimace horribly. It was a great way of discouraging unwanted groupies.

30 SEPT

A few weeks before he died in his crashed Porsche Spyder, he had filmed a TV public service promotion for road safety, warning viewers, 'Drive safely, because the life you save may be *mine!*' Beside his dead body were scattered speeding tickets, one issued only two hours earlier. He once told Lenny Bruce he'd once been given a ticket for driving too slowly! He explained, 'The cop caught up with me.'

Ether was first used by a dentist pulling out a tooth today in 1846. It had been used in childbirth a few months earlier. And as a general anaesthetic for surgery in 1841, four and three-quarter years before. My dentist has three ways of putting patients to sleep . . . injection, gas or watching 'Crossroads'.

Henry IV became king of England today in 1399. He rode to his coronation through 'a deluge of rain, yet arriv'd dry as God had preserv'd him from the elements.' Perhaps he wore his reign coat.

The Festival of Britain ended on this day in 1951 on the South Bank site where it had required one million tons of cement. Cement – that's the stuff that won't set until a dog runs through it.

Seven hundred sons and more than 350 daughters . . . and they all called him 'Daddy' . . . and he believed them! Nobody would risk losing his head on the block just for love – that's what the Moroccan King Mulay Ismail reckoned, so on this day in 1703 he made beheading the penalty for any lad caught fooling around with his wives. Mulay had more wives, concubines and offspring than any ruler in history. One wife was English and another an Irish-woman, Mrs Shaw. Forty sons are said to have been born to him within four months in 1704! By 1721 he was credited with over 1,050 offspring – and his last child is reported to have been born eighteen months after his death!

Henry Ford introduced the model T on this day in 1908 at a price of $850. Within eighteen years, his pro-duction tech-niques reduced that to $310. His slogan: 'You can have it any colour you want as long as it's black.'

A bankrupt building contractor, Aarno Lannin-Parras, hijacked an aircraft of Finnair today in 1978. He forced the pilot to fly to Amsterdam and back, released it in return for a ransom of $206,000; then went home, where he was arrested and the money recovered. Lannin-Parras said, 'Isn't there *any* safe way to make money these days?' Well, yes, to make a fortune today you just have to come up with something that's inexpensive, tax deductible and habit forming.

The first postcard was issued today in 1869 . . . in Austria. My pet postcard was sent by a neglected wife, left to spend her holiday alone in sexy Italy by her busy executive husband. She writes, 'Having wonderful wish. Time you were here.'

Remember for a few moments a day many Scotsmen would prefer to forget – 1878 and the failure of the City of Glasgow Bank. Huge crowds gathered in Aberdeen but the police quickly dispersed them by announcing a flag day. The bank manager did a braw bricht moonlight flit! And all the poor people of Glasgow were pounding on the portals of the Scottish pound! Thousands were literally ruined when this bank failed in its sporran exchange.

2 OCT

Who remembers this day in 1914, when the very first British mines were laid in the North Sea? The first enemy vessel to encounter them was an Italian battleship. The lookout shouted, 'It's a mine! It's a mine!' And the Captain shouted back, 'Hokay! You can-na have it!'

The City of London became a smokeless zone today in 1955. It was a matter of life and breath. Before this date the kids of London could play hide and seek without even moving.

THE FORGER WHO FORGED A HEAD

German Karl Becker, perhaps the greatest forger of all time, was arrested today in 1825. For ten years he had counterfeited ancient medals and coins so perfectly they were later prized by collectors and fetched huge sums at auction. He asked to be punished like the best coin forgers in China – given a job at the Imperial Mint! (His masterpiece was a head of David 'by Michelangelo' valued today at £75,000!)

THE 'MICKEY MOUSE CLUB'

was born on TV this afternoon in 1955 with twenty-eight members. Twenty-two years earlier, Mickey broke all fan mail records with an average of 66,000 letters per month, bringing his personally addressed communications to a 1933 total of 800,000! Walt Disney, his creator, received only 109 fan letters, but he wasn't too worried. He was busy setting another all-time record. By the time of his death in 1966, Disney had won more awards in any category, twenty-four established trophies plus six specials, than anyone else in the industry. After 118 Mickey cartoons, Disney ended the mouse's big screen career in 1953, explaining that Mickey was 'too sweet tempered for modern tastes'. TV took up Mickey's tail and found a new audience eager to accept the idea of an oversized rodent who owned a dog, befriended an angry duck and who talked as if a mousetrap had once nipped him in the bud and severed his connections.

3 OCT

All the riches of Rome couldn't save Marcus Crassus who was the wealthiest man in the entire Roman Empire and got bumped off by the Syrians today in the year 53 BC. An actual translation of a topical joke has survived from his day . . . 'Marcus Crassus is so rich he pays his taxes in one instalment!' A gag over 2000 years old is worth having. By my usual standards, that's new material.

'London Bridge Days' commence on this day in Lake Havasu City, Arizona, USA. That's where our dear old London Bridge was reassembled after we flogged it in 1968. London has plenty of historic sights left to sell yet . . . like the very first maternity hospital, built rather aptly in Pudding Lane.

Russia launched the world's first satellite, *Sputnik 1*, on this day in 1957. I was in New York and I remember how, after the news broke, citizens behaved as though each had been personally affronted. One paper, the *National Enquirer*, even went so far as to claim that the object in the sky was not Russian but a meteor caught in orbit. Asked if this were true, a Russian spokesman said, 'No comet'.

'BIG WHITE HOUSE SCANDAL' reports Dan O'Day. 'Today in 1860 President Buchanan's niece and the Prince of Wales sneaked out of a White House reception and went bowling!' Queen Victoria could well have taken this to be an indication of all the carefree exploits of young Edward's that were to follow. She never hid her disapproval of his wild behaviour. He once refused a final drink with friends, saying, 'I can't stay. I must go back home to the palace and explain to dear mama.' His friends asked, 'Explain what?' Edward said, 'How the devil do I know? I'm not home yet.'

4 OCT

When the six-month-old baby 'took a buster of a fall' down the boarding-house stairs, he got a name to remember! Comic genius Buster Keaton was born today in 1896 at Pickway, Kansas. That accidental tumble changed his first name from Joseph to Buster . . . and the man who gave him that label was the star who picked him off the floor, the great magician Harry Houdini.

THIS IS MY WEDDING ANNIVERSARY

In 1973 my second wife Jacqueline took me on. She has an electric personality. Everything that she lays her hands on, she charges.

5 OCT

The world's first 'bathing costume' to be put on sale as such was displayed in the window of J. W. Farley's outfitting shop, Baker Street in London on this morning in 1830. It was made of linen, muslin and a light worsted, covering the wearer from neck to ankles and wrists – but incorporated 'concealed vents to allow the passage of water' It's strange to think that once women wore swim suits down to their ankles, then down to their knees, then down to their hips. Now you can't be sure they'll wear one down to the beach.

Statistics published by the London Passenger Transport Board this morning in 1960 claim that during a normal day a bus conductor will walk eighteen miles. Peter Cagney asked, 'Why doesn't he catch a bus?'

Charlotte Addison, who died on this day in 1797, was the daughter of the famous poet Joseph Addison (his plays include *Rosamund* (1705) and *Cato* (1713) and Charlotte must have inherited some of his love for words). Although she was hopelessly insane, she memorized the contents of a 300-page dictionary and could repeat word for word any sermon she heard.

The Dalton Brothers died with their boots on today in 1892. Some say if they'd taken their boots off, everyone else would have died. All four infamous rogues were killed as they tried to rob a bank in Coffeyville, Kansas. Marshal Owen Patricks suggested their epitaph: 'Here lie outlaws so shifty they wouldn't even look a potato in the eye.'

This was the 1964 wedding day of Janice and Francis, fondly recalled by oddity lovers because of their surnames – Salt and Pepper. As lovers of painful puns, let's wish them the condiments of the seasoning.

In the year 1877 a curious incident befell three Lords of the Admiralty who went out for a sail. These masters of the sea collided with a lighter! Excuse me while I break into doggerel verse again . . .

6

OCT

'Rub a dub dub,
Three men in a tub!'
Was a rhyme I'd recite as a tot.
But I'm more than delighted
I never recited
A tale of three Lords in a yacht!
On the sixth of October,
Three Lords, none too sober,
Went out in the sea for a sail.
Getting tighter and tighter
Their yacht struck a lighter!
Like demons they started to bail.
Rum a dun dun,
Three Lords on the run!
All at sea as the waves rose so
    high . . .
Three Admiralty Lordships
Were boozing aboard ships
And waving a wave of good-bye!

The Post Office Tower opened in London today in 1965. A window cleaner fell off it and wound up in Middlesex Hospital. That must have been a hell of a bounce.

'You ain't heard nothing yet!' said Al Jolson – and how right he was. Tonight in 1927 'The Jazz Singer' opened in New York City's Warner Theatre. Talking pictures became a sensation overnight and we had talking pictures right up until the discovery of Marlon Brando. He introduced sterephonic mumbling.

Charles the Simple died on this day in the year 929. As King Charles III of France (the posthumous son of Louis II le Begue), he was a dreadful messer, getting crowned by an archbishop called Fulk when he was only fourteen years old. He ran around all over Europe trying to get support for five years but the magnates kept telling him, 'Grow up, mate . . . we've got Eudes.' Charles said, 'Anyone can get a silly name' and proved it by marrying a woman called Eadgifu. Eudes died in 898 so the magnates let Charles become king which was a duff move on their part. Charles gave Normandy to the Vikings and spent all his time trying to kill everyone in Lorraine. So the magnates took the crown back and gave it to Eudes's brother, Robert the Strong. Charles proved that was another silly name by rushing back from Lorraine and

knocking Robert the Strong down dead. The magnates went absolutely potty, chased Charles away to England and made Eudes's other brother, Raoul, into the king. Charles couldn't believe that France could have a king called Raoul and laughed so hard he died at Peronne on this day in 929. I told you he was simple.

Lunik 3 took the first photographs of the far side of the moon today in 1959. US comedian Joey Adams said, 'The American space plan is a little slowed down. We plan to send up three astronauts in one rocket, but there's still a little disagreement on who should sit by the window.'

Carbon paper was first patented in 1806. It was copied at once.

On this day in 1906 the Persian Assembly was opened by the shah. My wife fancied a visit to the centre of Iranian culture to observe the magic and mystery of Muslim life . . . so she went to Harrods for the day.

Aged eighty-four, he bent a steel bar across the bridge of his nose! Joe Greenstein died of cancer on this day at Brooklyn's Kingsbrook Hospital in 1977. World famous as the 'Mighty Atom', he was born in Poland of Jewish parents and was so sickly he was not expected to live. Adopted by a travelling strongman named Volanko, he never grew taller than five feet but developed the astonishing strength to bite through steel, tow trucks and hold back an aeroplane tied to his hair! Much more than a music hall freak, Joe's physical and philosophical

power inspired superhuman feats based upon simple human deter- mination. Each novel challenge – hanging by his scalp from a racing plane, bursting iron chains by muscular expansion to escape from the path of a speeding car (photo- graphed frame by frame in 1939) – and even the familiar foe of ad- vancing age, all were welcome opponents to be vanquished as long as God permitted and Joe's spirit responded. Joseph Greenstein's mental and physical powers were phenomenally youthful and vital right up to his last days, Although I can't really believe that at eighty he was so strong he could dribble a bowling ball. Or that his physique was such that he could wipe his nose without using his hands. Hell of a bloke, though, wasn't he?

Henry Fielding died on this day in 1754, aged forty- seven. Most famous for his brilliant picaresque novels *Tom Jones* and *Joseph Andrews*, he was also leading playwright of his day and, as a JP, he organized the detective force that became Scotland Yard! We've got a great police force. Some weeks they catch even more criminals than they employ.

Uganda became independent on this day in 1962. It took President Idi Amin to make them regret it. As his megalomania became apparent, a team of Ugandan psychiatrists tried vainly to find out what made him tick. And more especially, what made him go 'cuckoo' every half hour.

9 OCT

A breathalyzer was introduced on to British roads today in 1967. A policeman stopped me and said, 'Blow in this bag!' I said, 'Why?' He said, 'My chips are too hot.'

The king of Yugoslavia was assassinated on this day in 1934. He was Alexander I and when he became king of the Serbs, Croats and Slovenes in 1921, assassins began taking pot shots at him right away. So in an effort to make them feel as if they all belonged to one nation, Alex changed the name of the country to Yugoslavia on 3 October 1929, declaring, 'The best solution is Yugo!' 'Wrong,' said the assassins, 'Yugo!' – and he did.

WELL, DON'T TELL CHRISTOPHER COLUMBUS, BUT...

... Leif Erikson discovered America in the year 1000! Four hundred and ninety-two years later Columbus discovered it again but Leif was too busy preparing to play the lead in 'High Chaparral' to give a damn.

This is the anniversary of the introduction of the Korean twenty-four-letter phonetic alphabet in 1477. I studied Korean by listening to language lessons while I slept and it worked. Now I can speak Korean fluently. But only when I'm asleep.

10 OCT

The eighteenth Olympic Games began in Tokyo on this day in 1964. An athletic coincidence with this day in 1978, when the largest-ever field turned up for a cross-country run. The spot was Lidingöloppet in Sweden. The course was just over eighteen and a half miles. And the starters numbered 7036! Amazingly, 6299 finished! Popular among the front runners was US hippie Mal Rose who wore a T-shirt with 'Love Your Enemies' on the front side and, as he explained to Swedish TV viewers, 'Kiss Your Friends on the back side.'

Today the Labour Party won the *second* General Election of 1974! And Harold Wilson was safely back at Number 10. Mike Yarwood pictured Edward Heath taking Wilson out sailing on *Morning Cloud 2* – and Wilson throwing his cigarette end over the side, saying, 'Put your foot on that, would you, Ted?'

The contents of the tomb of the 'Boy King' were first photographed today in 1924. Tutankhamun's treasure was all gold – gold casket, gold death mask, gold funeral gifts – those Egyptian mummies sure knew how to live.

Marie Antoinette never said, 'Let them eat cake' – on this day in 1789 or any other! The yarn that she did so was invented after her 1793 execution by revolutionary propaganda merchants who wanted to make Marie appear to have been heartless. The tale of an uncaring princess who, on being told the starving people have no bread, gives this cynical answer, dates from Jean-Jacques Rousseau's *Confessions* in 1766, at least twenty-three years before poor Marie is accused of such royal disdain.

King John's baggage got lost in the wash today in 1216. His dad, Henry II, called him 'Lackland', because as the youngest son he owned no property. John was suspicious, vengeful and treacherous – and those were his good points. He had Arthur of Brittany murdered in captivity. And Matilda da Braose, the wife of a marcher baron who opposed John, was starved to death with her son in a royal prison. His elder brothers had a soft spot for him. It was a swamp at the back of the palace. (He was forty-eight when he died and was buried in Worcester where you can still see his effigy.)

Huldreich Zwingli was killed on this day in 1531, the spot where the great Swiss religious reformer fell being marked with an inscribed boulder near Zürich. His bold sacramental theology challenged accepted ecclesiastical politics and I'm all for that, aren't you? Our church is keeping up with the times. They've replaced the organist with a rock group, the evening meditation with a sensitivity session and the Sunday collection now takes American Express.

Today in 1911 the District Railway hired a man with a wooden leg. They'd just installed a moving staircase at Earl's Court and they employed Pegleg Pete to ride up and down it all day to give confidence to the passengers. When they caught him soliciting donations for a new false leg, they told him to hop it.

THE WORLD'S BANANA EATING RECORD WAS SET TODAY IN 1972

Michael Gallens of Cairns, Australia, ate sixty-three bananas in ten minutes – on a TV show! Viewers admitted he had appeal. (Back! Back! I say!)

Twenty-seven hours of belly dancing became the world record today in 1972. Pamela Ness of Kansas City shook her abdomen continuously 'without mechanical aid'. It was the greatest navel manoeuvre since Trafalgar.

12 OCT

Kruschev put the boot in today in 1960 – when the explosive Soviet leader pounded his shoe on the table and made a dramatic exit from the twenty-fifth anniversary meeting of the United Nations. The meeting was abandoned in pandemonium. No wonder. You should have smelled his socks.

Today in 1895 the first amateur golf tournament was played at Newport, Rhode Island. When I play golf I have such rotten luck. Once I missed getting a hole in one by only four strokes.

Everyone knows Columbus sighted America today in 1492 – but remember, he thought it was China. Also, in those days, everyone thought the whole world was flat. Now we know the rest of the world is round. It's only Britain that's flat.

ACTRESS BEA LILLIE WAS SNUBBED BY HER BEST FRIEND WHEN THE GIRL MARRIED INTO A SNOBBISH SOCIETY FAMILY--- BUT BEA SHOWED UP AT THE WEDDING TODAY IN 1922--- AS A TEMPORARY CLEANER!

BOB MOUSEHOUSE

Britain's first female prime minister was born today in 1925. While Margaret Thatcher's election was a milestone for sexual equality, it's sad to note that, according to the Population Reference Bureau Incorporated, 54 per cent of the world's 2.2 billion women are literate compared with 67 per cent of the men. Personally, I believe women should be equal. Mind you, I haven't found anything to equal them yet.

13 OCT

History's most expensive knickers were sold – they were second-hand – but they were Queen Victoria's! So they were knocked down for $3000 at an auction in British Columbia to a Houston pub proprietor, Jim Anderson, who hung them above his tavern bar. It was the first time her knickers had been up for ninety years.

Thurnby Lodge, a Leicester housing estate, was invaded today in 1967 – by millions of money spiders! I hope the residents didn't kill them. I can't bear to harm anything. I even use Teflon-coated flypaper.

Variety, the great US show biz paper, today in 1937 carried the sad ad, 'Lion Tamer – looking for tamer lion'.

SPEEDING... 1901 STYLE Edgar Cundy was summonsed for 'furiously driving' a motorcar in Brighton Road, South Croydon, today. 'The police evidence as to speed was conflicting, various estimates ranging from 16 to 153 mph.' Sounds like my wife's driving style. She's the type of motorist who gets angry over how close the fellow up ahead is driving to her.

They called it the Battle of Hastings in 1066 but that was only one of several mistakes. The punchup that decided the fate of England was supposed to have happened in July but Bill the Conqueror couldn't get all his lads together in time. When he finally landed at Pevensey it was 28 September and there was nobody

14 OCT

worth fighting. King Harold was up in Yorkshire bashing away at another invader called Harald Haardrada of Norway. Having lost men in seeing him off, King Harold came pelting southwards and began making mistakes. (1) His men were knackered and Bill's boys were rested, (2) his men were on foot with only spears and heavy axes while Bill's boys were mounted and had swords and archers to give them extra muscle, (3) he forgot the advice his mum gave him when she said, 'Harold, don't play with arrows, you'll have somebody's eye out one day.' The fight was held on a hill a good six miles from Hastings. After he'd won, Bill called the place Battle because he'd been to the battle there. Later he stopped at a spot in Cornwall and called it Looe.

Lovely true story (from Joe Hickman) – on this very day in 1838, workmen digging in Moundsville, West Virginia, USA, found a stone tablet inscribed with hieroglyphics. For ninety-two years experts from all over the world came to study the tablet, to decide if the inscriptions were Etruscan, Runic or some other ancient language. Then one day in 1930 a teenager walked up and simply read the message. It said in very poorly carved English: 'Bill Stump's stone, October 14, 1838'!

15 OCT

Jack Gardener retired today in 1947 after sixty years as a hotel porter – forty of them at London's famous Savoy Hotel. He was seventy-eight and loved to tell how he first got the job at the elegant Howards Hotel in Kensington in 1887. The manager told Jack, 'This job requires both politeness and tact. Are you sure you know the difference?' . . . 'Yes, sir, I do.' . . . 'Well, supposing you had to take a message to a lady's room and you found the bathroom door open and the lady sitting in the tub. What would you do?' Jack replied, 'I'd say, "Excuse me, sir" and get out fast – and the "excuse me" would be politeness – but the "sir" would be tact.' No wonder they hired him.

Labour was in – but Harold Wilson had a majority of only five – on this day in 1964. Wilson used to fascinate me. It was riveting to see him sign a piece of legislation – then wipe his fingerprints off the pen.

The first ascent by two men in a captive balloon was made over France today in 1783. They were good friends and seldom fell out.

The University College of Wales was founded today in 1872 at Aberystwyth. Within twenty-four hours the English-born dean disagreed with the Welsh-born governor, Lord David, Earl of Glamorgan, over the teaching of the Welsh language. The dean lost, demonstrating the error of arguing with a determined Welsh nobleman in his own territory. Or to put it another way, 'Never have a tiff on a tough toff taff's turf!'

J. Walter Thompson died on this day in 1928, twelve days before his eighty-first birthday. He started as an advertising space salesman for William J. Carlton in 1867 at a salary of $12 per week. Eleven years later he bought out Carlton and formed his hugely successful worldwide advertising agency. After he sold it and retired in 1916, the turnover in top personnel became heavy. One executive put on his hat and coat and called to his secretary, 'If my boss telephones while I'm out, be sure to get his name.'

16 OCT

THE HOUSES OF PARLIAMENT WENT TO BLAZES TODAY IN 1834 . . .

. . . and were almost totally destroyed. The mother of parliaments, our two famous houses in Westminster represent the greatness of democracy, compared with lesser political creeds. Socialism is when you have two cows and give one to your neighbour. With Communism you have two cows, the government takes both and gives you the milk. With Fascism you have two cows, the government takes both and shoots you. With a democracy, the government buys both cows, shoots one, milks the other, throws the milk away and buys butter from Holland.

Discussion of theory of evolution was banned from state textbooks – by the Texas State Textbook Board today in 1925. A million years from now the earth will probably be peopled by inhabitants who will sternly deny that they ever descended from man.

Oscar Wilde was born today in 1854. Welsh poet Lewis Morris once moaned to him that the press never published his work. 'It's a conspiracy of silence, Oscar. What should I do?' 'Join it,' said Oscar.

The Romulus and Remus of India were recaptured from the wolves today in 1920! The Reverend J. A. L. Singh heard villagers' tales of inhuman and malevolent 'devils' running with a she-wolf. Singh recognized them as human children and dug up the wolves' lair. The 'mother' was killed by arrows and the 'wolf children' were seized. One was only one and a half years old and died in hospital. The other, aged eight, lived to be seventeen, learning to stand upright, talk and eat normally. Oddly enough, shortly after I was born I was very nearly switched with another baby at the hospital. But one of the nurses caught my father just in time.

Anatoly Karpov defeated the Soviet defector Viktor Korchnoi today in 1978 – and remained world chess champion. The Russian grand master complained of the strangeness of Western customs: 'Over in America, you order hot tea, then put ice in it to make it cold, then put sugar in it to make it sweet, then put lemon in it to make it sour . . . then you lift your glass, say, "Here's to you", and drink it yourself.'

Saturn's seventh moon was discovered and named 'Mimas' tonight in 1789. Now we've photographed it. Judging from the huge craters, it's obvious there's life there even if it's only Sunday golfers.

Frederic Chopin died on this day in 1849, aged thirty-nine. The Polish child prodigy made his Vienna debut in 1829, his Paris debut in 1832, his London debut in 1837. Edward Lucaire writes, 'Because most of Chopin's audiences would only see one side of him during his recitals, he would sometimes shave only one side of his face.' Ah, so that might explain why he wrote his 'Piano Etude for Left Hand Only'. If they wanted him to take a bow, he could play and use his razor at the same time.

18 OCT

Scientists at Berkeley, California, announced that they had artificially created anti-protons, confirming the existence of anti-matter on this day in 1955. By causing a conflict between matter and anti-matter, enormous atomic energy is released. If harnessed, they explained, you could take a single lump of coal and heat an entire building for a year. So what's new about that? I had a landlord in Bayswater who did the same thing for eight years.

History's biggest newspaper was published this morning in 1965. The *New York Sunday Times* came out that day weighing 7½ pounds! Its 15 sections contained 946 pages. Half a million copies were printed, requiring 5000 tons of paper. Joe Hickman's comment: 'Sort of makes you want to run right out and plant a forest.' I love Joe's humour, it's so wry. He once said, 'The good news is – business is booming again. The bad news is – it's booming for businesses that paint "Going out of business" signs.'

The Belgian Congo was colonized by today in 1908. Missionaries were advised to argue with any cannibals they met. This was in the hope that they wouldn't want to eat anything that disagreed with them.

The first telegraph cable was laid today in 1842 by Samuel Morse. It ran from Governor's Island to the Battery across New York harbour and lasted twenty-four hours! It was tomorrow in 1842 that a ship's master, who'd never heard of Sam's cable pulled up his anchor and wrecked 200 feet of it! Well, we all make mistakes, as the octopus sighed, sliding off the bagpipes.

Marlon Brando's stage debut took place in 1944. Old Mumbles first trod the boards in the Broadway smash, 'I Remember Mama'. He isn't Italian, contrary to popular belief, but comes from the French line of Brandeau's. When he told Henry Fonda, a family friend, that he planned to study method acting in Lee Strasberg's experimental group, Fonda advised him, 'Always be extremely careful of the scenery, Marlon. There's no telling who had it in his mouth just before you.'

19 OCT

On this day in 1933 the Berlin Organization Committee voted to have basketball introduced at the 1936 Olympic Games – so having a profound effect on the growth of the game. I was a sort of guest on a basketball team once. Every player on the team was 6 feet 10 inches except me. I was 5 feet 10 inches. My job was to keep everybody else's socks pulled up.

Jackie spent today wondering whether she should wed Ari before tomorrow's 1968 wedding day. Onassis's death on 15 March 1975 left Jackie so rich she's had her navel removed and a wallsafe put in.

TODAY IS YORKTOWN DAY, marking the surrender of Lord Cornwallis to General Washington at Yorktown, Virginia, in 1781. George Washington had more wit than history gives him credit for. One day, as he sat at the table after dinner, he complained that the fire burning in the hearth behind him was too large and uncomfortably hot. 'But, sir,' his host chided, 'it behooves a general to stand fire.' The instant reply was, 'But it does not become a general to receive it in the rear.'

A house that just grew . . . and grew . . . and grew . . . is the bizarre Winchester House, near San José, California. Mrs Sara Winchester was quite certain that if she stopped building her house, her life would end. The construction went on for thirty-eight years! By this day in 1921, 10,000 windows had been put in and the 2000th door was fitted. The eight-storey house contained miles of secret passage ways and hidden halls, many leading nowhere except to blind alleys and blank walls. Mrs Winchester's house covered more than six acres and had grown to 160 rooms when a one-day strike by the builders brought the work to a halt . . . and on that day in 1922, eighty-five-year-old Mrs Winchester died.

My old classmates at Dulwich College gathered for our twenty-fifth reunion dinner tonight in 1970. We rediscovered each other from name tags bearing old school photographs. Gasps of disbelief filled the air. Suddenly I spotted a face I could recognize without having to read the name tag. 'Rimmel!' I yelled, pushing my way across the room, 'you haven't changed a bit!' 'Oh, no?' he smiled and then he bowed and tipped his toupee.

This was the night of the famous Watergate 'Massacre' in 1973 – when President Richard Nixon fired Watergate prosecutor Archibald Cox! Attorney General Elliott Richardson resigned and his deputy William Ruckelhaus was fired as a wild backlash to their refusal to carry out the order. Bob Orben said he had a crazy dream: 'President Nixon telling a bartender, "My country doesn't understand me".'

This morning's edition of the *Belleville Daily Advocate* in 1966 reported, 'The Civil Aeronautic Authority announced that a sentry and a mysterious gunman exchanged shorts on Saturday night near the Joliet airport.'

21 OCT

He's the first man ever to notch up 100 centuries in a test match. And in two separate seasons his average has been more than 100 runs per innings – that's record book stuff for Geoff Boycott, born today in 1940 in Fitzwilliam, Pontefract, Yorkshire. I once saw a newspaper headline that read '500 STEEL WORKERS MOUNT BOYCOTT!' and I thought, 'He'll never play cricket again.'

The self-cleaning oven was patented today in 1960. Right away my wife yelled, 'When do I get a self-cleaning oven?' I yelled back, 'Right after I get a self-mowing lawn.'

Thomas Alva Edison invented the electric light on this day in 1879. A hundred years later I was told that, because of all the burglars around, I should leave the lights on in my house. So I went away for two weeks and left the lights on. I came back and got robbed by the electricity board.

'WE ARE WAITING... SO ARE THE FISHES!' rasped Churchill as he broadcast his scorn at Hitler's invasion plans today in 1940. When the great World War II prime minister honoured the BBC's comedy success 'Much Binding in the Marsh' with a visit to the radio studio, the late Kenneth Horne greeted him with the show's famous catchphrase, 'Have you read any good books lately?' 'My dear Horne,' confided Churchill with his usual humility, 'when I want to read a good book, I write one.'

Halley's comet was sighted in 1909, just as predicted by the great English astronomer in 1758. He sat at his telescope for fifty-two nights in succession searching for meteors on Mars. His wife said, 'You're more likely to find asteroids on Uranus.'

22 OCT

Chinese peasants were terror-stricken on this day in 2136 BC – they believed a dragon was eating the sun! So they made as much noise as they could to scare it away . . . and it worked! You've no doubt guessed that this date marks the first recorded solar eclipse. Just another example of how differently those in the East react. In the Orient, when a woman walks behind her husband it means he is being respected. In Britain, when a woman walks behind her husband, it means he's being tailed.

'One of the most courageous acts in aviation history,' said Wilbur Wright of the first 'parachute' jump, made over Paris today in 1797. Yes, that's 1797 – the year André-Jacques Garnerin rode in a gondola beneath a 23-foot para-chute, released from a balloon at 2230 feet. Today the most courageous act in aviation is eating the airline food.

Pope John Paul II was in-augurated today in 1978. Roman Catholics accepted him as the Lord's repre-sentative on earth. As for me, I also believe that God is not dead. He's just waiting for us to negotiate.

Until this morning in 1864 police-men wore top hats. And until 1884 they carried football-fan rattles to summon help. They still don't carry guns, only whistles. When they chase a lawbreaker, they have to shout, 'Halt or I'll toot!'

The electrostatic copier was patented today in 1938 – by a US attorney named Chester Carlson. He promptly quit practising law, telling a fellow counsellor, 'As soon as I realized that it was a crooked business, I got out of it.' The other attorney asked, 'How much?'

The earth was created on this day in 4004 BC! All right, all right, don't take my word for it. This earth-shattering – or rather, earth-forming – fact is recorded in the *Chronology of the Bible* written in 1650 by no less an authority than Archbishop James Usher. According to the great man (who got it from you-know-Who), the earth was created on this very day – on a Sunday morning – at 9.00 am!

23 OCT

BRUTUS COMMITS SUICIDE!

That's tomorrow's big headline about today's big news in Rome, 42 BC. The honourable Brutus fell upon his sword. Ugh! Well, I suppose it's a better way to go than the Irishman who cut his throat with a razor. Of course, it mightn't have taken so long if he'd plugged it in.

Severinus Boethius was beheaded for treason in Italy today in 525. The legend says the Roman philosopher's comments annoyed Theodoric, King of the Visigoths . . . but that after Boethius was decapitated, he walked to the cemetery carrying his head. The coffin-maker persuaded Boethius to lie down flat at last by arguing that he could not measure the casket with his wooden rule unless the head was replaced on the shoulders and the entire corpse stretched out before him. And I thought you could only flatten a ghost with a spirit level.

'It's Chulalongkorn day in Thailand! Happy Chulalongkorns!!

W. G. Grace, record-breaking cricket hero, died this day in 1915. They say he always scored best with old bats. Personally, I'd rather bowl a maiden over.

Richard Burton bought his wife a diamond today in 1969. Elizabeth Taylor received a 69.42-carat goodie costing over a million dollars. Later on, married to US politician John Warner, she flogged it to pay for his campaign expenses. Burton's comment: 'If only I'd known I could have sent him the money in the first place and cut out the middle man.' It's the only time Elizabeth Taylor has been described as a middle man.

24 OCT

Christian Dior died on this day in 1957, aged fifty-two. The fashion designer from Granville in France created the 'New Look' popular after World War II and introduced the sack dress in the 1950s. He'd have found the 1970s pretty confusing. Well, I did. The girls wore hot pants to make them look like boys and see-through blouses to prove they weren't.

The world's oldest football club, Sheffield FC, issued its rules today in 1857. The rule that didn't really catch on was: 'If fog is anticipated, extra time will be played first.'

TODAY IS UNITED NATIONS DAY

Well, at least they can all agree about *something*.

TODAY IS ST CRISPIN'S DAY

Before you draw your sword and cry, 'God for England, Harry and all that!', note this as a day as much for swallowing rapiers as for brandishing them. For Alex Linton was born today in 1904 in Ireland – and Alex holds the world record for swallowing four twenty-seven-inch blades at the same time! Which recalls Ted Ray's sad tale of the three-foot high circus midget who swallowed a three-foot six-inch sword and pinned himself to the bench. Meanwhile, back at the historic heroics . . .

On this same October day that Henry V thrashed the French at Agincourt in 1415, the poor old Light Brigade rode into the Valley of Death at Balaklava in 1854. The order to charge was never given! The only command was to advance at a trot and that's what they did, riding at an even pace down the valley towards the guns that were never meant to be attacked, under rifle and cannon fire from three directions. Out of 675 men, 113 were killed and 134 captured or wounded. Blame Lord Raglan's ambiguous orders Lord Lucan's lack of comprehension, Captain Nolan's failure to explain and Lord Cardigan's blustering stupidity. 'Lord Cardigan,' asked Sir Wycliffe-Rudd, 'have you heard that joke about the Egyptian guide who showed some tourists two skulls of Cleopatra . . . one as a girl and one as a woman?' 'No,' replied Cardigan, 'let's hear it.'

26 OCT

The Beatles collected their MBEs at Buckingham Palace today in 1966. 'I'm not saying it's given them swollen heads,' said Arthur Askey, 'but now the boys think the initials on our pillar boxes stand for Eleanor Rigby.'

George III was crowned king of England today in 1760, to suffer one of the longest reigns in British history – sixty years of tremendous change during which the king went violently insane. Quite a lot of the world's most famous leaders have been unfit for even simple jobs – and if we'd had medical boards throughout military history, quite a few mighty soldiers would have been turned down cold! General George Washington had false teeth, General U. S. Grant was a confirmed alcoholic, Bismarck was dangerously obese, the duke of Wellington was seriously underweight, Nelson lacked an arm and an eye, Kaiser Wilhelm had a withered arm, Napoleon had stomach ulcers and piles, and Julius Caesar was an epileptic!

The shah of Iran was crowned on the Peacock Throne in 1967. Are you aware of the extent to which the Middle East has taken over our economy since then? Next time you're holding a pound note, look closely and you'll notice the queen is riding a camel.

In today's issue of the *St James's Chronicle* in 1776, this curious advertisement was published: 'Van Butchell (not willing to be unpleasantly circumstanced, and wishing to convince some good minds they have been misinformed) acquaints the Curious no Stranger can see his embalmed wife, unless (by a Friend or personally) introduced to himself, any Day between Nine and One, Sundays excepted.' Van Butchell's ad was a cunning come-on, an early example of the now familiar advertising technique of 'if you can't afford it, don't ask for it'. Butchell was a quack doctor and one of advertising's earliest and most original con men. People flocked to see his 'embalmed wife' – and pay hefty unexpected extras for refreshments and 'waiting room benches, curative and most easing to those in posterior discomforture'. I reckon my doctor's a con man too. For £25 all he does is send you a get-well card.

27 OCT

Theologian Michael Servetus was burned at the stake on this day in 1553. The execution of the forty-two-year-old Spanish physician led to severe criticism of John Calvin, although Calvin hadn't wanted Servetus burned at all. He'd wanted to cut his head off instead. A hard nut was old Calvin. He took confession with a spotlight and a rubber truncheon.

The world's busiest underground railway opened today in 1904 – between New York City's 154th Street and Brooklyn Bridge. A thousand million passengers are jammed into it per year. Comedian Bill Beckett was one of the straphangers when a girl next to him suddenly blurted out, 'There's something very pressing I've just got to get off my chest!' Bill asked, 'What?' She said, 'Your goddam hand!'

28 OCT

US investors had plenty to complain about today in 1929 . . . when bank stocks fell 500 points. Ten billion dollars were wiped off the Wall Street stock market. The head of a brokerage firm gave a pep talk to his staff: 'Remember that stock I was going to retire on when I was fifty-five? Well, I have good news. My retirement age is now three hundred and fifty.'

The Statue of Liberty was dedicated on this day in 1886. A light shone all night from the torch – it was a real bonfire fueled by charcoal and oil. Next morning the stewards celebrated with smoked beacon and eggs.

The dog that hated cats had his big day in 1953! J. P. Donleavy's Alsatian dog Sultan loathed every pussy in Dover Estate, Ottawa. He'd actually killed twelve. The court ruled that Sultan should be put down as a menace to public safety. As Mr Donleavy drove his Chevrolet to the veterinary centre, Sultan suddenly jumped down from the seat beside him and plonked his paw on the accelerator. The result: the Chevvy raced out of control and crashed into a building – killing six occupants – all cats! Donleavy's car had ploughed into the local cats' home. Sultan must have died happy.

I've heard of playing footsie . . . but really! Today in 1975 Faustino Collazo of San Antonio, Texas, USA, shoved a thirty-year-old woman across a car, pulled off her shoes, and covered her feet with kisses. He was arrested for pedic rape. (It's not true that he offered to make it legal by putting a wedding band on her third toe, left foot.)

The only fighter ever to have held three world boxing titles *at the same time*! He was Henry Armstrong and tonight in 1937 he k.o.'d Petey Sarron to win the world featherweight title. The next year he took the welterweight title from Barney Ross and the lightweight title from Lou Amers. 'In proportion to its size,' Armstrong told the *Ring*, 'my strongest muscle is in my eyelid!' The eyelid certainly has a strong muscle. Only the other Saturday night mine picked up an eight-stone redhead.

The Czolgosz family hangs a wreath around the fusebox every year on this day . . . to commemorate the 1901 electrocution of Leon F. Czolgosz, the twenty-six-year-old anarchist who assassinated US President William McKinley in Buffalo on 6 September. Asked if he had any last-minute advice to give, Czolgosz's lawyer told him, 'Don't sit down!'

29 OCT

It was also a black day for Sir Walter Raleigh who got the chop today in 1618. He was very nonchalant about it. First he took a stroll around the block.

IT'S A GOOD DAY FOR FIRE EATERS!

Jean Chapman put out 1921 flaming torches in her mouth, one after the other, today in 1977 at Stoke Poges, Buckinghamshire, in only 120 minutes. Relaxing over a meal afterwards, she burned her mouth on the soup!

Israeli forces invaded the Sinai Peninsula on this day in 1956. The Arabs and the Israelis both agreed that the Middle East was the promised land. They just can't agree on who it's promised to.

30 OCT

The world's first TV star was fifteen-year-old William Taynton of London! Who? Yes, well, this was in 1925 so perhaps you weren't watching at the time. But on this historic date, young Bill was paid to sit still while a primitive TV camera transmitted his image. John Logie Baird built his transmitter in his attic from cardboard boxes, a motorbike lamp, piano wire, a tea chest, old biscuit boxes, sealing wax, a mangle handle, a carpenter's motor and some darning needles. Since then, a lot of shows have looked as if they were built out of less sophisticated material. Sometimes radio did it better. For instance . . .

This was 'the night that America panicked' in 1938. Young genius Orson Welles broadcast his ultra-real documentary drama based on H. G. Wells's *The War of the Worlds*. Convinced that Martian monsters were invading the USA, many listeners ran for the hills. Some people actually believe the tale that two Martians came to earth at Christmas time and saw a lighted Christmas tree so one went into the house to investigate. When he came out the other Martian asked, 'How was it?' And his companion said, 'Lousy! Five colours and only one flavour.'

Muscle builder Charles Atlas was born today in 1893. I once sent for his body building course and as soon as it came I heaved and strained and sweated for an hour . . . but I still couldn't get the package open.

The first book was published in London bearing the imprint of a lady publisher. This blow for what was then called 'Freedom for the New Woman' was struck today in 1901 when Florence White published an obvious bid for the best-seller list titled *Smallpox: Its Prevention, Treatment and History*. Now there's even Women's Lib Rice Crispies. That's right. They go, 'Snap! Crackle! Mum!'

The Bloody Tower of London was almost destroyed by a fierce fire on this day in 1841. It had burned for twenty-two hours. My wife's very aware of fire hazards. While I was away last winter, she told me she had a guard in front of the fireplace every night. I'd feel better if we didn't live next to a barracks.

31 OCT

British planes bombed Egyptian airfields in preparation for an Anglo-French invasion on this day in 1956. I don't want to criticize our foreign policy at the time of the Suez crisis, but I suspect we had a leak in our think tank.

The great British music hall comedian Dan Leno died on this day in 1904. His biographer, J. Hickory Wood, wrote: '(His songs) were not really songs at all. They were diverting monologues in a style of which he was as undoubtedly the originator as he was its finest exponent.' In short, Dan was the first patter comedian, a calling which exerted such a strain upon the indefatigable perfectionist that when he died on this date he was only forty-four. In Dan's own words, 'Ah, what is man? Wherefore does he why? Whence did he whence? Whither is he withering?'

1 NOV

Tonight is All Saints Night. In 1600 vandals sacked All Saints Church in Sedlec, Czechoslovakia. It wasn't possible to replace all the superb ornaments and unique religious artefacts they had stolen. Instead, the Roman Catholic congregation exhumed the remains of nearly 10,000 dead to decorate what is now the strangest place of worship in all Bohemia. A bony chandelier made of thigh bones shines upon several hundred skulls arranged to form the Schwarzenberg family crest. Tourists wanting to look around this ghoulish chapel knock on the door . . . with a human hipbone! Of course, they don't always get an answer. The place has a skeleton staff.

His real name is 'Electronic Random Number Indicator Equipment' – but he's been personified as Ernie since his birth on this day in 1956. He's been called a 'sex maniac' because so many big prizewinners happen to live in Essex, Middlesex and Sussex. The odds against winning a prize at all are hefty 18,400 to 1!

Legislation was introduced for the preservation of Britain's waterfowl as long ago as this day in 1790! But it didn't make much difference. Everyone chose to duck the issue. Of course, the birds went on breeding anyway. They reckoned that one good tern deserved another. No wonder they were puffin. Wasn't that foul?

The Marques de Pombal went to the lavatory at 9.29 a.m. – and one minute later the palace collapsed. On this day in 1755, three massive earthquakes destroyed the industrious commercial seaport city of Lisbon. Museums, libraries, the opera house, convents and prisons, all came tumbling down. And the Marques de Pombal said, 'I don't know my own strength – all I did was pull the chain.'

A young Californian couple, Frank Belmo and Chrissie Nathan, won their appeal today in 1970 when the San Francisco court ruled that their public love-making on the bonnet of Frank's car in daylight on a crowded car park by Fisherman's Wharf was not 'lewd behaviour' within the meaning of the law. Chrissie was so overjoyed, she kissed the judge. Then removed her pretty frock, padded bra, blonde wig and revealed 'herself' as a man. the couple were re-arrested on the ground that their public behaviour now constituted 'an unauthorised political demonstration'!

2 NOV

This is the birthday of the world's first test-tube baby rabbit! The bunny-under-glass was presented to the New York Academy of Medicine today . . . in 1939! I wouldn't have thought rabbits needed any artificial help with that sort of thing.

The M1 motorway was opened on this day in 1959. It took you from London to Birmingham in ninety minutes – even if you didn't want to go.

The man they couldn't hold lay dead – riddled with police bullets. Jacques Mesrine, France's public enemy no. one, had driven into a carefully laid ambush. And he was executed as surely as if he had been blindfolded and pinioned in a prison yard. A squad of police sharpshooters opened up on Mesrine as he drove up to his lodgings in a small square near Montmartre, Paris, today in 1979. And he died in a hail of bullets as he had lived – with a sexy gun moll by his side. The craftiest crook France had ever known, they say he threw his wife off the balcony of the twenty-third floor in a multi-storey block of flats and got off. He dashed down and put a shammy in her hand.

Wired from snout to tail with electronic sensors, a Russian dog named Laika became the first living creature from earth to be shot into orbit today in 1957. Soviet scientists were able to observe the biological effects of space travel for ten days. Then – as planned – Laika became the first living creature from earth to die in space. Isn't that sad? I wish I had a rocket to shoot our dog into space. He barks all night for no reason. My wife thinks we should buy him a burglar.

3 NOV

This evening in 1962 I stood with a group of partygoers on the beach in Barbados, West Indies, and listened as the duke of Windsor told us how to keep our wives happy. 'Of course,' he added, with a reflective smile, 'I do happen to have a slight edge over the rest of you here. It helps in a pinch to be able to remind your bride that you gave up a throne for her.'

The world's largest glacier was mapped by Helmut Merten today in 1890. He had good ice sight.

This was the 1972 wedding day of James Taylor and Carly Simon. Zsa Zsa Gabor offered Carly a gem of advice: 'Husbands are like fires, darlink . . . zey go out when unattended.'

The adverts proclaimed, 'Garbo laughs!' Her first comedy had its US release tonight in 1939, co-starring Melvyn Douglas in 'Ninotchka'. Someone suggested they should reissue her 1936 film as the consumptive heroine of 'Camille' with the slogan: 'Garbo coughs!'

An Algonquin Indian chief named Fire-Eyes Broley was photographed at the cemetery in May Falls, Nebraska, six years before he actually visited the site. Because Broley was shown the photo of the funeral of another Indian spokesman in 1934 and could clearly identify himself as one of the group at the graveside, he left California for the first time in his life and travelled to the cemetery in 1940. On the way there, Broley fell and hurt his knee. The cane he was given to help him walk in the graveyard is clearly visible in the film exposed half a dozen years before! Nobody recalled noticing the cane in the photo before!

4 NOV

Iranian students stormed the US embassy and seized the American hostages today in 1979. They're simple creatures. They only set fire to the US consulate because someone shouted, 'You get free gifts if you light up an Embassy!'

The world's first air-conditioned car was exhibited in Chicago this morning in 1939 – a Packard. It also featured a host of money-saving gadgets . . . a carburettor that saved 50 per cent on petrol, spark plugs that saved 60 per cent, a pre-ignition system that saved 70 per cent . . . Sometimes if you drove the car too far, the tank started overflowing.

Soviet forces attacked and bombed Budapest, Hungary, on this day in 1956. The problems of the world have become so complex since then even teenagers haven't got an answer.

5 NOV

Two of America's earliest train robberies happened today in 1870 – to the same train! Earlier in Nevada, 'Big Jack' Davis and his gang of five stopped the Reno express and took $40,000 in coins away with them to Virginia City. Within ten hours, the same train was seized at Independence by half a dozen runaway soldiers who stole a further $4500 missed by 'Big Jack' and his boys. All the villains were caught – thirteen altogether – and all got long prison sentences of ten years or more. You have to be smart to be a thief. One bright soul wore a mask all his life. He only took it off when he was robbing a bank.

It's Guy Fawkes Day! I loved this day when I was a boy. I remember once my brother John and I were collecting bonfire material. We went up to one house and an old lady came to the door – and my brother said, 'Do you want this door?'

On this day in 1791 mighty Indian warrior Tecumseh took on heap big army – and left it in a big heap! Eleven hundred US soldiers were thrashed today at Ohio's Wabash River by the mighty Tecumseh and his Shawnee war party. I once met a Shawnee chief backstage in London. 'How!' I said. 'You mighty brave!' He said, 'Brother, I've just seen your act. *You* mighty brave!'

He's won the Epsom Derby eight times, the Irish Derby four times, the German Derby three times, the French Derby twice, the Oaks four times, the St Leger seven times and the Ascot Gold Cup nine times! With more than 3000 wins to his credit, he's the world's greatest Jockey – Lester Piggott, born today in 1935 at Wantage, Berkshire. I wish I had Lester's skill at choosing horses. I only bet on horses that are so slow they get arrested for loitering. Every time I go to the races, I lose everything I've got with me. Next time I'm taking the wife.

Tonight Pierre Gassendi made the first observation of the transit of a planet – as Mercury did its thing back in 1631. Mercury is the smallest of the major planets, about 3008 miles wide, and it's the one nearest the sun. It whizzes round the sun faster than any other planet with one side turned away all the time. Its backside is freezing . . . (Beware another joke about my first wife). So spotting the little beggar as it nipped across the sun – when it was 'in transit' – was quite a clever trick back in 1631. You can try it yourself on 14 November 1999, the next time it's due to go between the sun and us. Then you'll appreciate how clever old Gassendi was, especially since he began life in ignorance and poverty. He was descended from a long line of sailors. And he was eight before he knew what they were queueing for.

6 NOV

THIS WAS NOAH'S BIRTHDAY;

2948 years before the birth of Jesus – according to one biblical scholar. And Dan O'Day adds, 'Noah helped to save two of every known variety aboard that ark . . . and he had a pair of everything on board . . . two goats, two dogs, two cats, Dolly Parton, two butterflies . . .

President Eisenhower was re-elected over the Democratic candidate Adlai Stevenson on this day in 1956. Major John Eisenhower was an aide to his father during World War II and was once sent to a colonel in the front line. 'My dad says to watch your right flank,' he told the colonel. 'Thank you,' said the officer. 'And what does your mommy say?'

Tyburn welcomed the last of the real swingers today in 1783 – as the last criminal to be hanged there mounted the gallows. He was a careless forger named John

7 NOV

Austin, and he followed some distinguished and extinguished visitors to the Tyburn tree. Situated at the corner of Edgware and Bayswater roads, the 'Deadly Nevergreen' attracted huge crowds to its high-priced galleries to observe the executions of Perkin Warbeck (1499), the Holy Maid of Kent (1535), John Felton, murderer of Villiers, Duke of Buckingham (1628), and Earl Ferrers (1760). One flamboyant thief named Stock Vinson gave a thirty-minute concert of songs and dancing to the crowd before announcing, 'Please excuse my final dance for it is upon thin air and I have never attempted it before . . . and may never do so again!' The wit's widow was rewarded with £13 4s, 8d., collected from a delighted audience.

If you go down in the swamp today, you're sure of a big surprise!
If you go down in the swamp today, you'll never believe your eyes!
For every toad that ever there was
Will gather there for certain because
Today's the day reptileans have their orgy!

On this day in the swamps of Sungei Siput, Malaysia, tens of thousands of toads suddenly went sex mad. They mated nonstop for a week in a totally inexplicable frenzy of croaking lust. Got the picture? I don't think I'll ever be able to eat toad-in-the-hole again.

John Milton died on this day in 1674, aged sixty-five. One of the first jokes I ever saw in print came from *Will Hay's Book of Schoolboy Howlers* and was an English student's essay on the great English poet: 'Milton got married and wrote *Paradise Lost*. Then his wife died and he wrote *Paradise Regained*.'

8 NOV

'Ram a cucumber through the vicar's letterbox and yell, "Look out, the Martians are coming!"' encourages the Knotty Ash mayor. Ken Dodd was a plumshious baby today in 1927. Britain's most original and consistent clown, Ken is the creator of a comic world, with Diddymen, jam butty mines, a whole new dictionary of tattifalarious words, tickling sticks and never an unkind joke. Just goofy inspirations about ways to cheer us all up. 'Be bold!' he urges. 'Go up to a policeman and ask him to move along! Take your trousers off, stand on your head and shout, 'How's this for Kojak?''

The yeti walked . . . and the Everest mountaineers just missed him! On this day in 1951 mountaineers Michael Ward and Eric Shipton accompanied Sherpa Tensing Norkay (yes, *that* one) on an Everest expedition. Just above 21,000 feet they encountered the only really inexplicable hard evidence of the abominable snowman's existence – footprints, recently made! They photographed them carefully. The Smithsonian Institution's top expert on primatology and a bigfoot sceptic admitted that 'no known creature in the world could leave such a spoor like this.' The closest I've ever come to one was when I worked a week's cabaret in Cardiff and the impresario paid me with a bouncing cheque. He was the abominable showman.

Two hundred and thirty-five thousand dollars for a cow! That's the price paid to the cow's previous owner, Claude Picket of Hornby, Ontario, today in 1976, by a US–Canadian syndicate at the 'Sale of Stars' in Oakville. She was a Holstein-Friesian named 'Hanover Hill Barb'. To celebrate her high price, the cow drank a bucket of champagne. She felt great that evening . . . but the next morning she had a terrible hangunder.

9 NOV

The first airplane to go faster than 4000 m.p.h. flew today in 1961. Major Robert White piloted an X-15 over Edwards Air Force Base, California, at a speed of 4070 mph for 86 seconds. On his way home after this history-making achievement, Major White was stopped and summonsed for speeding! (And he wasn't even in his car. You know how it is when you work up a good velocity . . .)

A bombardment of ice blocks 'the size of dinner plates' fell out of the Devon sky! Today in 1950 the London *Evening News* reported a shower of frozen meteors up to fifteen ounces in weight crashing all over a Devonshire farm – and one of them beheaded a sheep! And the farmer said, 'This wether's turned cold.'

One of the worst and most lethal winters began today in 1812 – and defeated the mighty Napoleon. During the retreat of his First Army from Moscow, the suffering troops were ravaged by snowy temperatures as low as minus 35° F (that's minus 37° C) for twenty-seven deadly days. Troops reported seeing brass monkeys, all asking the way to the welders.

A purr-fect landing for the jumbo cat who survived a trip around the world in thirty-two days! Today in 1979 a two-year-old Siamese cat was found by Pan-Am baggage loaders in the hold of a flight from San Francisco. She had landed at Heathrow Airport after a month of air travel on a Boeing 747 – via Miami, Guam and nearly every major country in the world. How she escaped from her box and survived, hidden in the cargo hold machinery without food or water for so long, was a tiny miracle. When a tomcat told her, 'I love you so much I'd die for you', she was certainly entitled to ask, 'How many times?'

10 NOV

This was the first day of existence for the US Marines in 1775. Their slogan: 'Semper Fidelis' – 'Always Faithful'. You can tell that to the marines.

'Give me a lame dog,' said Sir Archibald Geikie . . . and his wife passed him his writing pad. The great Scottish geologist died on this day in 1924, still addicted to convoluted puns, like the relationship of a writing pad to a lame dog. 'My writing pad is an ink-lined plain,' he'd explain. 'An inclined plane is a slope up . . . and a slow pup is a lame dog.'

THE MOON MAN SAW STARS

– today in 1978 when astronaut Neil Armstrong lost a finger. The ring finger of his left hand was torn off by the door of an outbuilding and Armstrong was rushed to hospital where the detached digit was successfully sewn back on. 'Lucky I didn't rip off all my fingers,' he said later, 'because I wouldn't have been able to pick them up.'

It was the 1973 day of the cease-fire between Israel and Egypt. The Israeli cabinet met to agree on a further peace plan and it wasn't easy. In Israel when seven men go into conference, they come out with nine opinions.

11 NOV

It was also UDI Day in Rhodesia in 1965 – when Prime Minister Ian Smith made his Unilateral Declaration of Independence. Everybody knew the blacks had bigger majorities . . . but Ian thought that was just a very indelicate rumour.

Jacques Cousteau published new deep-ocean discoveries on this day in 1968 – among them: captive squids suffering from depression commit suicide by eating their own tentacles! (Later on Jacques crossed an electric eel with a jelly fish and got current jelly.)

Tycho Brahe astonished the world of 1572 on this day by discovering a new star! (Later, he changed his name to Hughie Green.)

THIS IS ARMISTICE DAY, 1918

– when the agreement ending World War I was signed on the eleventh day of the eleventh month – precisely at the eleventh hour! Ronnie Corbett's grandad fought in Flanders with the Scots Guards. 'He played the bagpipes so well in battle,' says Ronnie, 'that the enemy used to shout out requests.'

Our most famous royal paddler died on this day in 1035 – at Shaftesbury, Dorset. Canute (some call him Knut, but you could see he didn't like it) was the son of a bloke named Sweyn (they pronounced that funnily too) who was king of Denmark. Sweyn grabbed all England for himself in 1013 and promptly dropped dead. We asked our own homegrown king, Aethelred II, to come back but young Canute had himself declared king by his crews at Gainsborough.

Aethelred said, 'This isn't an election and, even if it was, Danish sailors don't count' – and he chased Canute back across the North Sea. Two years later Canute returned and, singing 'There is Nothing Like a Dane', thrashed the opposition at Ashingdon on 18 October 1016. And that's how he came to rule England, Denmark and Norway for the next eighteen years or so. Oh, yes, and as for that tale that he demonstrated his limitations to his courtiers by failing to turn back the tide, well, I'll bet he wouldn't try it today. All that oil slick round his royal sandals? No way! We've got to do something about the pollution and fast. Last summer I was on the beach and a bully kicked oil in my face.

12 NOV

The first gardening programme was seen on TV today in 1936. I ought to watch more of them and learn. My garden's so disgusting the toads wear wellies.

After her eleven-day kidnap ordeal, Mexican police freed Señora Brianda Rodriguez, daughter of the sherry magnate, Señor Pedro Domecq, today in 1978. A ransom of £1 million had been demanded – but nothing, not even an autographed photo of Orson Welles, did they get!

13 NOV

The largest animal on earth was shot on this day in 1955. A Hungarian big game hunter killed a huge African bush elephant in Angola. It was 13 feet 2 inches from foot to shoulder . . . 33 feet 2 inches from tail to trunk tip . . . and weighed 24,000 pounds! Libby Morris heard of a scientist who crossed an elephant with a callgirl. Got a callgirl who does it for peanuts but never forgets.

America's famous whisky rebellion was squashed by the army today in 1793 – forcing US citizens to pay a whisky tax of nine cents a gallon! Today that's been increased over 1000 per cent. I wouldn't mind so much if I could give the taxman 1000 per cent of my hangovers too.

Nell Gwynn died on this day in 1687, aged thirty-seven. the leading comedienne of the king's company from 1664 for five years, she became Charles II's mistress from 1668, living in seduced circumstances. But she didn't become lazy. She still worked flat out.

'BLOODY SUPERSTITIOUS RUBBISH . . .'

Gottfried von Leibniz died on this day in 1716. He was the German philosopher and mathematician who invented differential and integral calculus. He based his metaphysics on the theory of monads . . . distinct simple substances. I saw a stunning American comic named Charles Fleischer at the *Comedy Store* in Los Angeles, who based his entire act on the concept of monads, even selling tins of them to the audience, calling them 'Molides'. He used them to prove that 'Any order that can be misunderstood will be . . . and all orders are capable of being misunderstood.' And he went on to demonstrate that 'a fool is his own informer' – and 'if you're not part of the solution, then you must be part of the problem.'

Princess Anne married Mark Phillips today in 1973. When asked, 'Do you take this man to be your lawfully wedded husband?' she replied, 'One does.'

England's oldest man, Thomas Parr, died, aged 152 – today in 1635. Asked to what he attributed his great age, Parr said, 'Keeping regular.' 'Regular?' asked the diarist Samuel Meaton. 'You mean bowel movements?' 'No,' said the old man, 'I mean breathing.'

This morning in 1959 the *Manchester Guardian* ran a story with this heading: 'Crumbling piles. Owners held to blame. Country seats neglected.'

This is the annual elephant round-up day in Bangkok, according to John Fultz, author of *Phantastic Phunnies* of Kent, Ohio. His reliable assurance comes with the news that, in honour of US Thanksgiving, John has crossed an elephant with a turkey . . . 'the meat's less expensive – but the stuffing will cost you a fortune!'

15 NOV

Two hundred and fifty thousand people gathered in Washington to protest against the war in Vietnam – on this day in 1969. While they demonstrated outside the White House, President Nixon and his buddy, Bebe Rebozo, watched a football game on TV. Nixon became really conscious of his waning popularity when he was standing outside the White House and a couple ran up to him with a camera.

The man asked, 'Mr President, we realize you're busy, but would you mind?' Nixon smiled graciously and said, 'Of course not.' So they handed him the camera and posed by their car.

Christopher Columbus discovered tobacco today in 1492. It wasn't Sir Walter Raleigh, nor did Walt first bring it to Europe. That was Frenchman Jean Nicot. Columbus just happened to see an American Indian puffing away and asked, 'What are you smoking in that pipe-like device?' The Indian said, 'That's my business.' 'Really?' said Columbus. 'I thought it must be, but how do you dry it?'

One of my ten favourite films 'A Night at the Opera', was released today 1935. At the New York premiere, a lady autograph collector twittered at Groucho Marx, uncertain which of the famous brothers he was, 'Let me think . . . you're the ugly dumb one, aren't you?' Groucho replied, 'Out of the two of us, no.'

Here's a quote from today's issue of *Women's Own* in 1980: 'Why is it I wonder that butchers always seem so cheerful? It's not that their job is a specially enviable one for in winter meat must be very cold to handle. Maybe they get rid of any bad tempers by bashing away with their choppers.'

16 NOV

The dice game of 'craps' was first introduced in New Orleans as an 'official gambling pursuit' today in 1813. Bernard Xavier Philippe de Marigny de Mandeville returned from France and invited friends to join him in 'an evening of Hazards suited to the tastes of Johnny Crapaud'. Johnny Crapaud was a slang term for a Creole, but almost at once the dice game was called 'Crap's'. Poor Mandeville lost a fortune. Losses at the game forced him to sell off vast family property, even to building a road through his land in order to offer building lots either side. The road was shown on nineteenth century maps as 'Craps Street'!

They arrested Caruso today in 1906 – for pinching a lady's bottom! The world-famous opera star had been overcome by desire in the monkey house of the New York City Zoo. Enrico Caruso was the greatest and he was the first to admit it. He once complained to his manager that another well-known tenor was getting more press coverage. When the manager gently suggested that he was behaving with a trace of conceit, he replied, 'Me? *Conceited*? Not the Great Caruso!'

Today they discovered the northern-most island in the world – in 1978! Yes, we're still exploring this planet. This unnamed 200 square yards of frozen rock lies north of Greenland and 250 miles from the North Pole. And we're still puzzling over our largest satellite too, especially since . . .

The first moon rock went on display on this day in 1969. And the press started calling this the 'Space Age'. If you've ever tried to park a car in town during the past thirteen years, you'll know how absurd that was.

On this day in 1956 my car bumped into another that had a 'Just Married' notice on it. I apologized to the man inside. He replied, 'Oh, it doesn't matter. It's been one of those days!'

17 NOV

The Suez Canal opened today in 1869 with fireworks – and there have been fireworks over it ever since!

The Royal Astronomer saw a UFO today in 1882! From the Greenwich Royal Observatory E. Maunder witnessed 'a strange celestial visitor'. Jeremy Beadle reports, 'He claimed the circular object glowed green. On a breathalyzer test, that'd be well over the limit.'

During a NATO exercise today in 1967, bad November weather interfered with radio communication. The commanding officer of the main flying patrol gave urgent instructions to the other aircraft in his flight to increase their altitude. 'Get above this bloody awful weather,' he commanded. Through his headset came a slightly bewildered response, 'I'll do my best,' said the voice, 'but I anticipate a degree of difficulty. This is a submarine.'

The first airport designed for jets was opened on this day in 1962 . . . Dulles Airport, Chicago. It lost over $7 million in its first year of operation due, they said, to 'high overheads'. That's what made the Romans give up the Colosseum. The lions were eating up all the prophets.

William Tell shot the apple off his son's head today in 1307. Thanks, Bill! If it hadn't been for you and your legend, 'I'd never have had seven years on ATV with 'The Golden Shot', all of it inspired by the original Tell-Tale.

The Iron Duke was buried in St Paul's on this day in 1852. The last hand laid on his body was his valet Kendal's, who cut a lock of hair from his head 'whereupon the coffin was instantly soldered down'. The duke's hair was tied with a red thread in a bow and put in a gold bracelet at the request of the wearer – Queen Victoria.

18 NOV

The man who accurately predicted the 1936 US election results was born today in 1901. George Gallup founded the American Institute of Public Opinion in 1935 and so originated the famous Gallup Poll. His son asked him if he was going to vote. Gallup replied, 'Lord, no! There's nobody running that I'm for – and there's no way of voting against the ones I don't like!'

THE PARACHUTE HAT WAS INVENTED BY ZEKE HALEY OF BOSTON, MASSACHUSETTS, USA, TODAY IN 1879. IT WAS A PARACHUTE UMBRELLA FIXED TO A HAT WITH A CHINSTRAP --- TO PROTECT THE WEARER FROM RAIN & SNOW - AND 'TO BE WORN BY LINEMEN, CONSTRUCTION WORKERS AND THOSE WHO GO IN DANGER OF FALLING TO THEIR HARM'. IT MIGHT EVEN SUIT OTHER PEOPLE....

BOGMOUKHOUSE

Franz Peter Schubert died on this day in 1828, aged only thirty-one. The Austrian composer combined classical and romantic styles, created German lieder in 1814 (by setting Goethe's poem 'Gretchen am Spinnrade' to music) and, of course, owned a horse named Sarah. You must remember Goethe's other poem:

'Schubert had a horse named Sarah.
Drove her to the big parade.
And all the time the band was playing
Schubert's Sarah neighed.'

19 NOV

In Guyana on this day in 1978, over 900 members of the Californian sect known as the 'People's Temple' killed themselves in a communal ceremony by drinking a soft drink laced with cyanide. The leader, Jim Jones, died from a gunshot wound. He had bequeathed $7 million to 'benefit oppressed peoples all over the world' but he left it to the Soviet Union. Now they can afford to take out the Steppes and put in escalators.

The *Mayflower* arrived off Cape Cod, Massachusetts, today in 1620. In 1880, *Heritage Magazine* ran a survey of all the distinguished American families who claimed that one or more of their ancestors came over on this voyage. Their conclusion: the little *Mayflower* carried 14,642 passengers!

And I thought my wife was a loud lady . . . today in 1976 Mrs Grace Hall hit the female shouting record at Exeter, Devon, by yelling at a volume of 110 decibels. They're filming her life story: 'Deep Mouth'.

THIS IS FLAG DAY IN BRAZIL

Jack Douglas says he went to a real South American restaurant when he was in Rio de Janeiro. First you eat the meal, then you overthrow the chef.

20 NOV

On this day in 1917 the first tank-dominated battle took place. Three hundred and fifty British tanks rolled over German defensive positions at Cambrai in France. Although the Germans managed to knock out sixty-five of the advancing juggernauts, many deserted in terror at the sight of walls, barbed wire and trenches all crushed beneath the terrible caterpillar treads. My dad was there and he once told me, 'This old bible of mine saved my life in that war. See, son, here on the fly-leaf? That's the German for "I surrender", the French for "I never knew she was your wife" and a secret flap containing a white flag.'

11,333 bananas . . . 34,000 scoops of ice cream . . . 12 barrels of chocolate and pineapple syrup . . . 110 gallons of whipped cream . . . and 160 pounds of chopped nuts! That's what it took to make the world's longest banana split measuring a gooey one mile and ninety-nine yards in length and assembled in Australia by Cleveland High School students today in 1976, getting them a mention in *The Guinness Book of Records*. My brother-in-law volunteered to eat it at my suggestion. Anything to stop him eating my food. He's overweight but only because of an unusual physical problem with his feet. He can't keep them out of the pantry.

The world champion table tennis player in 1949 was Johnny Leach, born today in 1922. Sadly, after he could no longer hold his position as the greatest ping pong player, Johnny still suffered the occasional yearning for it. In the game, this is known as ping pong pang.

Today was Her Majesty's wedding day in 1947. Now they're suggesting that the queen should pay income tax! 'Good idea,' said BBC producer Mike Craig. 'She can pay mine for a start.'

Gaiety and triumph . . . but what tears were shed to achieve them! Tonight in 1934 Cole Porter's smash hit 'Anything Goes' opened at the Alvin Theatre in New York, to run for 420 performances – conceived in despair and rewritten in tragedy! Producer Vinton Freedley was desperate. Penniless from the flop 'Pardon my English', he begged, borrowed and bullied the finance for his one idea – a cast of unknown talents brought together by a shipwreck. On the eve of opening, tragedy struck. The SS *Morro Castle* was sunk on 8 September 1934. A musical based on a sea disaster was unthinkable. Almost suicidal, Freedley risked everything on a crude last-minute rewrite which cut the sinking but depended totally upon the skill of his inexperienced leading lady. The show made a star of Ethel Merman (and a lot of money for Mr Freedley!)

21 NOV

The man who invented the phrase 'Rock'n'Roll' was fired today in 1959. Alan Freed was sacked by US radio station WABC in New York City for refusing to sign a sworn statement that he'd never accepted payola for plugging records. I remember paying a bloke to plug my first records. But they never got a play on the air. Then I found out he was plugging the holes.

Composer Henry Purcell died on this day in 1695. A pious neighbour paid a bedside call to the dying man and asked primly, 'Henry, have you made your peace with God?' Purcell whispered, 'We never quarrelled.'

England's most devoted servant died on this day in 1807. As chief cashier of the Bank of England, Abraham Newland spent twenty-five years in the bank – sleeping there every night and personally signing every note! The pound note is now so worthless I'm beginning to enjoy paying alimony.

THE CONTROVERSY RAGES ON

– 'Who were the plotters? How many snipers? Why have so many witnesses died?' – but this day in 1963 is blackened by the fact of the assassination. The first US president born in the twentieth century, J. F. Kennedy, died from bullet wounds in Dallas, Texas. The striking coincidences in the assassinations of Abraham Lincoln and John F. Kennedy continually amaze me. Lincoln was elected president in 1860; Kennedy in 1960, just a century later. Lincoln was warned not to attend the place in which he was shot; so was Kennedy. Both men were shot in public view, seated beside their wives – and on a Friday. Both were shot from behind. In both cases the fatal bullet entered the back of the head. The men who succeeded both presidents were named Johnson. Both Johnsons were Southerners, former Senators, Democrats and their birth dates were a century apart – Andrew Johnson's in 1808, Lyndon B. Johnson's 1908. Booth shot Lincoln in a theatre and was found in a warehouse. Oswald shot Kennedy from a warehouse and was found in a theatre. And both assassins were shot down before they could be brought to trial!

Blackbeard was hanged on this day in 1718. The pirate's real name was Edward Teach, and he was so evil-hearted that he wore a big black beard so he could make faces at people without them seeing what he was doing.

The SOS was adopted as the international distress radio signal today in 1906. The famous call 'May Day' comes from the French for 'Help me' – 'M'aidez!' I know a French girl for whom the distress call has a special meaning, because she was the victim of an air disaster. Her husband came home by plane one night instead of by train.

Britain's greatest detector of forgeries began his career today in 1935 – by successfully forging a cheque for £5000! Julius Grant was aged thirty-four and working for a major British papermaker when he was sent to Amsterdam to demonstrate a new kind of paper to a Dutch bank. They told him they were quite satisfied with the paper they were already using. Grant made only one request – that they write him a small cheque. Finding his earnest and eager confidence amusing, the Dutch bankers obliged. Grant hurried back to his hotel and, using his skills as a trained chemist, erased the small amount for which the cheque had been written – then wrote it the equivalent in Dutch gulden of £5000! He returned to the Dutch bankers and stunned them with the 'forgery'. 'This is impossible with our paper,' he told them. 'Our paper reveals every eradication, every change!' Grant got the order for his firm – the first and last paper sale ever made personally by the man who then became the major international expert in more forgery investigations than any other man in the world.

23 NOV

The zoom lens was patented today in 1948 – by Dr Frank Gerard Back – a device of great value to the *paparazzi*, through whose stolen photos of the rich and famous 'the extraordinary are revealed as ordinary', wrote Anthony Burgess, 'and there is no diviner punishment than that'.

THIS IS THANKSGIVING DAY IN JAPAN

'I've met all kinds of girls but given my choice, I'd marry a Japanese girl,' said comedian Bobby Knutt. 'They're beautiful, obedient and quiet – and your mother-in-law lives in Tokyo.'

THE PIED PIPER OF HAMELIN NEVER PIPED

– on this day in 1284 or on any other! For centuries it was popularly believed that on this November day a piper named Bunting (because of his multi-coloured clothes) offered to get rid of the vast rat population plaguing the people of Hamelin in Westphalia. Having lured the rodents to a watery grave in the River Weser with his irresistible melodies, the piper was refused his pay. In revenge, the cheated piper returned on St John's Day to entice the town's 130 children away with his magic music, leading them off forever to a secret cave in the Koppenberg mountain. That's his story but it ain't history! This same tale occurs in the ancient literature of Persia, China, Greece and Arabia. The persistent parable with its obvious moral about broken bargains was most probably inspired by the terrible Children's Crusade of 1212 when a German youth named Nicholas led 20,000 young crusaders to their deaths.

'Frankly, there are times when I wished that Pied Piper guy would come back,' says harassed parent Mike Platt. 'I'd pay him to leave the rats and take my kids!'

Fred Astaire was voted one of the twelve best-dressed men in the world by *Esquire* magazine today in 1936 – yet he still wears an old bathrobe he bought in 1917 for $14! Fred's superstitious about it. Barry Cryer said his suits were all nearly as old so he went to a Berwick Street tailor and told him, 'What I'm looking for is something cheap, lightweight and double-breasted?' And the tailor said, 'Have you met the wife?'

25 NOV

Tonight in 1952 they gave the first performance of Agatha Christie's *The Mousetrap* at London's Ambassador Theatre. Critics tried to murder it – but the whodunnit out did 'em, didnit? It's still running – longest run in show biz, not counting the time six foot six inches newsreader Andrew Gardner got a ladder in his body stocking.

When my wife Jackie was my secretary, back in 1970, she took this afternoon off to attend a friend's wedding. In her carefully kept diary she always entered the reason for any of her absences, illness, holidays, funerals and so on. I found her entry for today read, 'Engaged in union activities'.

'Rock Around the Clock' by Bill Haley and the Comets made its first million dollars today in 1955. What a group they were! Eight boys with hearts of gold, wills of iron; and ears of tin.

And at the honeymooners' paradise, Niagara Falls began to fall again – today in 1969. It had been stopped for a disintegration study. Quite a few husbands on their second honeymoon have been stopped by their doctors for the same reason.

THE CLOCKWORK CAR FOR GROWNUPS!

Long before the price of petrol took off, the wind-up automobile was patented today in 1881. The driver sat alone in front of a gigantic coil spring. One hard-working passenger sat in the rumble seat, keeping the spring wound up with a big crank. 'It worked fine,' says Joe Hickman, 'but on long trips the passenger tended to get cranky . . . and it took him a while to unwind.'

Alice Liddle received a gift from mathematician Charles Lutwidge Dodgson on this day in 1864. God bless the little girl. She had inspired the greatest work of child's fantasy fiction ever penned. The gift was the Oxford professor's tale of a young girl's adventures beneath the earth – later known to the world under his pen name as Lewis Carroll's *Alice in Wonderland*. In this book, Carroll invented the word 'squawk' (a 'pormanteau-word' blend of squall and squeak). His Mad Hatter character emphasized the mental instability suffered by the felt hat makers of old England, who were poisoned by the mercury they used to stabilize the wool. A complex and curious man, Carroll travelled with a trunk in which every item had been meticulously wrapped by him in separate sheets of paper. He gave a page of mathematical calculus to his friend Professor N. B. de Lynge, who said 'Am I to read the holes?' 'I am sorry,' said Carroll, blushing. 'That paper was wrapped around my spare set of false teeth and they do gnash so!'

The world's first major tidal power station was opened today in 1966 at St Malo, France. Strikes and industrial action halted its operation for nearly a year. And the tide was out in sympathy.

WHEN HAYDN SHOULD HAVE GONE INTO HIDIN'!

This was the unlucky composer's wedding day in 1760. The marriage of the wheelwright's son to the wigmaker's daughter was a disaster. As a musical giant, Haydn was unmatched. As a husband, mismatched. His solicitor said, 'You can't get a divorce just because you say she's too fussy and fastidious.' Haydn protested, 'But the other day she insisted on washing my face!' The solicitor said, 'What's so bad about that?' 'Wait,' said Haydn, 'Then she ironed it!'

Today in 1865 Canada sold 40,000 bison to the US. Then America received a buffalo bill.

The first Handicrafts School for Young Ladies was opened in West Gate Street, Bristol, today in 1784. The widow in charge was a Mrs Stitch. I don't think I need to embroider on that. I used to love handicrafts at school, sewing and sewing away, all day long . . . always pleading with the teachers to give me more sewing to do. In fact, that's what they used to say about me . . . 'Here comes that pleading little sew-and-sew.'

The 'most protracted yodel' noted in *The Guinness Book of Records* was the one that came out of Don Reynolds for 7 hours, 29 minutes . . . in Brampton, Ontario, today in 1976. How that electric cowprod got jammed up there nobody really knows.

Carl Stommfelder died in Bern on this day in 1803.

FORTY-THREE YEARS IN THE BATH TUB!

The wealthy son of a banking family, Carl was born idle and at the age of 25 weighed over 290 pounds. He fell into a cesspool while evicting a farmer and couldn't get out until rope and tackle were brought. Obsessed with cleanliness, Carl began to bathe six or seven times a day and had a special tub made with 'waterproof' cushions made from sheep stomachs. In 1760 he climbed into the bath . . . and never left it again alive. He conducted business, ate his meals, slept – and even had a form of sex life with a housekeeper and local 'callgirls' – all in the tub. In his will he asked to be buried in the tub but, after his sanity was brought into question, Carl's body was interred normally in the Stommfelder family crypt. Funnily enough, my hobby is relaxing in the tub. I sit there for hours. Sometimes I even fill it with water.

27 NOV

120 HOURS OF GO-GO ON HIS YO-YO --- THAT PUT JOHN WINSLOW OF GLOUCESTER, VIRGINIA, USA, INTO THE RECORD BOOKS TODAY IN 1977. THE YO-YO WAS BORN IN THE 16th CENTURY AS A FIGHTING WEAPON IN THE FILIPINO JUNGLES. THE WORD MEANS 'COME-COME' --- BUT IF YOU'RE ON THE WRONG END, IT MEANS 'BYE-BYES'!

BOB MONKHOUSE

'Babyface' Nelson was gunned down by law officers on this day in 1934. Born Lester N. Gillis on 6 December 1908 in Chicago, he joined the John Dillinger gang to rob banks. Comedian Dave Ismay says, 'The crime rate is just as bad today! Last week I was playing a game of Monopoly and someone was murdered in one of my hotels.'

This is Republic Day in Chad! The country went independent from France in 1960, had a civil war from 1963 to 1972 and is still pretty short of money. The capital, Fort Lamy, is sometimes called 'Miracle City' because God only knows how the houses stay up. The local population's mostly shift workers. If you mention work, they shift.

28
NOV

The cat who lived to be thirty-six yesterday, died today in 1939. The tabby 'Puss' owned a human named Mrs. T. Holway of Clayhidon, Devon. Many cats live to be twenty or more, but 'Puss' went into *The Guinness Book of Records* without pussyfooting as 'The Oldest Cat Ever Recorded'. Throughout the last sixteen years of his nine lives, 'Puss' wore a Red Cross badge on his collar and tourists who called to meet him contributed a total of £714 to the Red Cross. I suppose 'Puss' was a sort of first aid kit.

29 NOV

He never lost a single fight . . . but never won a title! British lightweight Hal Bragwell fought his 180th bout today in 1948.

The first automatic packaging machine was patented in 1841 by Birmingham inventor Samuel Corbett. He made a bundle.

The undefeated Hurricane Hal was never given a crack at the title. Shame, because Bragwell really was a dedicated boxer. His mum had to count to ten every morning to get him up.

'The Duchess of Duke Street' died on this day in 1952. She was eighty-five-year-old Rosa Lewis (born Rosa Ovendon), the celebrated society caterer and proprietor of the Cavendish Hotel in the heyday of Edward VIII and the Churchill family. She had a wicked tongue. When she wore a fabulous string of pearls to one of her own banquets, a shrewish dowager approached to examine them. 'Mrs Lewis,' she said bitchily, 'I'm told that the best way to tell whether pearls are genuine is to bite them with one's teeth.' 'Bite away!' replied Rosa. 'Mind you, dear, it only works if the teeth are real too.'

JONATHAN SWIFT!?

It's Jonathan Swift Day – since his birth today in 1667 – and next time it pours down, give a thought to the great Irish satirist who wrote *Gulliver's Travels*. He invented the expression to 'rain cats and dogs' in his dialogue *Polite Conversations*, according to Edward Lucaire's *Celebrity Trivia*. Well, if that's true, he also enabled comedian Bernie Clifton to say, 300 years or so later, that following an explosion in a famous Japanese car factory, 'It was raining Datsun cogs!'

This was Sir Winston Churchill's birthday in 1874 at Blenheim Palace. My favourite from his many classic put-downs: 'Say what you have to say and the first time you come to a sentence with a grammatical ending, sit down!'

30 NOV

The world's first football international was a goalless draw today in 1872, when Scotland played England on the West of Scotland Cricket Ground! Personally, I gave up the rough and tumble of football when I was involved in a vicious foul and lost an important fixture.

That supremely witty Irish poet and dramatist Oscar Wilde died on this day in 1900. As he lay dying in a coma, his Parisian landlord whispered to an old friend at the bedside, 'Who on earth is going to put up the money for the poor devil's funeral?' Wilde's eyes flickered and he murmured feebly, 'I am dying as I have lived – beyond my means.'

1 DEC

King Henry I died on this day in 1135. Hank Mark One was the youngest son of Bill the Conqueror, with two brothers ahead of him in the queue fro the throne. So when Robert was off crusading in the east, Hank went on a hunting party with brother Rufus . . . and Rufus got shafted. Funny? Well, no one's ever proved that Rufus was turned into kebab on Hank's orders, but the bloke who fired the fatal arrow was looked after very nicely afterwards, thank you very much. As soon as Rufus was only lukewarm, Hank was getting himself crowned. He was in such a lather to put his bum on the boss's chair, he couldn't even wait for the right archbishops to turn up and had the whole coronation done by two bishops named Maurice and Gerard. They got him the crown wholesale. Hank begot more bastards any other English king – twenty of 'em! But he remained the biggest bastard of them all.

THE FIRST CREDIT CARD WAS ISSUED IN BRITAIN TODAY...

. . . in 1895! It was called 'The Golden Promise and Guarantee of Honour' and was limited to shops in Kingston upon Hull. People got quite a charge out of it.

The tomb of Egyptian King Tutankhamun was discovered today in 1922 by Lord Carnarvon and Howard Carter. King Tut's curse decreed that anyone entering his tomb will live to regret it. Dan O'Day tells me, 'That's nothing new. I get the same feeling every time I enter a voting booth!'

Today in 1903 they copyrighted the first movie to tell a story – Edwin S. Porter's 'The Great Train Robbery'. Now it's re-enacted every time you buy a ticket on BR.

On this day in 1805 the French army met the combined forces of Russia and Austria near the Moravian village of Austerlitz. The French were at a disadvantage – deep inside hostile territory, heavily outnumbered and faced with an aggressive and confident enemy. Yet – within a few hours Napoleon's *Grande Armée* had won its most spectacular victory – and Europe shuddered in horror! Napoleon went through his next fourteen battles without a scratch. He must've had some other reason for sticking his hand under his coat.

2 DEC

The safety razor was patented on this day in 1901 by King C. Gillette. He nearly went bankrupt! For the first year, he sold only fifty-one razors. The collapse was averted in 1903 when Gillette invented his slotted blue blade – and sold over twelve million. But, for a while there, it was a close shave.

Filippo Marinetti died on this day in 1944, aged sixty-seven. The founder of the 'Futurist' art movement, he was also a leading Fascist author and a fanatic about fast driving. When he died he owned eleven cars. Imagine that . . . having your very own traffic jam!

Fred Astaire's first film was released today in 1933 – but who was his dancing partner? No, not Ginger. Nor his sister Adele. The title, 'Dancing Lady', referred to Joan Crawford. As for Fred's screen test, it's a wonder he ever got into a movie. The studio's talent judge wrote, 'Can't act, can't sing, balding, can dance a little.'

Born on this day in 1795, the man who *didn't* invent sticky-backed stamps! Sir Rowland Hill is famous as the man who invented the adhesive postage stamp. Only he didn't. Of course he *was* knighted by a grateful sovereign, awarded £15,000 and buried in Westminster Abbey. But any Taysider could tell you

that he pinched the idea from James Chalmers. No, not the Scottish missionary also named James Chalmers who was eaten by cannibals at Dopima on Goaribari Island in 1901 (it was their first taste of religion). *This* James Chalmers was an Arbroath bookseller and a fierce critic of our postal system. In 1834 he came up with his new idea – gummed sheets of stamps cut into stamp-sized rectangles. Three years later he was still trying to promote his invention to the House of Commons when along came a Kidderminster school teacher touting the same notion – his name, Rowland Hill. Chalmers' claims faded although in 1853 his son Patrick demonstrated that Hill had never mentioned adhesive stamps until told of them in a letter from Chalmers. And having pinched the idea, Rowland Hill had then removed all the relevant papers from the official records!

Giovanni Battista died on this day in 1823. He was famous all over Europe as Belzoni the Great, the great strongman who could hold up a huge frame carrying ten grown men! His brother Marcello was hanged in Italy for being even stronger. He held up an entire train.

Dr Christiaan Barnard performed the world's first heart transplant on this day in 1967. And I think my tax inspector was the donor. It certainly had no sentimental value for him.

Today in 1961 a famous painting by Henri Matisse, 'Le Bateau', had been hanging in New York City's Museum of Modern Art for forty-seven days. One hundred and sixteen thousand people had passed through the gallery during that time – and not one, including the gallery staff, had noticed that the painting was upside down!

South Moluccan terrorists caught a train today. The two groups took over the Amsterdam railway and the Indonesian consulate in 1975. Hostages were terrified. Meanwhile, in a bid to avoid human suffering, the pope offered to take the place of an audience at a Les Dawson show.

4 DEC

'MONOPOLY' WAS BORN TODAY!

Wedgy Benn wasn't around to protest about property deals in 1935 when Charles Darrow, an unemployed engineer, saw *his* property deal exercise launched by Parker Brothers to become the world's most successful box game. At least 500 million sets have been sold!

Alfred Fuller, founder of the 'Fuller Brush', died on this day in 1973. I sold brushes from door to door once. I showed one housewife all my best stuff. Spread out my hair brushes and nail brushes and clothes brushes all over her doorstep. That's when I made my mistake. I showed her my broom and she swept them into the gutter.

Brighton Chain Pier was completely destroyed by gales today in 1896. The rain was so heavy, animals from Brighton Zoo were seen in pairs, carrying boat tickets.

Be grateful you're not like Dr John Irving Bentley. He overheated himself today in 1966 . . . and left only his right foot to baffle the world! There is no known way in which a person can generate enough heat to burn up totally . . . but people keep doing it. Old Dr Bentley just self-incinerated himself to powder, except for that right foot and its shoe – Mrs Mary Reeser spontaneously cremated in 1951 leaving only a little pile of ash and another foot in a satin slipper – Mrs Mary Carpenter self-destructed in 1938 in a boat on the Norfolk Broads – and the only clue is the coincidental local increases in the earth's magnetic field. Conclusions: if your compass starts waggling, have a cold bath.

5 DEC

Wolfgang Amadeus Mozart died in 1791. Nearly two centuries later the leader of the Amadeus String Quartet received a fan letter addressed to 'Mr Amadeus String'.

The post office has asked me to remind you that you have only five more days to post your Christmas parcels if you want them to arrive by Easter.

US PROHIBITION ENDED TODAY IN 1933

Not that it made much difference to my American Uncle Millhouse. He drank so much bathtub gin, he had cirrhosis of the loofah.

G.A. HOLMES SET A NEW RECORD FOR NAKED FLYING TODAY IN 1917.

STREAKERS ARE GITTIN' BOLDER EVERY YEAR, MA...

YEP, PA, AND KINKIER TOO.. ....NICE BOOTS...

TWO AMMO SHIPS COLLIDED IN HALIFAX HARBOUR, NOVA SCOTIA. HOLMES WAS BLOWN INTO A TREE TWO MILES AWAY! HE WAS ALIVE, BUT TOTALLY NUDE EXCEPT FOR HIS RUBBER BOOTS.
— Bob Monkhouse...

This is the Feast Day of St Nicholas! St Nick is the patron saint of sailors, pawnbrokers, merchants and children. Also, coopers, brewers, dock workers and scholars, Likewise those who unjustly lose lawsuits and the lands of Lorraine, Greece and Sicily. St Nick has always been a figure of giving, sharing, spreading joy . . . sort of like Britt Ekland with a beard.

6 DEC

True or false? That steam car companies were put out of business by the oil companies. Motoring nuts say it's true but it isn't. Steam cars burnt furnace oil, paraffin, kerosene or petrol *to make steam*! Oil companies loved 'em! They used more oil-based fuels than the new internal combustion engines did. Meanwhile, the world's first real motor-cab fleet began operating today in 1897 by the London Electric Cab Company . . . until they blew a fuse and went bust in March 1900. Well, these battery-powered taxis only moved at eight mph. Horses pulled cabs faster and did the rhubarb a power of good besides.

7 DEC

It was on this day in history that Captain Scott of the Antarctic discovered he could keep warm by shoving a live penguin down his trousers. Okay, okay, so I made that up. But here's a true bird's tale . . .

WHAT WAS A BIRD DOING IN SPARROW'S?

An early pioneer of Women's Lib, the handsome Mrs Frances Bird-Loughton put on her young brothers' clothes, stuck false whiskers on her face and a pipe in her mouth and blustered her way past the porters at Sparrow's Club this morning in 1898. And what did our Fanny do next but lock herself in the loo in this exclusively male establishment! She stayed in there for eighteen hours, pushing Women's Suffrage appeals under the door. By then the members were bursting with indignation at the very least. Four constables dismantled the lavatory door and conducted Mrs Bird-Loughton to the station. Nice touch of sexual equality: her husband was fined £25! Well, you can never please the Women's Libbers anyway. If they're in business with you and you treat them like men, they get angry. If you treat them like women, your wife gets angry.

Seventeen bananas in two minutes – that's today's greed record set in 1973 by a right nana named Dr Ronald L. Alkana of the University of California at Irvine. He felt so proud of what he'd done, he ran up a palm tree and threw coconuts at the crowd.

ON 7 DECEMBER 1761, MADAME TUSSAUD WAS BORN

Her mother left a candle by her cot . . . and when she next looked, the baby had made Charlie Drake and Ronnie Corbett out of it!

Today in 1960 the *Liverpool Daily Post* ran the headline: 'No water – so firemen improvised.'

On 8 December 1957, the first delivery was set down to enable the workmen to start the construction of the M1 motorway. It was a kettle and twenty-four cups! One of the lads said, 'De shovels haven't arrived, sir', and the foreman said, 'Den ye'll just have to lean on each other till they come.'

Did you know that on 8 December 1894, the wonderful American humourist and comic artist James Thurber was born? So give thanks for that. He was the man who said, 'Everywhere I look today there are dirty streets, dirty books, dirty movies, do you know I think we're living in the Nineteen Dirties!' How he loved his dogs. He once said in a restaurant – to the waiter – 'Would you put the rest of my steak into a bag for my dog? And you'd better put in two slices of bread in case he wants to make a sandwich!'

Today in 1973 'Peterborough' of the *Daily Telegraph* saw a card pinned to the coat of a violin-playing busker in London's Oxford Street which read: 'DOING MY BEST I AM NOT A WELFARE FIDDLER'

James Thurber lost the sight of his left eye when he was six years old after one of his brothers accidentally shot him with an arrow. Yet he went on to be one of America's best-loved cartoonists, squinting through his good eye which wasn't too good either. He found life wonderfully laughable, but had his own rules for it, for example. 'Early to rise and early to bed makes a male healthy and wealthy and dead.' He died in 1961.

Marconi made the first transatlantic radio signals . . . from Poldhu, Cornwall . . . to a kite on aerial wire flown from Signal Hill, Newfoundland. The Anglo-American Telegraph Company threatened him with legal action if he persisted, saying they owned the exclusive rights to operate electrical communications in the colony. I love being on radio. Hell, I'd still do it even if the BBC paid me for it! Doing radio for the money is like joining a monastery to meet girls.

9 DEC

'Coronation Street' was born today in 1960 – due for only a six-week run. Well over 2000 episodes later, TV's longest-running serial is still a top rated crowd-pleaser. Its original title was 'Florizel Street' . . . but the production chiefs thought that sounded too much like a disinfectant! What a coincidence! They tell me my show doesn't *sound* like a disinfectant – it just *needs* one.

The world's first dolphin rustler was convicted today in 1977. Kenneth Le Vasseur of Honolulu stole two dolphins from the Hawaii Institute of Marine Biology and set them free in the Pacific Ocean. He admitted that his decision was not accidental. It was on porpoise. (Now let him set that joke free! Better still, let it die in peace.)

Roller skates were patented today in 1884 – by Levant M. Richardson of Chicago. He advertised them as a health aid, 'giving most beneficial stimulation to the soles and heels and so aiding in the perfect maintaining of strong legs, as our doctors advise'. I heard of two specialists on holiday in Spain, watching the girls in their swimwear. 'Beautiful legs, eh?' said the orthopaedist. 'I hadn't noticed,' said the other, 'I'm a chest man myself.'

The first issue of *Playboy* magazine went on sale this morning in 1953. It featured the famous nude colour-calendar photo of Marilyn Monroe. Dan O'Day says that Dolly Parton has finally agreed to pose for a *Playboy* centre fold-out: 'It'll appear in the January, February and March issues.

THIS IS HUMAN RIGHTS DAY

People in some countries who haven't got human rights call it 'oppression'. John Fultz says, 'Some other people just call it "marriage"'.

The Royal Academy was founded in 1768. Two hundred years later, they turned down my painting called 'Nude Chorus Girl in my Flat'. It was a primitive affair. But I reckon it's better to have had a primitive affair than never to have loved at all.

Cuba became an independent state today in 1898! Sixty-four years later, Robert Orben was saying, 'When it comes to Fidel Castro, there's only one thing that keeps him from being a bare-faced liar.'

HIS BUSINESS WAS BOOMING !

Alfred Nobel died in 1896. He invented dynamite. Then he invented prizes for anyone who survived it.

Sentenced to hang for stealing sheep on this day in 1539 – but he couldn't even afford to die! That was Will Kelly of Ramsey on the Isle of Man. His punishment was commuted to exile because Will was too poor to pay for his execution. He had patches on everything he wore. As a lad Ken Dodd says he was the same: 'Patches on my jacket, patches on my trousers, on my cap, my underpants . . . I once walked into a fancy dress ball and won first prize as a quilt.'

11 DEC

This is Republic Day in Upper Volta. Yes, that's right; it's the bit of the map between Togo and Mali in West Africa. Eric Morecambe showed Ernie Wise a snapshot of himself exploring West Africa: 'See? That's me, drifting across a river on a log.' Ernie gasped, 'That's not a log, it's a crocodile!' 'Oh,' said Eric, 'I wondered why my legs kept getting shorter.'

King Edward VIII abdicated today in 1936. Can you imagine giving up your country for a woman? I know blokes who won't even give up their darts night.

He spat a melon seed 59 feet 1½ inches! That's how Brian Dunne spat his way into *The Guinness Book of Records* in Yeppoon, Queensland, Australia, today in 1976. There's a portrait of Brian at the Savemore Centre, showing him in action. As you'd expect, it's the spitting image of him.

Only twelve days to remember where the hell you stored the Christmas decorations.

The lone yachtsman arrived in Sydney, Australia, today in 1966. It was a welcome halfway harbour for Francis Chichester on his round-the-world solo journey in *Gipsy Moth IV*. But this day marks the conclusion of an even longer solo journey in 1976, when . . .

12 DEC

Walter Stolle concluded what *The Guinness Book of Records* calls 'the longest cycle tour' . . . 402,000 miles! The itinerant lecturer set out on 24 January 1959; covered 159 countries, suffered 231 robberies – plus the theft of 5 bicycles – and endured over 1000 punctured tyres, before packing it in, today in 1976 – a ride of all but 17 years! Asked if he had any regrets, Stolle told the *Sheffield Star*: 'I regret having remained a bachelor all these years.' Well, he should have forked out the extra twenty quid and bought a tandem.

Today is National Ding-a-Ling Day, observed every year on Frank Sinatra's birthday. He was born in 1917. 'In spite of his youth,' reports Joe Hickman, 'Frank has already achieved the rank of Grand Exalted Senior Ding-a-Ling.' He tested for the role as Maggio in 'From Here to Eternity' at Clark Gable's suggestion. Harry Cohn, the studio's boss, favoured Eli Wallach for the part and wouldn't pay Sinatra more than $8000 to play it. 'Old Blue Eyes' accepted the 8000 bucks – and, later, the Academy award. Sinatra wasn't in the least bitter about Harry Cohn after that. He said, 'Harry just happens to be the type you like better the more you see him less.'

The Battle of the River Plate took place today in 1939, reaching its climax with the sinking of the German battleship, *Graf Spee*. What a scene aboard that huge ship! The first mate said, 'I gotta leak in der engine room' . . . and the captain said, 'Vell, if you gotta, go right ahead!'

13 DEC

'No man is a hypocrite in his pleasures!' said the great doctor. And: 'Patriotism is the last refuge of a scoundrel!' And also: 'Let me smile with the wise, and feed with the rich!' The flow of that unique mind stopped today at Bolt Court, London, with the death of Samuel Johnson in 1784.

Jan Vermeer died in 1675. The great Dutch painter's last words were, 'For ever awaits me'. If they ever make a film of that they could call it 'Vermeer to Eternity'.

William Caxton produced the first example of printing in England today in 1476. He began to ignore his wife and was said to be 'wedded to his work'. She said, 'William, what's wrong with me?' – and he said, 'Nothing . . . you're just not my type.'

SIX THOUSAND COPIES OF A CHRISTMAS CAROL WERE SOLD TODAY IN 1843

But after this promising publication date, Charles Dickens received an absurdly small sum from its phenomenal sales around the world. His publisher was a real-life Scrooge. 'He went on holiday with a clean shirt and a ten-pound note,' said Dickens, 'and when he came back, he hadn't changed either.'

'Let me go quietly . . . I cannot last long,' he said, then, an hour later, 'Doctor, I die hard . . . but I am not afraid to go.' At last, with a sudden smile of what appeared to be delight, George Washington died of damp underwear on this day in 1799. He'd refused to change his sodden clothes after a ride in freezing rain. Health tip: at the first sign of a ticklish throat or tight chest, go to bed at once with a warm nurse. Get tight and tickle *her* chest.

14 DEC

The first screw was patented in 1798 – by David Wilkinson of Rhode Island. His wife told friends, 'Not only does he think he's the first, he thinks he invented it, for God's sake!'

Norwegian explorer Roald Amundsen reached the South Pole today in 1911. His party of five travelled eight weeks by dog-sled, starting out with fifty-two dogs and eating thirty-six. Most of us have eaten hot dogs but he's one of the few to eat them cold.

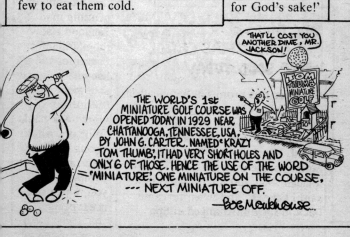

THAT'LL COST YOU ANOTHER DIME, MR. JACKSON!

TOM THUMB MINIATURE GOLF

THE WORLD'S 1st MINIATURE GOLF COURSE WAS OPENED TODAY IN 1929 NEAR CHATTANOOGA, TENNESSEE, USA, BY JOHN G. CARTER. NAMED "KRAZY TOM THUMB", IT HAD VERY SHORT HOLES AND ONLY 6 OF THOSE. HENCE THE USE OF THE WORD "MINIATURE". ONE MINIATURE ON THE COURSE, --- NEXT MINIATURE OFF.

—Bob Monkhouse...

Queen Salote died in 1965. Her lovely smiling face beamed from every newsreel and daily paper at Queen Elizabeth II's coronation. Tonga, the Friendly Islands, received independence after seventy years of British protection, four months ahead of Fiji, its more advanced neighbour. My wife and I visited there in 1972 and adored it. I'd like to have been born in the Friendly Islands, where the girls are all friendly. I'd even like to have been born in the Virgin Islands, but I'm not sure that's technically possible. (Curious fact: The office of commissioner of education in the Virgin Islands was once held by a man whose name was A. Moron. That's not a joke, it's true. If it was a joke, it would have to be a bit funnier.)

WALT DISNEY DIED IN 1966 ON THIS DAY

He won more Oscars than anyone else in the film industry, seventeen in all, some posthumously. Sir Alfred Hitchcock had a nice remark about the great animator: 'Disney, of course, has the best casting. if he doesn't like an actor, he just tears him up.'

SITTING BULL LAY DOWN AND DIED ON THIS DAY IN 1890

His squaw said she would spend her life mourning his passing but remarried three months later. Her name was Lying Cow.

Billionaire J. Paul Getty was born born in Minneapolis, Minnesota, today in 1892. If he'd bought a resort hotel, would they have called it 'Spa Getty?' Sorry. Only asking.

THE BOSTON TEA PARTY HAD NOTHING TO DO WITH THE TEA TAX!

Numerous history books sustain the false belief that 150 rebels dumped 342 chests of tea into Boston harbour on this night in 1773 as a protest against the British tea tax. Certainly the harbour water tasted of Ceylon and Darjeeling for a while but the boozed-up insurgents didn't care about the piddling tax. That amounted to only $300 *per year*!

No, what got Paul Revere and the lads angry enough to raid the three tea ships was the crafty stroke pulled six months earlier when Parliament in London saved the British East India Company from going bust by letting them flog a gigantic seven-year surplus supply of tea to the world without duty charges. That meant they could undersell anyone, especially the American tea merchants. As a result of the bold insurgence of such rebels, the America we know today is a great and free country where anyone can grow up to be a taxpayer.

16 DEC

The Battle of the Bulge began today in 1944. That was *Hitler*'s Battle of the Bulge. Mine began in 1978 when I bought my first girdle.

'I love criticism just so long as it's unqualified praise' . . . so said Sir Noël Coward, born today in 1899 at Teddington, Middlesex. He died 26 March 1963. In the days of the 2p phone call, Coward was sitting in the Ivy, a favourite theatrical restaurant, with a group of London wits. Henry Kendall spoke of a producer who was less than well loved: 'Oh, he's crude and crass I know, but he'd really give you the shirt off his back.' 'Quite,' agreed Coward, 'but who'd wear it?'

Napoleon divorced Josephine on this day in 1809 – because she had been unable to bear him a son. And he was unable to bear her too.

Ely Culbertson died on this day in 1955, aged sixty-four. The American bridge expert from Poiana de Verbilao invented the system of contract bridge and, in the early 1930s, established the game as the world's most popular pasteboard pursuit. I play it for fun, I just make bets in my mind. That way I don't lose any money. I just lose my mind.

17 DEC

In 1977 the *Hindustan Times*, which nets a neat £1000 a page from matrimonial adverts, today ran this item from a 'pleasant Delhi' family who offered: 'A charming 24-year-old daughter who can paint, decorate and mend plugs, a 26-year-old daughter who has herself always busy, and 2 daughters both 20 and 21, with the same body and large dowries.'

The first reward for communicating with extraterrestrial beings was announced today in 1900. 'The 100,000 franc prize excluded Martians who were deemed too easy to contact,' says Jeremy Beadle. Remember the one about the Martians who land their spaceship in a deserted London street? One of them aims his laser-gun at a pillar box. The other raps him on the antenna and says, 'There's no need to shoot, you fool! Can't you see it's only a woman?'

WATCH THIS SPACE!

Arab terrorists killed thirty-one people at Rome Airport on this day in 1973. Six years later the Arabs tried injecting mercury into Israeli oranges, ready for Christmas delivery. 'Those Israelis were no mugs,' said Dutch scriptwriter Fred Mooten. 'They sold the oranges back to the Arabs as novelty thermometers.'

MOTHER GOOSE WAS HATCHED, TODAY IN 1719

Well, she made her first appearance in an English-language book anyway – *Mother Goose's Melodies for Children*, published by Tom Fleet of Boston, Massachusetts. She'd flown before but only in French, when Charles Perrault brought out *Tales of Mother Goose* in 1699 – but here's the odd thing about it: Tom Fleet had never heard of the French book. He'd collected the nursery rhymes and fables from his mother-in-law! She was born Elizabeth Foster of Massachusetts, and became a grandmother with an inventive flair for stories and verses to keep her grandchildren amused. So where did Tom Fleet get the name from? It was his mother-in-law's married name – Elizabeth Foster Goose! This means that two children's books were created within twenty-two years of each other, on either side of the Atlantic, attributed to two totally different Mother Gooses. Or Mother Geese. It's uncanny! Just telling you about it has given me Mother Goosepimples.

18 DEC

Slavery was abolished in the USA today in 1865. And on this same day in 1975 there was a race riot in Detroit, Michigan. One black motorist had a white pillowcase flying from his car radio aerial. A patrolman stopped him: 'What's that for?' 'It's to show I'm neutral,' said the driver. The cop frisked him and found a loaded gun in his pocket: 'Neutral, huh?' Then what's this pistol for?' 'Mister, that's in case somebody don't believe it,' said the man.

On this day in 1900 Sir Alfred Tennis invented the elbow which bears his name.

Louis Antonio de Bourbon was made a cardinal today in 1735. What made it a bit unusual was . . . Louis Antonio was only eight years old. By a childish coincidence . . . Scotland's Margaret Fleming died today in 1811, famous for her prose, her poems, her epitaphs and diaries. And what made that a bit unusual was . . . Margaret was only eight years old too.

19 DEC

The world's first Christmas greeting from outer space! US President Eisenhower wished peace and good-will to all mankind from a satellite transmission today in 1958, actually passing over the North Pole where Santa Claus lives. Well, Santa doesn't really *live* at the North Pole, children. He just maintains a residence there for tax purposes.

William Pitt the Younger became prime minister of Britain today in 1783 at the age of twenty-four! He kept the job till 1801 and did it again in 1804–5, reorganizing the country's finances. We need him again now. The only people whose business is picking up are street cleaners.

SIXTY-SIX AND A HALF MILES PER HOUR – ON A SKATEBOARD!

That's the stunning record set today in 1977 when Peter Clarke achieved that speed over a course in Johannesburg, South Africa. Peter was fourteen years old and proud to be in *The Guinness Book of Records*. Asked how he chose to lubricate the castors on his skateboard, he answered, 'With castor oil!' And he wasn't joking. That's what he actually used. It just goes to prove – truth is stranger than friction.

Today in 1901 a locomotive reached Lake Victoria – and the Uganda railroad was at last completed – after five and a half years of disease and death among its builders – 'Coolies from Hindoostan'. They were the great-grandfathers of the same Asians thrown out of Uganda by President Idi Amin seventy-three years later. The British bosses imported the Indian work force as 'the only tropical people capable of supplying 582 miles of railway for £1 per month per man'. They weren't proof against the African coast climate, malaria and lions though. Seventy per cent were killed or disabled. The other thirty per cent spent their wages buying railway tickets back to the depot.

THE LONGEST DOG SLED TRIP EVER MADE BY A WOMAN BEGAN TODAY IN 1938

– when Mary Joyce left Taku, Alaska and mushed all the way to Fairbanks in three months, a journey of 1000 miles. Not once was the temperature higher than 34 degrees below zero. Joe Hickman writes, 'Mary said the whole trip was a little disappointing. Besides almost freezing to death, she didn't sell much Avon either.'

20 DEC

Film stars Stewart Granger and Jean Simmons wed today in 1950. The marriage lasted ten years. I was married for ten years before I told anyone. I like to keep my troubles to myself.

A weight of 3239 pounds – that was the load lifted today in 1885. The toughguy who did it was a professional strong man, William Curtis. His prize – 100 gold guineas (just enough to pay for the hernia operation).

The world's first animated cartoon in technicolour of feature length with sound opened tonight in 1937 – at the Cathay Circle Theater, Los Angeles, California . . . and every cent Walt Disney could raise, beg or borrow was riding on the success of 'Snow White and the Seven Dwarfs' . . . the story of a girl who lived alone with seven little old men. She used to got to bed feeling Sleepy and Dopey and Grumpy . . . and wake up feeling Happy. Later she urgently needed Doc.

21
DEC

Benjamin Disraeli was asked the difference between a misfortune and a disaster. He answered his publisher's question: 'If Mr Gladstone fell into the Thames, that would be a misfortune. But if someone pulled him out, that would be a disaster.'

Students at Cambridge were not permitted to keep dogs in their room . . . so Lord Byron kept a bear. Lord Wernham asked him, 'What about the stench?' Byron answered, 'The bear will just have to get used to it.'

'DIZZY'
WAS BORN
TODAY
IN 1804

The Pilgrim Fathers landed in 1620 in the New World . . . and nearly became extinct, the silly old puritans. They were so narrow-minded, they re-fused to sleep with their wives because they were married women.

Ceasefire for Zimbabwe – on this day in 1979 – when Lord Carrington, Robert Mugabe and Joshua Nkomo agreed a constitutional settlement. They signed the agreement today at Lancaster House together with Bishop Muzorewa and Sir Ian Gilmour. 'Talks almost broke down,' said comedian Roy Hudd. 'During a coffee break someone asked, 'Black or white?' – and none of them could agree.'

Extinct for sixty-five million years – then he got caught! A smart fisherman knew he'd got something unusual in his net this morning in 1938. Instead of throwing the ugly fish back in the South African sea, he took it to the town's museum. There was a world-wide sensation. He'd hauled in the fishy equivalent of a caveman – the prehistoric coelacanth, older than man. I suppose our ancestors fished for them too. In those caveman days, a husband would show his mate how much he loved her by hitting her on the head with a club and dragging her home by the hair. You could always tell a happy wife. She was lumpy and bald.

22 DEC

Last of the mightiest movie moguls, Darryl F. Zanuck died on this day in 1979, aged seventy-seven. As chief executive of 20th Century Fox Corporation from 1962 till his death, he inspired fierce loyalty. A writer on his payroll answered a job offer from a rival studio, 'My heart belongs to Fox . . . lock, stock and Darryl.'

The world's fastest jet plane made its first flight today in 1964, the Lockheed SR-71. Even the automatic pilot was scared.

'SAILOR JOE' DIED ON THIS DAY IN 1965 IN TORONTO, CANADA. THE 77-YEAR-OLD TATTOOIST'S REAL NAME WAS VIVIAN SIMMONS. HE HAD 4,831 TATTOOS ON HIS BODY!

BOB MONKHOUSE...

WHO COULD MAKE A TWO-PIECE WOOL SUIT IN 1 HOUR AND 52 MINUTES?

No, not a sheep! This was a full-size man's suit, made from square one – actually shearing the sheep! Today in 1931 Bud Macken of Mascot, New South Wales, Australia, spent 19 minutes carding and teasing the wool, 20 minutes weaving the cloth and 72 minutes cutting and stitching the suit together – a total of 111 minutes, plus an odd 25 seconds. That leaves 35 seconds from the total record time of 112 minutes. And it took Bud 35 seconds to shear the sheep! Of course, a Hong Kong tailor can make a suit in 30 minutes – and that's how long it lasts on your back too. While we're discussing the crown colony . . .

23 DEC

Due to a printing error a Hong Kong manufacturer's agent in the Channel Isles was lumbered with 50,000 unsaleable tea towels today in 1980. The commemmorative design on them read: 'William the 1st: Duck of Normandy'.

The annual 'Feast of the Radishes' is held today in Mexico. The annual 'Feast of the Radishes' is held today in Mexico. Sorry to tell you that twice. Those bloody things always repeat on me.

The 'Falling Man' on a pillar within the cathedral of Tournai, Belgium, is a likeness of the architect fashioned by his own hand just before he plunged to his death from a scaffold of the structure on this day in 1030!

Hansom cabs were patented by Joseph Hansom today in 1834. He immediately sold his rights for £10,000 – but never got paid! 'Whoever catches the fool first,' wrote Ed Howe, 'is entitled to shear him.'

On this Christmas Eve in 1801 Richard Trevithick climbed Camborne Beacon in Cornwall. The Cornish engineer and pioneer of the high-pressure, non-condensing engine made the climb with seven or eight pals – aboard England's first full-scale wheeled vehicle moved by steam! On the way down again a passing drunk inquired, 'What happened, Santa? Did your reindeer die?'

24 DEC

Vasco da Gama died in 1524. The Portuguese navigator led an expedition round Africa to India, opening a sea route to Asia. He had a woodmaker carve the Ten Commandments around the base of his ship's mast, and his pet expletive was, 'Moses guide me!' he told the Jewish diarist Immanuel da Malta, 'We Gentiles may have taken much from the Jews but, in the instance of the Ten Commandments, you cannot say we have kept them.'

'NO MORE IMMORAL FILMS IN NEW YORK CITY' said the headline today in 1908. Boy, had that newspaper got a wrong number! The major revoked the licences of 550 cinemas in a successful bid to force them to stop Sunday performances and the showing of 'improper photoplays'. Last week I saw a movie in a New York cinema that was so dirty, if they ever show it on TV they'll have to use Swedish subtitles.

Tonight Santa Claus goes on the tiles with that loaded old bag again. I wonder if Mrs Claus ever stops to consider – her husband has the names of all the bad little girls.

25 DEC

Christmas cards are a charming old English custom, aren't they? Except for the fact that they were first engraved by Louis Prang in Roxbury, Massachusetts, for export to London! They weren't introduced to American trade until a year later in 1875. Of course, some people hate anything to do with Father Christmas. That's just Claus trophobia.

This was Humphrey Bogart's birthday – on 23 January! Warner Brothers studios changed Bogie's birthday to Christmas Day, 1899 – a publicity department trick to (a) shave nearly a year off the age of an increasingly important romantic star of the early 1940s, but also (b) to lend some holiday glamour to his conventional background. Bogie, who died of lung cancer, smoked five packs of Chesterfields a day. He said, 'I drag on a cigarette so hard I've got nicotine toes.'

SOME MUMS RECEIVED BUMPER BUNDLES FOR CHRISTMAS! SHARING THE BIRTH DAY OF JESUS ARE: DAME REBECCA WEST – 1892, PRINCESS ALEXANDRA, KENNY EVERETT – 1944, ANWAR SADAT – 1918, STUART HALL – 1934, NOELLE GORDON – 1923, AND COUNT DRACULA'S BLOOD BROTHER, NOSFERATU!

ROG Monkhouse...

Well, only 364 days to Christmas! Here it is: Boxing Day . . . the day when you can punish the kids by sending them to their room without any batteries . . . when the only Ghost of Christmas Past that starts to haunt you is the cold turkey . . . and you begin to dread the task of unstringing all those Christmas tree lights. That little job is on my list of favourite things to do just below having my inside leg measured by Captain Hook. How about a drink? I've got a good one for your Christmas Party – it's one part snowball, two parts brandy and six parts prune juice – and its called the 'Christmas Rush'. Know why we call it Boxing Day? Because of the 'boxing of the church', when boxes are placed around it to receive casual offerings. And most families like to gather on Boxing Day – for a punch-up. Well, even the strongest of men become emotional about family ties . . . especially if they have to wear the one they got for Christmas. So let's see what else happened today.

26 DEC

On Boxing Day, 1959, a Soviet Antarctic expedition reached the South Pole. They went there because they couldn't stand another Russian winter.

And on Boxing Day, 1904, a Swiss scientist called Helmut Schneer experimented on herself with a peroxide solution and found the first harmless hair bleach. Later his condition was described as 'fair'.

On Boxing Day, 1787, at Spithead into the water for the first time went the *Bounty*. And in no time at all the harbour was clogged with wet chocolate and soggy coconut.

Radium was discovered on this day in 1898, by Pierre and Madame Curie. Their pet cat Tabitha nosed her way into the cupboard where the Curies kept their experiment and was poisoned by the acid . . . thereby coining the phrase, 'Curie-acidity killed the cat.' (Don't you threaten me!)

Christmas holiday quiz question: Which bird became the US National Bird today in 1960? Did you say the bald eagle? Wrong. No, not the turkey either. Try again.

Would it help if I told you it had the less-than-enchanting name of '*Turdus migratorius*'? No wonder the poor bird changed it to Robin. Batman was *so* proud.

27 DEC

Trotsky was chucked out of the Soviet Communist Party today in 1927. His last public act in Moscow had been to open an art exhibition. One picture was a big success . . . a painting of a loaf of bread, a sausage and a bottle of vodka. Everyone wanted to know the artist's name and address.

THE FARMHANDS OF OKEHAMPTON ARE ALL PUCKERED OUT...

. . . at the end of this day. Tradition has it that any farm lad visiting the Devon market town has the right to offer any girl a kiss without fear of annoyance. One extravagant romeo swore he'd give the town's beauty queen a diamond for every kiss – so she let him kiss her twice! And true to his word he bought her a double diamond.

Charles Lamb died in 1834. The great essayist wrote *Elia* in 1823, and the year before his death, *Last Essays of Elia*. His last words were, 'My bedfellows are cramp and cough – we three all in one bed.'

Lord Macauley died in 1859. His last words were, 'I shall retire early . . . I am very tired.' Queen Mary II of England also died on this day 165 years earlier. Her last words were to Archbishop Tillotson who broke down while praying for her: 'My Lord, why do you not go on? I am not afraid to die.' Two composers died on this day: Maurice Ravel in 1937 (his last words, looking at his bandaged head in a mirror: 'I look like a Moor'), and Paul Hindemith in 1963, while planning to write an opera with Peter Ustinov. His last words were, 'Now I shall collaborate with the undertaker.'

28 DEC

John Everitt, the outlaw who invoked the law! On this day in 1725, the notorious 'Highwayman of Hounslow Heath' brought a lawsuit against a confederate in a London court. Everitt was demanding his share of the loot from a robbery they had committed together! The magistrates dismissed the case and no action was taken against Everitt for his confessed crimes. I was never that lucky in a law court. Maybe I should change my solicitor. Once I had a parking ticket and he got it reduced to manslaughter.

The oldest minute of any masonic lodge was recorded on this day in 1598. I remember the first time I went to see one of those stag nights. My little daughter woke up and asked her mother to tell her a fairy story. And my wife said, 'Wait till three o'clock when your father gets home . . . and he'll tell us both one!'

Charles Mackintosh was born today in 1766 in Scotland. Charles invented the raincoat, gave his name to it and, says Joe Hickman, 'created a sensation at a fashion show when he demonstrated that it could be worn with anything . . . or with nothing.'

Parliament legally destroyed sex as the difference between men and women on this day in 1975. The Sex Discrimination Act became law, taking upon itself a task that many people think would be better left to moralists and educationalists. It's given the bigoted, the humourless and the totalitarian a legal opportunity to waste millions of taxpayers' pounds. As far as I'm concerned, the Sexual Revolution is like any other revolution if it wasn't for TV, I wouldn't know any of it was going on.

29 DEC

Becket kicked the bucket on this day in 1170. Henry II had his beloved friend Thomas murdered in Canterbury Cathedral. Oddly enough, it was on this day last year that my brother-in-law pointed out the archbishop of Canterbury to me in our local. I said, 'Are you sure he's the archbishop of Canterbury?' He said, 'Of course, it says so on his T-shirt.'

The US tyre pioneer Charles Goodyear was born today in 1800. John Fultz said, 'Rough birth . . . left skid marks on his mother.'

Parliament ordered the closing of all the coffee houses in Britain today in 1675! It was believed that they provided gossiping scandal-mongers with centres from which to spread malicious rumours about His Majesty's government. Actually I think our democratic system today is so simple it leaves nothing to argue about. Parliament passes the bills . . . the queen signs the bills . . . and us, we only have to pay the bills.

'TRY, TRY AGAIN!'

was the motto of *Never Mind the 2nd* . . . and it worked today in 1945. The handsome horse gave up at the fourth fence in today's steeplechase, then remembered: 'If at first you don't succeed . . .' As all the other horses in the race fell or became disqualified, he ran again – and won! He wouldn't have done it if I'd bet on him. I bet on a horse and it was so slow the jockey kept a diary of the trip.

Grigory Rasputin was his name. Was he an evil genius, a saint or a martyr?

THE MAD MONK WAS BUMPED OFF TODAY IN 1916

He was known to be 'a child of nature' in his early life, able to heal sick or injured livestock with a touch. Tales of his sexual exploits certainly confirm the idea that he was superhuman. He had a remarkable anatomy, that's clear. Able to crawl through the snow on all fours and leave five tracks. Even his wife, a blond and blue-eyed village girl totally under his spell, went on record as saying, 'He has enough for all.' And, by God, he gave it to them! Then, on this fatal morning, Rasputin sat up late drinking. The wine was poisoned, the cakes he ate had enough cyanide in them to dissolve an elephant, but the 'Holy Devil' felt no ill effects. Growing impatient, his enemies shot him. He staggered outside and they shot him again. Then they stabbed him nine times. When his body was found, trussed up like a turkey under the ice of the Neva River but with one arm worked free, it was clear that Rasputin had been alive when submerged and only drowning had killed him. He was forty-four. 'If I die,' he had prophesied, 'the Emperor will soon lose his crown.' Cue the Russian Revolution please!

30 DEC

Gaston VII was crowned ruler of Bearn, a province of France, and reigned for forty-one years . . . all because, when the barons watched him and his twin brother sleeping in their nursery today in 1174, Gaston was contented and peaceful – but his twin was sleeping with clenched fists!

31 DEC

Composer Sergei Rachmaninoff died on this day in 1944, aged sixty-nine. The Russian-born piano virtuoso settled in the USA. Performing at NYC's Carnegie Hall, he became painfully aware of a man in the front row rhythmically tapping his foot. Rachmaninoff contained his irritation although, from his seat at the piano, the metronomic shoe was directly in front of him. But as he moved from the allegro to the andante, he became 'scherzo-phrenic' about it. He held up his hand, stopped the orchestra, rose and crossed the stage to glower down at the amazed offender: 'I'm sorry, sir, but what with this conductor, his baton and his fifty musicians forcing themselves upon me, I cannot always keep time with your foot.'

Was Jack the Ripper's body found floating in the Thames today in 1888? Many people believe so. The corpse was identified as that of a 'depraved lawyer' named Montague John Druitt. His mother was insane. His cousin was a surgeon – and his surgery was only a ten-minute walk from the district of the Ripper murders. Druitt vanished after the last slaying – whether to commit suicide or to become a murder victim himself, no one knows.

And on 31 December 1600, the Honourable East India Company was given its charter by Queen Elizabeth I. Their first venture was a complete failure. They tried to get their own back on the Indians by sailing to Bombay and opening a take-away fish and chip shop.

The chimes of Big Ben were first broadcast on this New Year's Eve in 1923 . . . together with a BBC reminder:

> Refuse that extra glass,
> Let it pass,
> When you drive,
> Arrive alive.

(Pretty snappy stuff for 1933, eh? And true too – on New Year's Eve, nobody should drink and drive. Driving isn't that important.)

Diane Simone Michelle von Furstenberg was born today in, 1946, in Brussels, Belgium; from 1971 she developed a one-woman dress-designing venture into a multimillion dollar international giant, marketing ready-to-wear garb, handbags, cosmetics, shoes, lots more. She launched the trend towards the simple, sexy, body-hugging jersey shirt-dress; dislikes bras because they are 'like a kind of bondage'. I'll always remember the time my wife bought a bra that was two sizes too small. Every time she took it off it sounded like two champagne bottles being opened. Which reminds me – it's time to uncork the bubly right now . . . so . . .

. . . HAPPY NEW YEAR! AND HERE'S TO MANY MORE 'HAPPY DAYS'!

SAVAGE SURRENDER

Natasha Peters

A woman of passion . . .

A man of cruel desires . . .

An explosive story of turbulent love . . .

From the luxury of a French chateau to the black nightmare of a slave ship, from sweeping romance as a pirate's wench to unspeakable degradation at the hands of brutal men, Elise Lesconflair meets her destiny as a woman of daring . . . a woman of bold desires . . . a woman of love.

'A rousing historical filled with breathless action and tempestuous romance.' Jennifer Wilde, author of *Love's Tender Fury*

£1.60

A SERIES OF DEFEATS

Barry Norman

Henry Tyson is floundering in the widening gap between expectation and achievement as he approaches middle age. His wife leads such a busy, successful life as a writer that he has to cook his own dinner on returning hom frome a dreary day's reporting for the *Daily Journal*. He's been passed over for promotion and the executive editor is out to get him. Dismayed, he takes a mistress and his wife consequently leaves him. He's already been beaten up by another woman and Henry's misogyny is becoming as rampant as his sense of failure.

But Henry's defeats – from being locked in the lavatory to being coolly appraised by his wife and mistress as though he were not in the room – and his wanderings through the jungles of television and journalism, London and the permissive society, are recorded in a chronicle of brilliant hilarity and acute observation, and *A Series of Defeats* will delight Barry Norman's present fans, and make him many more.

85p

THE UNLUCKIEST MAN IN THE WORLD
and similar disasters

Mike Harding

Born in the picturesque spa of Lower Crumpsall, he spent his early years in the brooding shadow of a cream cracker factory. At the age of seventeen he bought a set of Mongolian bagpipes and joined a rock and roll band. Much of his manhood has been spent waiting for a girl wearing red feathers and a hulu skirt to come into his life. He is the incorrigible, irrepressible and slightly mad Mike Harding.

The Unluckiest Man in the World takes us into the world of Mike Harding with an inimitable collection of happy, sad, ridiculous, profound and simply hilarious songs, poems and stories.

£1.00

A LITTLE ZIT ON THE SIDE

Jasper Carrott

He's been a delivery boy (the terror of Solihull), a toothpaste salesman (for four hours), a folkie (repertoire – two songs) – and the most unlikely and original comic superstar for years.

Now Jasper Carrott reveals more of the outrageous talent that has taken him from the Boggery to a series of one-man shows that won him I T V's Personality of the Year Award.

Discover the do-it-yourself man, how to become star of Top of the Pops and the Carrott guide to dog-training. Relive the simple pleasures of The Magic Roundabout, Funky Moped and the Mole.

£1.00

METROPOLITAN LIFE

Fran Lebowitz

The cult bestseller from America's funniest writer!

'A wonderful new book. . . . We have waited too long for a writer who is willing to point to her reader and warn "You are under arrest for being boring." Truly the woman deserves a place of honour in a troubled time . . . she should be treasured as an endangered species.'

Newsweek

'The funniest woman in America'

The Observer

'Glorious moments of unforced laughter'

Sunday Telegraph

95p

BESTSELLERS FROM ARROW

All these books are available from your bookshop or newsagent or you can order them direct. Just tick the titles you want and complete the form below.

THE GRAVE OF TRUTH	Evelyn Anthony	£1.25
BRUACH BLEND	Lillian Beckwith	95p
THE HISTORY MAN	Malcolm Bradbury	£1.25
A LITTLE ZIT ON THE SIDE	Jasper Carrott	£1.00
SOUTHERN CROSS	Terry Coleman	£1.75
DEATH OF A POLITICIAN	Richard Condon	£1.50
HERO	Leslie Deane	£1.75
TRAVELS WITH FORTUNE	Christine Dodwell	£1.50
INSCRUTABLE CHARLIE MUFFIN	Brian Freemantle	£1.25
9th ARROW BOOK OF CROSSWORDS	Frank Henchard	75p
THE LOW CALORIE MENU BOOK	Joyce Hughes	90p
THE PALMISTRY OF LOVE	David Brandon-Jones	£1.50
DEATH DREAMS	William Katz	£1.25
PASSAGE TO MUTINY	Alexander Kent	£1.25
HEARTSOUNDS	Martha Weinman Lear	£1.50
SAVAGE SURRENDER	Natasha Peters	£1.60
STRIKE FROM THE SEA	Douglas Reeman	90p
INCIDENT ON ATH	E. C. Tubb	£1.15
STAND BY YOUR MAN	Tammy Wynette	£1.75
DEATH ON ACCOUNT	Margaret Yorke	£1.00

Postage

Total

ARROW BOOKS, BOOKSERVICE BY POST, PO BOX 29, DOUGLAS, ISLE OF MAN, BRITISH ISLES

Please enclose a cheque or postal order made out to Arrow Books Limited for the amount due including 10p per book for postage and packing for orders within the UK and 12p for overseas orders.

Please print clearly

NAME ....

ADDRESS...

....

Whilst every effort is made to keep prices down and to keep popular books in print, Arrow Books cannot guarantee that prices will be the same as those advertised here or that the books will be available.